20-00

Mid and Late Career Issues

An Integrative Perspective

SERIES IN APPLIED PSYCHOLOGY

Jeanette N. Cleveland, Colorado State University
Kevin R. Murphy, Landy Litigation and Colorado State University
Series Editors

Edwin A. Fleishman, Founding Series Editor (1987–2010)

Gregory Bedny and David Meister
The Russian Theory of Activity: Current Applications to Design and Learning

Winston Bennett, David Woehr, and Charles Lance
Performance Measurement: Current Perspectives and Future Challenges

Michael T. Brannick, Eduardo Salas, and Carolyn Prince
Team Performance Assessment and Measurement: Theory, Research, and Applications

Jeanette N. Cleveland, Margaret Stockdale, and Kevin R. Murphy
Women and Men in Organizations: Sex and Gender Issues at Work

Aaron Cohen
Multiple Commitments in the Workplace: An Integrative Approach

Russell Cropanzano
Justice in the Workplace: Approaching Fairness in Human Resource Management, Volume 1

Russell Cropanzano
Justice in the Workplace: From Theory to Practice, Volume 2

David V. Day, Stephen Zaccaro, Stanley M. Halpin
Leader Development for Transforming Organizations: Growing Leaders for Tomorrow's Teams and Organizations.

Stewart I. Donaldson, Mihaly Csikszentmihalyi and Jeanne Nakamura
Applied Positive Psychology: Improving Everyday Life, Health, Schools, Work, and Safety.

James E. Driskell and Eduardo Salas
Stress and Human Performance

Sidney A. Fine and Steven F. Cronshaw
Functional Job Analysis: A Foundation for Human Resources Management

Sidney A. Fine and Maury Getkate
Benchmark Tasks for Job Analysis: A Guide for Functional Job Analysis (FJA) Scales

J. Kevin Ford, Steve W. J. Kozlowski, Kurt Kraiger, Eduardo Salas, and Mark S. Teachout
Improving Training Effectiveness in Work Organizations

Mid and Late Career Issues

An Integrative Perspective

Mo Wang
University of Florida

Deborah A. Olson
University of La Verne

Kenneth S. Shultz
California State University, San Bernardino

Routledge
Taylor & Francis Group

NEW YORK AND LONDON

First published 2013
by Routledge
711 Third Avenue, New York, NY 10017

Simultaneously published in the UK
by Routledge
27 Church Road, Hove, East Sussex BN3 2FA

Routledge is an imprint of the Taylor & Francis Group, an informa business

Library of Congress Cataloging in Publication Data
A catalog record for this book has been requested

ISBN: 978-0-415-80495-0 (hbk)
ISBN: 978-0-203-09647-5 (ebk)

Typeset in Sabon and Optima
by EvS Communication Networx, Inc.

Printed and bound in the United States of America by Sheridan Books, Inc. (a Sheridan Group Company).

I dedicate this book to my wife, Jing Zheng,
and my daughter, Zoe Wang

— Mo Wang

We dedicate this book to our children Benjamin and Amanda Shultz who,
we hope, have long and fulfilling careers
—Deborah A. Olson and Kenneth S. Shultz

Contents

SECTION I: INTRODUCTION

SECTION II: CAREER ISSUES UNIQUE TO MID AND LATE CAREERS

SECTION III: TOPICAL ISSUES RELATED TO MID AND LATE CAREERS

SECTION IV: CONCLUSION

List of Figures, Table, and Text Box

Figures

Table

Text Box

Series Foreword

There is a compelling need for innovative approaches to the solution of many pressing problems involving human relationships in today's society. Such approaches are more likely to be successful when they are based on sound research and applications. The Series in Applied Psychology offers publications that emphasize state-of-the-art research and its applications to important issues of human behavior in a variety of societal settings. The objective of this series is to bridge both academic and applied interests.

In *Mid and Late Career Issues: An Integrative Perspective*, Wang, Olson, and Shultz review over 40 years of research and organizational practice and develop a critical framework for understanding the unique challenges of understanding and improving mid to late careers. Given the rapid aging of the workforce, the many changes in employment systems and models throughout the world, and the evolving economic and social environment in which work is performed, this volume is both timely and provocative.

The study of careers has evolved considerably over the last several decades, but there has been too little systematic work on the middle and late stages of careers. The Wang, Olson, and Shultz book fills this critical gap. Their book starts by reviewing the current state of career research and theory, and noting its heavy emphasis on the early phase of establishing a career. In this section, the authors show how the changing nature of work poses particular challenges for individuals who are in the mid and later stages of their careers.

In their second section, the authors review the individual, job, and organizational-level factors that are unique to mid and late careers. The section that follows highlights the individual and organizational strategies that show the most promise for helping individuals manage and progress through the later stages of their careers, and that can provide help in making the transition to retirement. This section also highlights the unique issues involved in the intersection or work and nonwork spheres of people in the later phases of their career.

The volume closes with a description and elaboration of a resource-based dynamic perspective on mid and late careers. This model integrates and synthesizes much of the research reviewed in the first several sections of this book, and it provides a valuable springboard for advice on both research and practice in this emerging area.

Mid and Late Career Issues: An Integrative Perspective shows how research and practical experience in organizations can be combined to strengthen the reach, relevance and realism of research on careers. This book will appeal to social scientists and students, but it is also highly relevant to managers and executives in organizations. We are extremely happy to add *Mid and Late Career Issues: An Integrative Perspective* to the Applied Psychology series.

Kevin R. Murphy
Jeanette N. Cleveland
Series Editors

Preface

A significant amount of research has been conducted over the past several decades focused on the transition from school to work by young adults, and the establishment phase of their careers. However, there is relatively little empirical and theoretical work on the unique career issues faced by those workers in their mid to late career stages, particularly with regard to the psychosocial dynamics of mid and late careers. With the aging of workers worldwide, we need a deeper understanding of the unique challenges and issues as well as the practical implications related to the shifting demographics to an older workforce, particularly the aging of the baby boom generation. Thus, a major goal for us in writing this book was to review, summarize, and integrate the extant literature on a wide variety of issues and the organizational realities related to workers in their mid and late careers. In addition, we offer recommendations for future research, practice, public policy, and worker interventions regarding the specific issues related to mid and late careers that we address in this book. Further, we have also included numerous case studies based on one-on-one interviews we conducted with a wide variety of individuals progressing through their mid and late career. These case studies provide illustrative examples of the key concepts we discuss in various chapters throughout the book. In doing so, we hope this book will have a profound influence on the next generation of students, scholars, organizational decision makers, and public policy professionals, as well as provide useful knowledge and information for workers who are in their mid and late careers.

Coverage

The book consists of four parts. Part I is the introduction and includes three chapters. The first chapter introduces key concepts, lays out the rationale for the book, and provides an overview to the rest of book. The second chapter briefly reviews the major career theories and discusses the evolution of career theory with a particular eye toward how this evolution has impacted mid and late career issues. Chapter 3 discusses the changing nature of work, workers, the workforce, and organizations, and how these changes have impacted mid and late careers in the 21st century.

Part II of the book has three chapters covering career issues unique to the study of mid and late careers. We take a multilevel approach with Chapter 4 focusing on individual level factors, Chapter 5 on job level factors, and Chapter 6 on organizational level factors that impact mid and late career. Part III consists of five chapters discussing a series of topical issues particularly relevant to the study of mid and late careers. Chapter 7 covers career renewal in mid and late career. Next, Chapter 8 covers performance management concerns with regard to mid and late career, while Chapter 9 covers training, development, and mentoring issues. Chapter 10 covers work and family issues, while Chapter 11 discusses the transition to retirement. Part IV consists of a single chapter (Chapter 12), which provides integration and summary of the book by introducing a resource-based dynamic model of mid and late career development and adjustment.

Unique Features

This book has four unique features. First, this book is the first to focus solely on advancing research in understanding and designing meaningful organizational practices that address mid and late career issues. In this sense, we provide a more comprehensive integration of theories, empirical knowledge, and organizational practices related to mid and late career issues than in any previous volume. Second, most topics that we cover in this book (e.g., performance management, leadership development, career renewal) have not been systematically reviewed and examined in other existing works. Third, we conclude each chapter by providing recommendations for future research on the topics covered in that chapter. Finally, we also provide numerous case study examples from more than a dozen structured case study interviews we conducted with workers (or recent retirees) regarding mid and late career issues. These case studies illustrate the application of knowledge and information included in the corresponding chapter. This unique feature helps in translating the knowledge into practice for employees, organizations, and policy makers, which has not been offered by previous books that are related to mid and late career issues.

Related Works

A variety of books have addressed various aging and work issues. Most of these volumes, however, suffer from one of three shortcomings. First, many current books only discuss a limited number of issues related to mid and late career (i.e., only have a chapter or two on the topic). Second, previous books tend to adopt a somewhat narrow and discipline specific focus (e.g., economics, sociology, occupational health). Finally, many of the texts are now dated or even out-of-print, reviewing primarily literature several decades old. Thus, given the shortcomings of existing works and the inevitable demographic and societal shifts as the baby boomers age, this book was written to fill the current void regarding research and theory related to the mid and late career issues.

Intended Audience

The primary audience for this volume is advanced undergraduate and graduate students, as well as researchers in both academic and applied settings. The disciplines of industrial and organizational psychology, developmental psychology, counseling psychology, vocational psychology, gerontology, sociology, economics, and social work would serve as the primary audience. In addition, organizational decision makers, public policy makers, human resource professionals, employee assistance programs, and older worker advocates (e.g., AARP) will also have an interest in this book. Media professionals will also use the book as a reference with regard to the implications of the shifting demographic and societal trends associated with mid and late career issues that are often reported in media. Further, given that most chapters include a section that illustrates the application of the knowledge and information included in the corresponding chapter, this volume will be useful for workers and soon to be retirees who are in their mid and late careers to achieve better productivity and work-related well-being. We have integrated the concepts of using talents to optimize performance for workers who are in their mid and late career. In doing so, our goal was to assist individuals in making decisions with regard to work that allows them to engage in meaningful activities in order to contribute at their highest level. In taking this approach, our focus is on how individuals, and the organizations they work in, can focus on maximizing the performance of their workers in mid and late career. Both previous research and biases that exist against older workers often reinforces the assumption that performance will inevitably decrease with age. Our focus was to assist individuals in finding ways to use their talents at work in both paid and volunteer roles and to encourage organizational leaders to engage in practices and design systems that optimize the use of employees' talents regardless of the age of the individual.

Acknowledgments

The authors would like to thank Anne Duffy at Taylor & Francis for guiding us through the arduous process of completing a book such as this. In addition, we thank Casey Arakawa, Julie Crippin, Donna Miller, and Shachipriya Tripathi for their assistance in conducting many of the interviews and case studies that are woven throughout the book. We also thank Gabby Burlacu for her help in organizing and checking all the references in the book. Finally, we are indebted to those who reviewed various chapters at several different points in the book writing process.

Mo Wang, PhD
Deborah A. Olson, PhD
Kenneth S. Shultz, PhD

About the Authors

Mo Wang, PhD, earned his MA and PhD degrees in Industrial/Organizational (I/O) Psychology and Developmental Psychology from Bowling Green State University in Bowling Green, Ohio. He is currently a tenured Associate Professor at University of Florida's Warrington College of Business Administration, specializing in research and applications in the areas of retirement and older worker employment, occupational health psychology, cross-cultural HR management, leadership, and advanced quantitative methodologies. He has received numerous research awards for his research in these areas, including the Early Career Achievement Awards from Society for Industrial and Organizational Psychology—SIOP (2012), Academy of Management's Human Resources Division (2011) and Research Methods Division (2011), and Society for Occupational Health Psychology (co-sponsored by the APA and NIOSH, 2009). He currently serves as an Associate Editor for *Journal of Applied Psychology* and the Editor for the *Oxford Handbook of Retirement.*

Deborah A. Olson, PhD, earned her MA and PhD degrees in Industrial/Organizational (I/O) Psychology from Wayne State University in Detroit, Michigan. She is currently an Associate Professor of Management and Leadership at the University of La Verne (ULV) in La Verne, California. Prior to joining ULV, she was a leadership development management consultant for over 25 years. She was the Vice President of Organizational Effectiveness and Management Development for Hay McBer and owned her own consultancy. During her time as a consultant, she worked with over 350 organizations, from both public and private sectors across North America. Her current research focuses on the areas of career development, leadership and team development, human resource management practices, positive organizational behavior, and the use of talents to optimize the effectiveness of older workers. In fall of 2011, she received the McElwee Excellence in Research Award from the College of Business and Public Management at the University of La Verne for her track record of research since completing her PhD in 1986.

Kenneth S. Shultz, PhD, earned his MA and PhD degrees in Industrial/Organizational (I/O) Psychology from Wayne State University in Detroit, Michigan. He also completed a year-long National Institute on Aging (NIA) funded post-doctoral research fellowship in social gerontology at the University of Southern California (USC). Ken has been a professor in the Psychology Department at California State University, San Bernardino (CSUSB) for over 20 years. He has presented over 100 papers at regional, national, and international conferences, and also published more than 50 refereed journal articles and book chapters focusing on aging and work related topics, including bridge employment and the transition to retirement. He has also published two other books, including *Aging and Work in the 21st Century* edited with Gary A. Adams.

INTRODUCTION

Chapter 1

Understanding Mid and Late Careers
Transformations and Challenges

Career paths and practices have evolved dramatically over the past several decades. New opportunities have been created by changing organizational structures and processes, life choices, and social entrepreneurs. When compared to organizational changes and traditional career trajectories prior to the 1980s, the breadth of changes and level of turbulence that has occurred since the 1980s were unpredictable and unprecedented (Harrington & Hall, 2007). As late as the 1980s, organizational leaders still made significant investments in establishing career paths and developmental tracks that would allow individuals to be identified early in their careers and move quickly through key developmental assignments to facilitate and nurture their growth (Davis, Skube, Hellervik, Gebelein, & Sheard 1992; Kaplan, 1991; McCall, Lombardo, & Morrison, 1988). In this context, organizations "owned" the career paths, and individuals looked for opportunities to keep themselves on the right career track. With economic recessions, the dot.com bubble, Y2K, and overall global economic turmoil, more individuals have taken charge of their own career paths and the evolution of their careers over the last several decades. The concepts of the boundaryless career (Arthur & Rousseau, 1996) and the protean career (Hall, 2002) emerged with the focus on individual's assuming full responsibility for the nature and course of their careers as a result of the impact of organizational dismantling of traditional human resource processes (e.g., careers for life) in the early 1980s, along with the impact of globalization. Taken together, these trends foreshadowed how careers today evolve in complex and dynamic ways that reflect the diverse life paths and choices that individuals make as their needs change (Benko & Weisberg, 2007).

Throughout each of the subsequent chapters, we integrate research and practice to provide an up-to-date perspective on the opportunities and challenges faced by workers as their careers have unfolded. We have not only reviewed the literature that focuses on the experience of work for people over 40, but we have interviewed numerous individuals who are 50 and over (some are still working, while others are engaged in volunteer work and have retired in the traditional sense from paid employment) and incorporated their experiences and perspectives in many of the chapters that follow. What we have found from these many interviews is that no one traditional mid and late career worker framework exists. Instead, consistent with the lifespan perspective on careers, there are many pathways to a successful career and many of those are forged based on the unique approaches taken by the individual as they progressed through their respective careers. We also have found that some mid and late career workers have continued to stay on a traditional corporate track, working in their area of technical and professional expertise until they retired, either through downsizing or personal choice. Thus again, it became evident to us that no single model can be used to fully describe individuals in their mid and late careers.

As a result of the many options that individuals have forged, we have referred to "mid and late career" and "older worker" in some areas interchangeably. The reason for this is that some individuals in their early 60s (traditionally defined as an older worker) are just beginning new positions and, in the traditional sense, could be called an "early career" worker. They made the choice to change career paths without regard for their chronological age. Our intent was to reflect the reality that exists at this point in time, not to muddle "age" and "stage," since those traditional career distinctions are no longer relevant for some people. Since organizational leaders have made choices to downsize and rightsize to optimize economic returns and growth, individuals have had to respond, either by choice or necessity, to adapt their careers to create something new and different that may have been unanticipated when they were in their 20s. Thus, our approach is consistent with the process model of careers that focuses on how people make choices to construct their careers over time based on their shifting personal needs, as well as the needs of family, work, and their community to create careers paths that are unique and integrated over their life course (Lee, Kossek, Hall, & Litrico, 2011).

Perspectives and Career Realities Reflected in this Book

Sullivan and Crocitto (2007) discussed how traditional career theories emerged after World War II when professionals and managers were predominately White men who worked in one or two organizations for the duration of their work years. With the more recent changes that have occurred, the first reality reflected in our writing is that the experience of mid and late career workers today is very different than it was post-WWII through the early 1980s. In the 1980s, individuals in blue and white collar jobs still had the traditional view of working until retirement age and then engaging in leisure pursuits to find contentment and enjoyment. At that time, retiring from full-time work in one's 50s was often a goal and carried a sense of prestige with it. This was true for the automotive worker who was able cash in on the "30 and out" rule, as well as the technology entrepreneurs who built companies and sold them for a substantial sum of money so they could retire very young. Now the focus of retiring when one turns the magic age of 65 seems outdated.

CASE STUDY

In our interview with Sara, she emphasized the point that many social and economic factors have changed compared to the 1980s. People are living longer now, and even though she is in her 60s she is in great health and does not have any specific age in mind regarding when she will retire. Sara loves what she is doing and wants to keep working as long as she feels like she makes a difference in what she does every day. Sara changed jobs when she was 59 and, from a career perspective, would traditionally be considered in her "early career."

We also interviewed Mary, who began working full time in a hospital at age 51. Prior to that time, she had been a full-time, stay at home mother. Mary was just starting her career even though she was in her 50s. Mary described how she had to learn how to communicate effectively with others in a business context and how different it was from her communications with family at home or while she was completing her degree at college while in her 40s. When Mary was 65, her manager at the hospital asked her if she was going to retire. At that time, Mary saw no need to retire, she liked having somewhere to go every day and work helped her structure her time. It was not until the hospital was purchased by a larger healthcare system in the area that Mary felt forced to take a retirement package. She was 69 when this happened and was devastated that the decision to retire was taken out of her control and imposed on her by the executives in power. Now almost 80, she still misses the daily structure that work provided, as well as the interactions with her friends at work, neither of which she has been able to fully replace in her daily routine since she stopped working full time.

Ultimately, chronological age is indeed distinct from career stage. However, the choices and experiences that individuals have before they are 50 have a clear impact on how they perceive their present choices and options, as well as what risks they are willing to take. For example, many individuals decided (like Sara) not to have children, while others (like Mary) had children in their 20s and early 30s, so that by the time they are in their early 50s they may have more interest in pursuing full-time work. Sara's early choices and the exceptional career success that she had achieved by the time she was in her 40s allowed her to take different risks and make different choices than Mary. However, both women ultimately were in new careers in their 50s and working in positions that they did not dream of when they were in their 20s. Each however, had different talents and different ways of demonstrating those talents. Both found ways to integrate their talents into their work to be effective in achieving their goals as older workers who were in their early career stages. Thus it is clear that priorities, challenges, and self-confidence are all impacted by the accumulated choices, successes, and experiences earlier in life (Feldman, 2002b; Mainiero & Sullivan, 2005).

The circumstances of both Sara and Mary illustrate the second perspective that is reflected throughout this book. Namely, chronological age and career stage for many individuals no longer correspond. As a result of this new reality, in the chapters that follow we discuss some of the implications and issues that are related to age and stage for mid and late career workers. However, it is virtually impossible to discuss all the possible configurations that have been created based on individuals' choices to weave the tapestry of their careers into their life course. Thus, in each chapter, we provide illustrative examples and discuss some of the implications of the intersection of age and stage for mid and late career workers.

We have also taken the perspective throughout this book that traditional career theory and research can provide insights and needs to be integrated given the reality that age and stage are increasingly less likely to converge in the career paths of workers over 50. This is consistent with the work of Lee et al. (2011) who state that as a result of the significant upheavals that have occurred over the past few decades, new ways to reflect on careers and illuminate the challenges and opportunities that individuals face need to be synthesized. Valcour, Bailyn, and Quijada (2007) developed the concept of the customized career which captures the wide range of individual needs as well as environmental opportunities and challenges that create a multitude of career paths that individuals select from as they seek to meet their personal and professional needs over the life course.

With that backdrop we begin by reflecting on where the field of careers began and the seminal work of Super (1957, 1980) to set the stage for understanding the new realities that need to be synthesized to develop more clarity on the challenges and opportunities of mid and late career workers. Litricio, Lee, and Kossek (2011) recently noted that "Careers have been defined as a window through which we can see how individuals' choices and constraints over the life course play out and interact with developments in society, organizations, and personal lives (Moen & Han, 2001)" (p. 1682). This definition makes clear that we can only truly study careers in retrospect or at best as they unfold over time. Thus, our focus on mid and late career in this volume takes a decidedly lifespan approach to the study of careers. In Chapter 2, we outline the history of career theory and then focus on the more prominent modern day theories that are particularly pertinent for studying mid and late career. However, we briefly review Super's highly influential work on careers here to set the stage for much of what follows.

Super's (1957) career stage model discussed five primary stages that individuals typically progress through during their career. First was the *Growth Stage* (birth–age 14). In this stage, thinking about careers starts with fantasy thinking, based on needs and fantasy role play. Next, individuals progress to the *Exploration Stage* (ages 15–24). In this stage, the person experiments (ages 15–17) with tentative choices, such as courses in school, part-time work, and discussions of various career options with family and friends. Next, there is a transition period (ages 18–24) when the person enters the labor market or professional training and attempts to enact an occupational identity that was forged earlier during this second stage. During the *Establishment Stage* (ages 25–44), the person attempts to make a permanent place for him or herself. There is first a trial period (ages 25–30), which may or may not be successful and which might include job changes before a good fit is found. Then, when the right fit is found, there is a period of stabilization (ages 31–44), as the person settles down in their chosen work and becomes secure. During the fourth *Maintenance Stage* (ages 45–64), the now middle aged individual has become established in his or her work, and thus the focus is on preserving the position attained. In the final, *Decline Stage* (age 65 and on), physical and mental capabilities decline, and, as a result, the person's work activities change. New roles must be found to replace the role work has played in their life. The substages here are deceleration (ages 65–70), when the person may shift from full- to part-time work or job duties may change, and retirement (71 and on), when the person stops occupational work altogether. However, there is great variability here, with some people stopping completely and easily, and while others continuing employment until death.

Super's model of career development served as the dominant model of careers for much of the second half of the 20th century. However, by the 1970s, Super himself was starting to realize that individuals were increasingly beginning to recycle through various career stages that tended to be shorter and more concentrated. Thus, his earlier age graded stage model was being replaced with a series of shorter career cycles that were less likely to be tied to specific ages (as the case studies of Sara and Mary presented earlier), thus resulting in his more recent lifespan-life space model of careers (Super, 1980). This newer model also placed greater emphasis on the numerous contextual factors that shape careers. Thus, many of the classical assumptions of how individuals progress through their respective careers were beginning to be challenged by the 1980s. In their place, new assumptions were evolving. For example, a key assumption of all of the contemporary career theories we present in the next chapter is that *individuals have critical learning experiences in their earlier stages of their lives that have long-lasting effects in later career. Particularly important are varied experiences and developmental relationships with family and friends* (Feldman, 2002b).

A second key assumption is that later career workers have increased freedom of choice and also have the resources to make personal choices and search for self-fulfillment. Again, most careers during the middle 20th century were orchestrated by the organization. Individuals in management roles took accountability for "moving" people into positions to optimize organizational outcomes. Organizations also invested a significant amount of time and resources in creating career ladders that managers would "climb" one wrung at a time. If individuals wanted to progress in their career, they followed the prescribed career paths and ladders that they wanted to pursue and which were delineated in the organizational chart. In addition, at the end of one's career, retirement ages were dictated by the organization. It wasn't until amendments to the Age Discrimination in Employment Act (ADEA) in the United States in the mid-1980s that workers were able to have more freedom in deciding when to retire. However, today's organizations still have significant influence on retirement decisions with early retirement incentive packages or less than desirable late career job reassignments, for example, but at least in theory the decision to extend or exit one career should be up to the individual. Extending one's career through a process of bridge employment is discussed extensively in several of the chapters that follow.

A third assumption reflected in this book is that contemporary careers and the choices that individuals make as their careers unfold have a "trapeze-like" moment of possibility that includes the anxiety that occurs when individuals make choices to explore something new. The more radical the change, the more apprehension that individuals can experience as they step into the uncertainty and possible chaos that could surround them as a result of their actions and choices. Sometimes, the uncertainty can immobilize the person rather than creating feeling of challenge and ongoing development. As part of our work in gathering data for this book, we conducted a series of interviews with workers who were over 45 and at different stages in their career (early, mid, and late). We have woven their comments, reflections, and perspectives into the chapters to provide a personal perspective that illustrate these "trapeze-like" moments in individual's careers.

The Approach of this Book and Topical Coverage

In this book we start with an industrial/organizational psychology perspective, given that all three authors hold PhD degrees in I/O psychology. Given this perspective, we consider both industrial/personnel psychology research (e.g., career choice and renewal, performance management, training) and organizational psychology research (e.g., work motivation, leadership development, work-family issues, mentoring). However, instead of emphasizing a particular theoretical orientation, we review, summarize, and integrate the interdisciplinary literature related to each content area by incorporating different theories as appropriate from multiple disciplines including sociology, economics, social work, as well as other areas of psychology such as lifespan developmental, vocational, and counseling psychology. We also cover issues involving mid and late career that focus on the individual worker, as well as their employing organizations and the broader social changes that impact the nature of work and careers overall. Therefore, we take a multi-level perspective and address each specific issue by synthesizing research, practice, and individual experiences of mid and late career workers.

We now provide a brief overview and introduction to the various sections of this book. Section I includes two chapters through which we provide an introduction and lay the groundwork for the other chapters. In Chapter 2, we provide a detailed review on the evolution of career theory, particularly as it relates to mid and late career workers. We then outline several contemporary career theories, including the boundaryless career, protean career, career and occupational mobility and embeddedness model, kaleidoscope career model, and the lifespan developmental career model. We also provide informative case study examples from the individuals we interviewed to illustrate how these various career models play out in the careers of individuals in their mid and late career. We conclude Chapter 2 with an agenda for future research on career models that would be particularly important for mid and late career workers.

In Chapter 3, we focus on the changing nature of work, workers, the workforce, and organizations. We detail how jobs in the 21st century have become less physically demanding, while becoming more cognitively and interpersonally demanding, and the implications of these changes for mid and late career workers. These job level changes highlight the shift in focus from individual level knowledge, skills, and abilities (KSAs) to broader meta-competencies such as emotional intelligence and adaptability. We also highlight how work today is more team based, often virtual (technology driven) so as more individuals telecommute and need to coordinate with colleagues in different regions of their country and often from around the world. Next, we review in detail the changing nature of workers in terms of both demographic and other forms of diversity, and evolving family contexts (e.g., dual career couples, child and elder care demands, single working parent households). The implications of increasing education levels of workers, as well as the shift in the implicit psychological contract between employee and employer from a long term relational contract to a short term transactional contact are also discussed.

Next, we move beyond the individual level to examine broader workforce transformations impacting careers. For example, we focus on the shifting trend to an older workforce as the baby boomers move through mid and late career. We also look at how workers in their late career are choosing to extend their careers through self-employment instead of retirement. The changing psychological contract also has implications at the broader workforce level. We then discuss how the prominent organizational level changes such as globalization, rampant downsizings, as well as the shift from a manufacturing based to a service and knowledge based economy, have important implications for those in their mid and late career. Issues of unemployment, underemployment, and career plateauing that are becoming more common with the changing nature of organizations are also detailed. Throughout Chapter 3 we again provide several illustrative case examples through our interviews with workers over 45 which highlight and elucidate how these various factors, at multiple levels of analysis, are playing out for workers in their mid and late career. We again conclude with an agenda for future research on how the multitude of contextual factors at multiple levels plays out in shaping individuals career experiences, particularly at mid and late career.

In Section II, which also consists of three chapters, we look in more detail at individual level factors (Chapter 4), job level factors (Chapter 5), and organizational level factors (Chapter 6) that are impacting workers in their mid and late career. Specifically, in this part of book, we aim at applying three types of analytic perspectives that exist in the literature to synthesize the relevant research findings. First of all, we recognize that career stage differences still exist among early mid career workers, late mid career workers, and late career workers (Shultz & Wang, 2008). Second, we recognize that multiple career-related criteria exist for mid and late career stages (e.g., subjective vs. objective career success, work-life balance, career change, relocation, and retirement decisions). Third, although there are a wide variety of factors that may impact mid and late careers, we recognize that they can largely be organized into three categories: individual-level factors, job-level factors, and organizational-level factors. This categorization helps us to better understand the common theoretical mechanisms behind the effects of these factors. In Chapter 4, we review both individual dispositions and individual attributes. Although both dispositions and attributes denote individual differences, dispositions are usually viewed as being stable and relatively free from environmental influence (Mischel & Shoda, 1995), whereas attributes may change rather easily over time and across different situations (Barnes-Farrell, 2003). In particular, we review cognitive ability, cognitive aging, and personality factors as important individual dispositions that may impact mid and late careers. Here, in addition to summarizing previous literature on cognitive ability and aging, we are among the first to explicitly link specific personality traits, such as core self-evaluations, extraversion, conscientiousness, openness to experience, and resilience to mid and late career issues. We also review physical health, physical aging, experience and expertise, and age-related motivation as important individual attributes that may impact mid and late careers. Drawing on the Socioemotional Selectivity Theory (SST), we particularly emphasize the unique role of age-related motivation in terms of work-related learning and emotional self-regulation. We end the chapter by noting that individual dispositions are often viewed as distal factors in theoretical models focusing on career issues. As such, we suggest future research examining individual attributes as mediators (or proximal factors) that link individual dispositions to mid and late career outcomes.

In Chapter 5, we discuss job-level factors that may impact mid and late careers. In particular, we apply two perspectives to organizing our discussion. The first perspective focuses on examining how job patterns influence one's mid and late careers. In other words, we are interested in understanding whether features of job patterns, such as the frequency of employment, the duration of employment, and the types of employment, would influence one's mid and late career. To facilitate this analysis, we use the notion of "job cycles" that are analogues to "career cycles" advanced by Hall (2002) to characterize one's job history. Following this notion, we analyze different types and features of job cycles and illustrate how they may influence mid and late careers, as well as how these cycles may themselves manifest in one's mid and late career stages. The second perspective we rely on to discuss job-level factors is based on theories of job design. Here, we mainly focus on delineating the job factors specified by job characteristics theory, the sociotechnical systems theory, as well as the contextual factors at the job-level. Our discussion of this perspective also explores the implication of the recent advancements in relational job design to the mid and later career stages. We end the chapter with several future research directions, such as calling for more explicit research on the independent and joint impact of various job cycle factors on mid and late career workers, applying various job characteristics models and study how their stated components work together, exploring how Selective Optimization with Compensation (SOC) strategies may best be implemented in the job cycles and job characteristics models we discussed, as well as examining the impact of work team structures on mid and late career workers.

In Chapter 6, we review the important organizational-level factors that may impact mid and late careers to address the fact that most people's career experiences are linked to one or multiple organizations. We also applied two perspectives in this chapter to organizing our discussion. The first perspective is built upon the notion of employee-organization relationship (EOR). We recognize that workers in mid and late careers may expect different types of obligations from the organization compared to workers in their early careers and may use their perception of EOR to inform mid and late career-related decisions. As such, we first discuss the general theoretical framework of EOR and then the details regarding how EOR may be linked to important mid and late career-related decisions. In this discussion, we review empirical evidence that links two EOR indicators, perceived organizational support (POS) and organizational commitment, to career-related decisions.

The second perspective we rely on to identify organizational-level factors that may impact mid and late careers is the strategic perspective of human resource management (HRM). We recognize that an organization's HR practice often entails financial and motivational consequences and is likely to trigger the sense making process for its employees. Specifically, we first review the concept and relevance of strategic HRM to mid and late career workers. We then discuss how different HR practices may influence mid and late career workers' financial situation, knowledge transferring activities, motivation and performance, and eventually their retention and recruitment. We end Chapter 6 by calling attention to several future research directions. Specifically, we argue that it is important to connect the EOR perspective and strategic HRM perspective by examining a meditation model, where *the desirable retirement-related HR practices and policies are likely to increase the perceived quality of the EOR, which, in turn, will align employees' retirement decision with organizations' strategic goals for the workforce.*

In Section III of the book, we explore a variety of applied issues which address the challenges and opportunities for mid and late career workers in terms of career renewal (Chapter 7), performance management (Chapter 8), training, development and mentoring (Chapter 9), work and nonwork issues that individuals in their mid and late career confront (Chapter 10), and the transition later career workers make to retirement (Chapter 11). In Chapter 7, we begin by discussing how choices individuals made in their 20s are reexamined and often result in actions that individuals take to change their career to align their work with their talents in order to find meaning in their work. We discuss how career renewal for mid and late career workers is often associated with taking positions that are less stressful and demanding in order to engage in work that they find more meaningful (even when the change results in making less money and holding positions that have "less prestige"). We also discuss how personal characteristics (i.e., emotional stability) impact the choices individuals make as well as the economic costs associated with career changes (i.e., reduced pension, lower pay, changes in benefits). We also explore the skills (technology and interpersonal) that facilitate individuals' ability to make successful career changes. We end the chapter with a detailed discussion of the importance of self-understanding (i.e., knowing one's talents) and finding meaning in one's work and the value such work brings to the people and the communities individual's serve as an important source of renewal for those individuals in their mid and late career. We end the chapter with proposed areas of future research to facilitate ongoing career renewal by exploring the importance of ongoing learning and development, having meaningful work, and being fully engaged (finding flow) for mid and late career workers to facilitate ongoing career renewal.

In Chapter 8, we focus on the performance management process and begin with a general discussion of the significance of the performance management process for both individual and organizational success. We discuss in general some of the issues related to poor implementation of the performance management process and then specifically discuss the importance of the relationship between the manager and the mid and late career worker in order to make the process effective. The quality of that relationship has a significant impact on the performance of the mid and late career worker, especially if the manager is younger than his/her employees. We provide a review of the research on age bias in performance ratings and the impact of biases on mid and late career workers. We provide recommendations on how to design a process to facilitate the performance of mid and late career workers and build a strong relationship between older workers and younger managers to build trust and ensure effective feedback is exchanged. We then present research and recommendations about how to design and implement a performance management process that optimizes the use of mid and late career workers' talents so that they can contribute at the highest levels to their organizations and the customers that they serve. We end the chapter by articulating ideas for future research to be conducted on how to identify the talents of older workers and assign them work that optimizes the use of those talents, to untangle the relationship between age and use of talents at work, and to further explore the nuances of the relationship that unfolds between older workers and their younger managers and how to optimize the effectiveness of these reverse age management reporting relationships.

In Chapter 9, we discuss the importance of training, development, and mentoring for workers in their mid and late careers. We begin the chapter with an overview of training and development systems and the biases that often exist that limit the training and development opportunities for workers over 50. We explore in detail how to design training and development opportunities that are meaningful and engaging for workers in their mid and late careers. We then transition to a detailed discussion about the importance of mentoring (both being a mentor and having a mentor) for people over 50. We discuss how, while not all people are cut out to be mentors, building networks of support to help optimize one's career is essential for ongoing development and growth for individuals in their mid and late career. We end the chapter by summarizing the areas of future research which includes: (a) furthering our understanding of how mid and late career workers integrate new knowledge and information, and transfer training content to enhance work performance; (b) age differences impact the mentoring relationship (e.g., do workers over 50 years old need different forms of support from their mentor when compared to individuals in their 20s); and (c) how individuals over 50 have built their networks and use them to facilitate their ongoing training and development.

In Chapter 10, we explore the complex work and nonwork demands that individuals who are 50 and older confront. We focus on how workers over 50 create balance in their work and nonwork roles and address the challenges posed by role overload and conflict. We discuss in detail the Cornell Couples and Career Study (Moen, 2003) and the implications of the research for mid and late career workers. We also discuss the important ways in which the "meaning of success" evolves for workers in their 50s compared to the definitions of success those same workers held when they were in their 20s. Then, we discuss the coping strategies that mid and late career workers use to address work nonwork conflicts. Finally, we discuss the approaches organizational leaders can use and policies they can implement to reduce the conflict between work and nonwork needs for individuals over 50. We end the chapter with recommended future research directions to expand our understanding of the unique challenges that individuals over 50 face as they seek to optimize the balance between work and nonwork demands.

In Chapter 11 we shift our focus to the transition later career workers make to retirement. Within this chapter we begin by defining what retirement is and how it is becoming increasingly difficult to have a single definition of retirement. We also discuss the various definitions of retirement currently being used and explicate the rapidly changing nature of retirement. The key question to ask has evolved from simply *when* to retire and has now also increasingly become *how* to retire and *what* to retire to. The process model of retirement from Wang and Shultz (2010) is discussed and detailed. We examine how retirement starts with a pre-retirement planning phase, moves to the retirement decision making phase, and finishes with a post-retirement adjustment phase. This temporal sequence of events unfolds amidst a wide variety of context factors at the individual (e.g., attitudes toward retirement, personality characteristics), job and organizational factors (e.g., employment history, career attachment), family factors (e.g., spousal support, marital quality), and socio-economic factors (e.g., social norms about retirement, current economic trends). We next discuss how the context for retirement in many countries is changing with a shift from "pro-retirement" to "pro-work" and the extension of careers with bridge employment and other late career options. The various major theories of retirement, including rational choice theory, role theory, continuity theory, image theory, the theory of planned behavior, and the life course perspective are laid out and the basic premises are discussed. Finally, as with all the other chapters, we conclude with an agenda for future research on retirement, with a particular emphasis on how retirement is no longer synonymous with the end of one's career.

Finally, Section IV consists of a single chapter (Chapter 12) where we summarize common themes that need to be considered to fully comprehend the experience of mid and late career workers. We do this by introducing a resource-based model of mid and late career development and adjustment. In addition, we also provide a synthesis of the chapters, showing areas where we have made significant progress, and defining areas which need further exploration, including those areas that are not likely to be resolved anytime soon. We also discuss the key implications for older workers, policy makers, organizational decision makers, and society more broadly.

Chapter 2

The Evolution of Career Theory

There is ample theory and research on how young individuals make the transition from school to work and the establishment phase of their careers. On the other hand, there is much less theory and research on the middle and late stages of workers' careers. However, it is clear from past research (cf. Feldman, 2002a) that experiences early in one's life and career affect mid and late career development. Thus, while the major focus of this chapter will be on career theories most relevant to the study of mid and late career, we must look more broadly at how career theory has evolved over time in order to understand its implications for those currently in their mid to late career stages.

The Evolution of Career Theories

Theories on careers were scarce before the Industrial Revolution of the late 1800s as most men followed their father's occupational path (e.g., in agriculture or trades), and the majority of women became mothers and homemakers (Baruch, 2008). Thus, the initial research and theorizing on career issues in the organizational and social sciences can be traced back to the late 1800s when organizational theorists (e.g., Weber) looked at promotional ladders and early psychologists (e.g., Binet, Galton) looked at individual differences in predicting school and work achievement (Feldman, 2002a). At about the same time that *Fortune* magazine writer William Whyte (1956, 2002) was discussing the "organization man" back in the 1950s, the study of careers as a distinct discipline began in earnest when educational and counseling psychologists (e.g., Super, Holland) began to study vocational preferences and instituted the use of interest assessment in career development and counseling. In the last 60 years, scholars from a wide variety of disciplines, including human development, psychology, sociology, and the organizational sciences have examined a wide assortment of both career development and career management issues.

However, much of what was proposed from the 1950s through the 1980s may no longer be germane to the study of careers, as both the organizational and individual contexts for careers have changed dramatically in the last several decades. For example, the organizational context has been permanently and inextricably altered by increased globalization; greater use of part-time, temporary, and contract workers; outsourcing and off-shoring of many job functions; rapid changes in technology advancements; and increased gender, racial, ethnic, and age diversity in the workplace (Sullivan & Baruch, 2009). In addition, the individual context of work careers has also transformed considerably in the last quarter century. For example, individuals are living longer, starting families later in life, experiencing both more dual career and single parent households, and increased eldercare demands (Cascio, 2007). Thus, the amalgamation of changing organizational and individual contexts for the enactment of careers over time has made many of the stage-based career models from the mid to late 20th century seem archaic. In fact, Moen (2005) has even come to label attitudes associated with these now outdated models as the "Career Mystic." We will provide much more detail on the changing trends in work and the workforce in the next chapter. However, for now we review and summarize several more contemporary career theories and models that are particularly relevant for studying and analyzing mid and late career issues given the changing organizational and individual contexts of the 21st century.

The Evolution of Career Theories with Respect to Mid and Late Careers

Sterns and his colleagues (e.g., Sterns & Huyck, 2001; Sterns & Kaplan, 2003; Sterns & Sterns, 2005; Sterns & Subich, 2002) have noted in several of their writings that career theory has evolved dramatically over the last century from initially ignoring mid and late career workers, to focusing on middle-aged and older workers only maintaining or exiting their careers, to more recently having a much greater appreciation with regard to the potential for continued growth at mid and late career (see Table 2.1 for a summary of

TABLE 2.1 The Evolution of Career Theory Relevant to Mid and Late Careers

Historical Period	Treatment of Midlife and Older Workers	Example Theories (and Authors)
Early 1900s	• Essentially ignored mid and late career issues	
Mid 1900s	• Saw mid career as a time of maintenance and late career as a time of decline	Life-Span, Life-Space Approach (Super)
Late 1900s	• Began to see potential for continued growth in mid and late career	
2000 to present	• Fundamental redefinition of what constitutes a "career"	Boundaryless Career (Arthur) Protean Career (Hall) Developmental Model (Feldman, Sterns) Bridge Employment (Wang, Feldman, Shultz)

this evolutionary process). The initial career models from the early 20th century focused exclusively on career exploration, entry, and establishment, while mid and late career workers were essentially ignored.

By the middle of the 20th century, theorists such as Super (1957) had proposed a fixed set of age-graded career stages that most workers were said to follow. For example, in Super's model the five stages included growth (ages 0–14), exploration (ages 15–24), establishment (ages 25–44), maintenance (ages 45–65), and decline (ages 65+) stages. Thus, mid career workers were mostly in the maintenance phase, moving predictably toward decline. However, it should be noted that Super (1980) later extended his earlier stage theory to acknowledge that the five stages may occur at different times in individuals' lives and may in fact occur several times throughout one's life as individuals change careers or what he referred to as micro-cycles (Shultz & Wang, 2008). Thus, it appears Super was foretelling some of the changes that have occurred more recently in the theorizing about the nature of careers over the last few decades, which we discuss in the next section.

Schein (1990) proposed a three-stage model of socialization, performance, and obsolescence versus development of new skills. Thus, mid and late career workers were essentially relegated to working merely to maintain their career until they eventually became obsolete to the point of decline and disengagement in the form of retirement. Younger workers, on the other hand, were said to be actively searching for an appropriate fit (sometimes referred to P-V fit, or Person-Vocation fit) during the exploration stage. Once this fit was found, they moved their way up the corporate career ladder during the socialization and performance stages.

Other career models from the mid to late 20th century also focused on establishing how well workers fit within a given organization (Person-Organization fit, P-O fit) or career path (P-V fit). For example, Holland (1985) wrote about the career congruence of workers. He talked about six finite work environments: realistic, investigative, artistic, social, enterprising, and conventional (his well-known RIASEC model). His, and similar theorists', major contention was that to be successful in one's career there needed to be a match between one's primary personality and motives, and one of the primary RIASEC work environments. So, for example, someone who is investigative by nature would fit best in a career that required investigative talents and skills (e.g., scientist). While Holland's work focused primarily on career selection by young adults, it was implicitly assumed that middle-aged and older workers would only find happiness and contentment at work when their own personalities and values were properly matched with the corresponding work environment.

The 1970s represented a time of transition, when authors such as Sheehy (1976), Valliant (1977), Gould (1978), and Levinson et al. (1978) began to question whether mid and late careers were simply a time to maintain the status quo. These authors helped to popularize the idea that midlife can in fact be a time of considerable transition and thus they helped to reshape both researchers' and societies' view of midlife career issues (Shultz & Wang, 2008). In addition, they also began to question the validity of existing models, based predominantly on the careers of White men, for explaining the career development of women and minorities, who have traditionally experienced very different career patterns from White men.

Mid and Late Career Models for the 21st Century

More recent career models that have evolved over the last quarter century (e.g., the protean career model, the boundaryless career model, career mobility and stability model, the kaleidoscope career model, and the lifespan developmental model) have a much greater appreciation for the continued potential for growth and renewal of workers in their mid to late careers. These models also mark a clear move away from the traditional linear career progression (i.e., organizational careers), recognizing that most workers' careers, particularly today, do not follow a lockstep, linear, and age-graded path that is predominantly dictated by the organization one works for. Instead, these models acknowledge extensive individual differences in aging, which impact mid and late career workers. In addition, there is a greater acknowledgement in more recent career models of the need to look at both subjective career factors (e.g., career satisfaction), as well as objective career factors (e.g., salary growth or promotional patterns) when examining the concept of career success.

CASE STUDY

In a recent interview with Lupe, a 68-year-old Hispanic female and mother of seven children, it was clear that her career did not follow the linear, lockstep, age-graded path predicted by many of the earlier career models discussed above. Lupe began her professional career in her mid 30s, after her children were in school full time. She finished her undergraduate degree in the medical field and worked in a doctor's office until retiring for the first time at age 53. Within a year however, Lupe was back working in a different doctor's office in a similar role. She then retired a second time at age 60, only to again find another job within a year, this time as a receptionist at public sector agency. She is now planning to retire a third (and she says final time) within a few months after conducting the interview.

The lifespan developmental model in particular puts forth the idea that individuals are influenced by a wide variety of factors, including biological and environmental influences that affect physical and cognitive aging, historical and generational events such as wars and economic recessions/depressions, as well as an assortment of unique individual factors and events that interact to determine an individual's unique career progression (we discuss these factors in detail in Chapter 5). Individuals are seen as beginning with different potentials in various characteristics and progressing at differing rates in their development based on a unique set of life circumstances. Thus, it is not surprising that workers who are the same age may be at vastly different points in their respective careers.

CASE STUDY

Clarice, a 59-year-old African American female, had recently decided to accept an offer of early retirement. Clarice had served as a secretary (23 years) and help desk technician (8 years) for over 30 years with the same company. This public sector agency was offering a "one time only" early retirement incentive offer to workers over age 55 with 20 or more years of service. While Clarice had anticipated working at least another three to five years, she had decided to make her part-time, side job as an Internet travel consult full time. She is looking forward to the decreased work hours overall and the increased flexibility in scheduling her time. Yet, Clarice does not anticipate fully retiring until her younger husband retires in at least eight to 10 more years.

Another important facet of the contemporary career models is an acknowledgment of a changing psychological contract between employees and their employers (Rousseau, 1995). Traditionally, the psychological contract between employees and employers was that if the worker is loyal to the company, the company will be loyal to the worker. However, with the structural changes to the economy starting the 1980s (e.g., mass layoffs, downsizings, and the use of more contingent workers), the psychological contract has evolved to where employers are expected to provide challenging work and developmental opportunities to their employees, while employees are expected to provide their full effort and attention to their current tasks. Nonetheless, the employee should not expect, nor the employer offer, any sense of a long-term loyalty or commitment to each other that was often implicit in the psychological career contract of the 20th century. Namely, all work is becoming like the free agency market in sports, where both employees and employers should be searching for the "best deals" they can get (Cappelli, 1999). However, as Zeitz, Blau, and Fertig (2009) recently noted, the playing field is clearly not the same for different types of workers (e.g., blue collar vs. white collar). Namely, well-educated, white collar workers are the superstars of the free agency market and have much more leverage in negotiating what their psychological career contract will look like. Meanwhile, most blue collar workers' psychological career contract is heavily dependent on the whims of organizations for which they work.

Next, we briefly summarize several contemporary career models and theories that have been proposed over the last few decades that are particularly relevant for workers in their mid and late careers. While we do not provide an exhaustive list of models (e.g., see also Peiprel & Baruch's, 1997, post-corporate career model) nor a meticulous review of each model, we do discuss and highlight some of the key defining features, with a particular eye toward how these models and theories have the potential to impact theorizing, research, and professional practice in the area of mid and late careers. We begin by discussing two of the most influential contemporary career models according to Sullivan and Baruch (2009), the boundaryless career model and the protean career model.

The Boundaryless Career Model

Arthur and Rousseau (1996) note that "The boundaryless career does not characterize any single career form, but, rather, a range of possible forms that defies traditional employment assumptions" (p. 3). By "traditional employment assumptions," Arthur and Rousseau were talking about how up until the mid 1980s most individuals' careers were "bounded" by the organization that they worked in. That is, their careers were largely controlled and directed by their paternalist employer. Terms such as "fast track," "promotion ladders," and "plateauing" were all common place, and well understood, up until the mid 1980s. Today, these terms have much less relevance for how many workers' careers unfold and develop over time. Instead, according to Arthur and Rousseau, we see a boundaryless set of potential paths that individuals can take as they themselves create and play out their careers.

However, while Arthur and Rousseau's (1996) edited text on the boundaryless career model has received extensive attention in the theoretical and research literature on careers (e.g., cited well over 700 times according to Google Scholar), recently, Zeitz et al. (2009) questioned whether the pendulum may have swung too far from the organization driven career to the individual driven career. That is, Zeitz et al. suggest the terms *boundary crossing* or *boundary converging* may be better metaphors for the changing nature of careers. In particular, the near exclusive focus on individual resources, particularly in professional level career paths, to the exclusion of needed institutional resources eliminates a large portion of the working population who do not have access to such needed career resources.

Sullivan and Arthur (2006) recently helped to solidify the boundaryless career concept by delineating the interdependence between physical (or objective) career changes and psychological (or subjective) career changes. A basic premise of the boundaryless career is the lack of boundaries evident in present day careers. Arthur and Rousseau (1996) emphasized that the boundaryless career represents the independence from traditional career arrangements, where individual's perceptions of the boundaries regarding professional networks, organizations, information, and family life are paramount. In addition, individuals can transcend not only organizational boundaries, but also cultural and occupational boundaries. However, most researchers have focused primarily on physical boundary spanning (i.e., transitioning across boundaries represented in jobs, employers, and industries), while a few others have emphasized psychological boundary spanning (i.e., the perception of the capacity to make such transitions). Sullivan and Arthur, conversely, emphasize the need to examine the interdependence between the two dimensions.

Sullivan and Arthur (2006) present a model of the boundaryless career that varies along two primary dimensions. The first dimension represents physical mobility, while the second represents psychological mobility. While Sullivan and Arthur acknowledge that there is a continuum of boundarylessness in terms of careers, they discuss four "pure types" of careers depending on whether the individual is high or low on the two dimensions. The first quadrant is represented by individuals with careers that are low on both the physical and psychological mobility dimensions. Individuals in this quadrant may range from the unskilled worker who sees few alternatives to his current work arrangement, to the highly skilled professional who has high levels of firm-specific knowledge and enjoys the challenge that his current employer provides. In both cases, the individuals are unlikely to perceive boundary spanning opportunities and thus unlikely to subsequently engage in actual boundary crossings.

Quadrant two represents individuals with careers high in physical mobility but low in psychological mobility. For example, individuals who regularly change employers because their spouse receives frequent job transfers or the young adult with experience as a waiter wanting to travel and thus changes employers frequently in order to travel the world. In both cases, these individuals are experiencing high levels of physical mobility; however, the psychological mobility remains the same as they are not seeking additional psychological benefits from their frequent job changes.

In the third quadrant we see individuals who have careers represented by high psychological mobility, but low levels of physical mobility. These individuals sustain high expectations for their employability, but do not necessarily act on these perceptions by changing jobs or employers. For example, a highly skilled professional may continue to develop her skills outside the workplace (e.g., by serving important roles in professional organizations) and be prepared for change if needed, but remains with her employer because of the autonomy the present position provides.

Finally, the fourth quadrant is represented by individuals who have careers where both physical and psychological mobility are high. A wide variety of scenarios can be represented in this quadrant. For example, the consultant who frequently changes employers to gain new experiences and expertise, hoping to one day start her own consulting firm. Alternatively, an individual may decide to "downshift" in order to pursue less demanding work and travel schedules, but that allows more time for renewal and personal reflection. As another example, individuals described as compulsive learners may decide to change jobs frequently in order to gain new knowledge and skills that will provide even more psychological and physical mobility in the future. Thus, it is clear, within each quadrant there are varying levels of psychological and physical mobility which may result in positive, neutral, and/or negative long-term outcomes for individuals with regard to their ultimate career success. As a result, the fourth quadrant may not always be the most desirable quadrant to strive for.

Sullivan and Arthur (2006) also provide several propositions for future research based on their model of the boundaryless career. These include, "Those with greater career competencies are more likely to have experienced more, and have more opportunities for, psychological and physical mobility than those with lower career competencies" (p. 25). These "career competencies" can be in the form of motivation and identity (knowing why), skill and expertise (knowing how), as well as relationships and reputations (knowing whom). In addition, they propose that "Individuals, through enhancing career competencies, are more likely to increase their opportunities for either psychological or physical mobility than to increase both simultaneously" (p. 25). Sullivan and Arthur note that changes in psychological and physical mobility often occurs sequentially rather than simultaneously. For example, in order for career changes (physical mobility) to be seen as career enhancing, individuals would need to establish career competencies that increase psychological mobility, prior to engaging in physical mobility.

A third proposition presented by Sullivan and Arthur (2006) is that "Men are more likely to have greater opportunities for physical mobility whereas women are more likely to have greater opportunities for psychological mobility" (p. 26). They support this proposition by noting differential cultural gender roles and expectations, as well as the gender based experiences that men and women have in the workplace (e.g., sexual harassment and discrimination, opportunities for mentoring). Their fourth proposition stated, "People in individualistic cultures are more likely to change work groups or organizations, and to exhibit physical mobility; in contrast, individuals in collectivist cultures are more likely to stay in their work groups or organizations and to exhibit psychological mobility" (p. 26). This makes sense given individualistic cultures' emphasis on personal goals, social networking, and promotion, while the emphasis in collectivist cultures is on group goals and job security. Their fifth, and final, proposition states that "People with individual orientations are more likely to recognize opportunities for and exhibit physical mobility; in contrast, individuals with collectivist orientations are more likely to recognize opportunities for and exhibit psychological mobility" (p. 26). Thus, even within certain cultures, individuals will have distinct individual orientations, thus it is important to look not only at the cultural level, in terms of the individualistic-collectivism continuum, but also at the individual differences level.

According to a recent review of the career literature by Sullivan and Baruch (2009), thinking on the boundaryless career has also permeated related areas to career research including mentoring, plateauing, work/nonwork conflict, retirement transitions, and expatriate assignments. That is, the shift from the traditional, linear, paternalistic career to the more individualized, boundaryless career has affected many other areas of study from when and how workers decide to retire to our integration of work and family roles. Thus, the concept of the boundaryless career has broad potential implications for the organizational and social sciences. However, more empirical work is needed in order to test and confirm (or disconfirm) the propositions presented by Sullivan and Arthur (2006).

The Protean Career Model

Hall (2004) traces the concept of the protean career back to his 1976 text, *Careers in Organizations*. However, as Sullivan and Baruch (2009) note, the protean career concept didn't firmly take hold in the literature until Hall's (1996b) book *The Career Is Dead— Long Live the Career* and his *Academy of Management Executive* article in the same year (Hall, 1996a). The concept of the protean career (based on the Greek god Proteus who was capable of assuming many forms) was envisioned to address many of the organizational and contextual changes we briefly mentioned earlier in this chapter, and will discuss in much more detail in the next chapter. Specifically, careers of today need to be adaptable, versatile, and flexible to the ever changing context in which they are enacted. They are individually driven by one's personal values rather than organizational rewards, and they focus on serving the "whole person" (Hall, 2004). In addition, career satisfaction is more a matter of how satisfied you feel about your work and life, not how much you make or the number of promotions you have obtained. The key attitudes focus on work satisfaction and professional commitment, rather than organizational commitment, with core values focused on freedom and growth, as opposed to promotional ladders (see Table 1 in Hall, 2004, for a direct comparison of the protean and traditional career models). With the increased emphasis on professional commitment, relational components such as career networks and mentoring (which we discuss in more detail in Chapter 9) are becoming more important for individuals looking to enact a protean career (Higgins, 2001).

Briscoe and Hall (2006) note that there are four primary categories of career orientation according to the protean career model. These four categories are based on the two orientations of self-directedness and values driven. Thus, an individual who is neither self-directed nor values driven in terms of a career orientation is labeled as "dependent." Meanwhile, a person who is not values driven, but is self-directed in terms of career management would be labeled as "reactive." Conversely, someone who is values driven, but not self-directed would be identified as "rigid." In both previous cases, these individuals will have a difficult time shaping their own careers, the former due to a lack of perspective, and latter due to a lack of adaptability. Finally, those individuals with a protean or transformational career orientation are both values driven in terms of defining their career priorities and identity, and also self-directed, in terms of being adaptable to changing environmental demands. Thus, the ideal of the protean career orientation is someone who is both values driven and self-directed.

Hall and Mirvis (1995) took the concept of psychological contracts, discussed earlier, a step further by discussing the concept of career contracts. Specifically, they delineate the "new career contract" that began to evolve in the 1980s. Namely, the shift from an organizationally driven career to the employee driven career (i.e., the protean career model). The protean career model is particularly relevant to mid and late career workers as the two meta-competencies (i.e., skills for learning how to learn) that Hall and Mirvis state are required to survive under the new career contract, namely adaptability and identity growth (i.e., self-reflection and self-learning), may be more difficult for older workers to acquire and develop. That is, older workers who spent a large part of their career developing a single set of skills and an organizational based identity, may find it difficult to suddenly have to demonstrate adaptability and engage in continuous learning of new skills. Hall (2004) notes that individuals need to possess both of these meta-competencies in order to fully enact the protean career, in that just having adaptability can lead to one being a chameleon, while just being self-aware can lead to paralysis by analysis (i.e., avoidance behaviors).

Hall and Mirvis (1995) note that the psychological contract between employees and their employer has shifted from a relational contract, where long-term relationships develop and hopefully flourish, to more transactional contracts, where short-term transactions and current performance are key. As a result, mid and late career workers must develop the meta-skills noted above through a process of "mid career routine busting." That is, instead of the traditional one-life one-career notion where the relational psychological contract allows for temporary imbalances to balance out over time, careers will consist of a lifelong series of learning stages (or what Hall and Mirvis call "mini-stages" of exploration-trial-mastery-exit) using much shorter transactional psychological contracts that will be necessary for true career development to occur at mid life and beyond. On the other hand, Hall and Mirvis argue that the increased flexibility and autonomy found in the protean career model may well suit older workers just fine, given their likely reduced external constraints (e.g., the need to pay for children's education) and internal drives (e.g., the desire to become a senior level executive) often begin to ebb as they progress through mid career and into their late career.

In addition, within the protean career the "career space" begins to broaden as one progresses through mid and late career to include both work and nonwork roles. For example, career fulfillment and satisfaction may be found more in mentoring roles outside one's own organization than in one's current work role. Thus, how individuals define career success and satisfaction evolves as one progresses through their career. In addition, it will be more appropriate in the 21st century to discuss one's career age rather than using chronological age as a proxy for career stage. Accordingly, being in one's career for say 10 to 15 years would represent mid career rather than simply assuming someone in their 40s would necessarily be in their mid career.

Combining the Boundaryless and Protean Career Models

Briscoe and Hall (2006) delineate, clarify, and then combine the various dimensions of both the boundaryless career and protean career models in order to identify eight likely career profiles. They use Sullivan and Arthur's (2006) physical and psychological mobility dimensions for the boundaryless career model (i.e., emphasizing a sense of opportunity) and then examine the protean career model in terms of the degree of self-directed and values driven career orientation an individual demonstrates as we discussed earlier (i.e., emphasizing a sense of agency). The protean career orientation is similar to an attitude, thus it has a cognitive, evaluative, and behavioral component. However, the protean career model does not imply a particular behavior (e.g., changing jobs), as in the boundaryless career model, but rather a mindset that focuses on making career decisions based on one's sense of self-directedness and personal values.

Combining the various orientations identified by Briscoe and Hall (2006) for the boundaryless and protean career models results in 16 possible combinations. However, some of the combinations are illogical or highly unlikely (e.g., an individual who is highly values driven and self-directed but lacks psychological mobility). Thus, Briscoe and Hall combine the various categories in the boundaryless and protean career development models to identify eight "likely" career profiles. First is the "Trapped" or "Lost" individual who is low on all four dimensions (self-directed, values driven, psychological mobility, and physical mobility). These individuals are unable to react quickly to opportunities and need to clarify their priorities and develop their career management skills. At the other end of the continuum are the "Protean Career Architects," who are high on all four dimensions and are thus able to leverage their capabilities into meaningful career management. In between these two extremes are the "Fortressed" (low on self-directed, psychological, and physical mobility, but high on values driven), the "Wanderer" (low on self-directed, values driven, and psychological mobility, but high on physical mobility), the "Idealist" (low on self-directed and physical mobility, but high on values driven and psychological mobility), "Organization man/women" (low on values driven and physical mobility, but high on self-directed and psychological mobility), "Solid Citizen" (low on physical mobility, but high on the other three dimensions), and "Hired Gun/Hired Hand" (low on values driven, but high on the other three dimensions). Briscoe and Hall go on to discuss in detail the career development and personal challenges that individuals in each of these career profiles is likely to face.

While numerous books and theoretical articles (including an entire special issues in 2006 of the *Journal of Vocational Behavior* and in 2010 for the *Journal of Organizational Behavior*) have been dedicated to the boundaryless and/or protean career models, one of the major complaints with regard to these contemporary career models is that, until recently, there were no measures that allowed for empirical tests of these models. However, Briscoe, Hall, and Frautschy DeMuth (2006) recently developed and validated multiple measures for each of the two models. For the boundaryless career model, they developed two scales (totaling 13 items), one measuring boundaryless mindset, and the other organizational mobility preference. For the protean career model, the two scales (totaling 14 items) were labeled self-directed career management and values-driven predisposition.

Based on three empirical studies using the scales, Briscoe et al. (2006) found strong support for the factor structure of the four separate scales, as well as compelling reliability evidence. In the third study, the authors also found convincing convergent validity evidence for their scales. Specifically, a strong positive correlation was found between self-directed career management and boundaryless mindset, with proactive personality tendencies. In addition, the Big Five personality dimension of openness to new experiences was correlated with boundaryless mindset, as well as with self-directed career management, values-driven perspective, and organizational mobility. Finally, the authors found that the number of employers per year and job changes did not correlate with any of the measures developed. Thus, while previous researchers have used frequent job changes as a proxy for measuring boundarylessness, this does not appear to be the case. This is good news for employers wishing to foster these career attitudes, as they don't need to fear that doing so would encourage some of their best employees to leave. Overall then, strong psychometric evidence and a nomological network of relationships is beginning to emerge for these newly created measures that will provide future researchers wishing to empirically investigate the boundaryless and protean career models with sound tools for doing so. However, more empirical research using these scales to predict relevant outcomes (e.g., career success) is needed.

Segers, Inceoglu, Vloeberghs, Bartram, and Henderickx (2008) examined data on over 13,000 working adults in Europe to match data from their Motivation Questionnaire to the four dimensions of the boundaryless and protean career models. As a result of their analysis, four motivational groups were identified. These included Protean Career Architects (30%), Trapped/Lost (22%), Hired gun/Hired hand (21%), and Curious/Wanderer (27%), similar to Briscoe and Hall's (2006) conceptualization, thus providing empirical support for some of the most recent theorizing with regard to the boundaryless and protean career models.

While the boundaryless and protean career models have added much to contemporary thinking with regard to career development and management, there are still some unknowns with regard to these models. For example, what obstacles are there to successfully implementing these models in practice (e.g., age, gender, and race discrimination; lack of individual competencies; organizational and cultural barriers)? Despite these unknowns, Sullivan and Baruch (2009) note, "The boundaryless career concept offers a foundation for exploring how careers are evolving in today's complex work environment" (p. 1554) and thus serves as a useful framework for studying contemporary careers. In addition, other present day models are also particularly relevant with regard to workers in their mid and late careers stages. Therefore, below we discuss several of these additional modern day models of careers or what Sullivan and Baruch refer to as "the next generation of career concepts" (p. 1554).

Career and Occupational Mobility and Embeddedness Model

Feldman and Ng (Feldman, 2007; Feldman & Ng, 2007; Ng & Feldman, 2007) discuss the concept of career and occupational embeddedness with relation to mid and late careers. Building on the concept to job embeddedness (Mitchell, Holtom, Lee, Sablynski, & Erez, 2001), Feldman and Ng discuss how individuals in their mid and late career become entrenched in a particular career or occupational path due to *fit* (i.e., the match between personal and occupational characteristics), *links* (i.e., the extent of social and personal ties individuals have within their occupation), and *sacrifices* (i.e., the totality of losses one would incur if they left their occupation or career). In addition, one's mobility is dependent on both *motivation* to change careers and *ability* to change careers. Thus, career change in mid and late career is a function of internal forces as well as external forces related to fit, links, and sacrifices. Specifically, Feldman (2007) hypothesizes that career mobility at older ages is a function of (1) older workers' social and professional networks, (2) their degree of fit with their present career path, (3) the sacrifices that would be incurred with leaving their current career path, and (4) the obstacles to gaining entry into a new career path.

Importantly, Feldman (2007) distinguished related concepts such as job change, career change, organizational change, and bridge employment in mid and late career workers. For example, job change refers to staying in the same career field within the same employer (e.g., moving from one department to another). Career change, however, involves entering a new occupation requiring fundamentally different skills and daily routines, as well as a different work environment. Changing organizations, however, may or may not involve a career change. For example, being a professor in the same discipline at one college versus another would normally not be considered a career change. However, moving from being a consultant to being a professor would involve a career change assuming there was also a change in the daily routine, work environment, and requisite skill set.

For mid and late career workers, the additional option of bridge employment is possible. Bridge employment involves leaving a career job and reducing the accompanying psychological commitment to work through temporary or part-time work in the same or different field, which allows one to eventually bridge to full-time retirement (Shultz, 2003). The key to designating this transition as bridge employment is the clear transition being made toward retirement at the end of one's career. Thus, while career change (and conversely embeddedness) is related to similar concepts such as job and organizational change, as well as bridge employment, it can also be clearly distinguished from these related concepts.

CASE STUDY

A recent interview with Hiro, a 60-year-old Asian American dentist, showed that during his first five years out of dental school (from ages 28 to 33) he worked for a practicing dentist in a private dental office performing dental procedures. However, at age 34 he transitioned to work for a community mental health foundation providing dental care to community patients. While this would constitute a job and organization change, it was not much of a career change, as he was still performing the same basic patient dental care as he did previously in the private dental practice. Then, at age 45, Hiro started his own private practice. This would again represent a job and organization change, but also a bit of a career change in that he was now also a small business owner thus necessitating some change in his daily routine, work environment, and requisite skill set. He did still see patients, but his duties were significantly expanded beyond patient care as a small business owner. Finally, at age 57 he sold his private practice and transitioned to a bridge job serving as an administrator in a county level comprehensive medical facility. Thus, as before, this represents a job and organization change, and also a career change in that his daily routine, requisite skills, and work environment have changed; he no longer sees patients on a daily basis. However, because this transition occurred very late in his career, and after what he consider "retiring" from private practice, this most recent transition would also be considered a move to bridge employment. This was also evident by the fact that Hiro viewed this as a job that he was likely to hold for only the next five to 10 years, so there was a clear end in sight for him. He also viewed his current job as less demanding (e.g., he didn't have to work weekends), which is typical of most bridge employment transition jobs, as bridge employment represents the transition phase from late career to full retirement.

Feldman (2007) takes a multilevel approach to career embeddedness by discussing individual, job, and occupational level factors that influence whether mid and late career workers remain with or change career paths. For example, at the individual level, enduring personality traits, such as openness to new experiences and self-efficacy, are likely to strongly influence individuals' motivations to change careers at mid and late career stages. Similarly, poor health and strong finances (i.e., wealth) can also be compelling factors for career change at older ages, as might life circumstances (e.g., the loss of a spouse). In addition, job related factors such as job stress, boredom, or a perceived lack of appreciation may also influence older workers to seek out alternative careers. Of course, organizationally based job related factors such as downsizings or termination (i.e., involuntary factors) might also force mid and late career workers to seek out new occupations and/or careers.

At the occupational level, changes in the work context and skills required for a given occupation over time may also motivate mid and late career workers to seek alternative careers, in that the careers these workers entered some 20 or 30 years ago no longer resembles the career they find themselves in now. Feldman (2007) provides a poignant example of a teacher who entered teaching several decades ago with wild enthusiasm to share knowledge and mentor kids but who must now deal with a work context that includes metal detectors, rampant drug use, and violence in her school, and all the while her creativity is being stifled by state and federal mandates on how and what to teach.

Feldman and Ng (2007) note that occupational embeddedness and mobility may be differentially related to objective career success (e.g., promotions, higher salaries) and subjective career success (e.g., career satisfaction, occupational commitment). Specifically, Feldman and Ng suggest that occupational mobility is much more likely to lead to subjective career success, than objective career success, particularly in the short run, due to the retraining costs and the lost income incurred during that retraining period. Individuals are also more likely to experience higher subjective career success when changing occupations due to the higher affect toward the new career, higher expectations for job satisfaction, which may become a self-fulfilling prophecy, and the cognitive dissonance that may occur to justify leaving the former occupation. Nevertheless, there are a wide variety of factors, at multiple levels (i.e., labor market factors, organizational policies and procedures, work group level factors, personal life factors, and personality and personal style differences) that need to be considered when examining occupational mobility and embeddedness, and their relationship to various measures of objective and subjective career success.

In addition, Ng and Feldman (2007) discuss how the factors that affect occupational embeddedness can change, depending on an individual's career stage. Specifically, in the early or establishment phase of one' career, generalizable occupational skills, as well as the development of social ties within the occupation, will be important to foster occupational embeddedness. However, during the maintenance or middle phase of one's career, accumulation of career attainments, career plateauing, and family status are likely to be more prominent in promoting occupational embeddedness. Finally, during the final or disengagement phase of one's career, leadership roles within the profession and general risk aversion are likely to be the most significant factors influencing occupational embeddedness. These proposed differences by career stage have important implications for both individuals and organizations.

While Feldman (2007) and Feldman and Ng's (2007) introduction of the concept of career or occupational embeddedness is relatively recent, some empirical studies have already begun to examine these concepts. For example, Adams, Webster, and Buyarski (2010) recently described a four part study they carried out in order to develop a measure of occupational embeddedness (i.e., the collection of forces that bind people to their occupation). Their study established the reliability, content validity, as well as predictive, convergent, and divergent validity of their newly developed measure of occupational embeddedness. Specifically, occupational embeddedness was represented by two primary factors: internal (i.e., from within the occupation) and external (e.g., family, community). In addition, the occupational embeddedness scale was negatively correlated with occupational withdrawal intentions, while positively correlated with occupational commitment. However, it was uncorrelated with social desirability. The occupational embeddedness scale also demonstrated incremental validity, beyond occupational commitment, in predicting occupational withdrawal intentions.

In an empirical study of 162 employees in multiple jobs and organizations, Ng and Feldman (2009) found that occupational embeddedness was positively correlated to both task performance and creativity, while being negatively related to counterproductive work behaviors, even after controlling for the effects of organizational embeddedness. In addition, occupational embeddedness was more strongly related to counterproductive work behaviors when negative affect was high, but more strongly related to creativity and organizational citizenship behaviors when positive trait affect was high. In terms of the various components of occupational embeddedness, fit had its strongest relationship with core task performance, while links were most strongly related to creativity and sacrifice had a small positive relationship with organizational citizenship behavior. Thus, it is clear that the three components of occupational embeddedness (fit, links, and sacrifices) have differential relationships with a wide variety of organizationally valued outcomes and thus should be examined individually.

In summary, it is clear that the occupational and career mobility and stability model is one of the first to specifically address the unique issues faced by workers in their mid to late careers. While many of the models discussed in this chapter implicitly address mid and late career issues, the career mobility and stability model is one of the first to explicitly address many of the unique issues that individuals in their mid and late career are likely to confront. Feldman (2007) does this adeptly from multiple levels and perspectives, however, like most of the newer models of career development, more empirical evidence for the proposed relationships is needed in order to implement these models in practice.

The Kaleidoscope Career Model

Mainiero and Sullivan (2005, 2006) began their investigation of mid career issues to study why women were "opting out" of the traditional workforce in larger numbers than men. Based on their research, it was clear that women and men do approach their careers from different perspectives. Women typically focus on relationships when making career decisions, factoring in the needs of children, their spouse, aging parents, friends, as well as coworkers and clients. Men, meanwhile, were more likely to keep their work and non-work lives separate, examining career decisions instead from the perspective of achievement goal orientation. Men's stronger career focus was possible, as it was often the women in their lives who managed the work and family interplay for them. Regardless of these differing perspectives by gender, Mainiero and Sullivan soon realized that both men and women desired something beyond the traditional corporate career. Through a series of five studies (in-depth interviews, focus groups, and three surveys of more than 3,000 working men and women) they found three key parameters or themes, which they refer to as the A, B, Cs of the evolving career landscape, where A stands for Authenticity, B for Balance, and C for Challenge. Specifically, *authenticity* refers to being true to oneself and being who you are, while *balance*, as the name implies, refers to the ability to balance various life roles within one's career. Finally, *challenge* represents the ability to stretch and develop higher level skills and abilities. These three themes serve as the lens through which careers develop, much like the three lens or mirrors of a kaleidoscope work together to create a pattern that is unique as the kaleidoscope is turned. When individual's circumstances change, much like when a kaleidoscope is rotated, the pattern of individual's careers shift in new ways as well. Thus, their ABC Model of Kaleidoscope Careers was born.

The Kaleidoscope Career Model is particularly relevant to mid and late careers as it suggests that, particularly for women, the equilibrium among the three key A, B, C components shifts as individuals move through their career. All three components are present at each stage however one component tends to move to the forefront for a given stage. For example, Mainiero and Sullivan (2005) propose that at early career the Challenge component is the focal issue, with Authenticity and Balance, while still relevant, having lesser importance. However, as individuals move into mid career (and often midlife) Balance becomes the dominant component. Finally, as one approaches late career, Challenge and Balance issues become less prominent, while Authenticity becomes the key driving factor. Thus, how individuals perceive and make career decisions changes as they move through their careers and their life circumstances change.

Sullivan, Forret, Carraher, and Mainiero (2009) recently used the ABC Model of Kaleidoscope Careers to examine generational differences in work attitudes. Surveying more than 900 professionals from across the United States, Sullivan et al. found that members of Generation X reported higher Authenticity and Balance needs than members of the Baby Boom Generation, while no differences were found in the need for Challenge across the two generational cohorts. However, because the research design was cross-sectional, differences across cohorts could be due to a variety of factors, including aging or differences within the cohorts. Thus, more research is needed to determine how the Kaleidoscope Career model my play out different for individuals from different generations.

The Lifespan Developmental Career Model

Feldman (2002a) noted that while stability has been replaced by the need for flexibility in workers' careers, career interests remain remarkably stable over one's life time, and that such interests begin to be formed and shaped very early in one's life. The first few jobs we hold greatly shape our work skills and personal values with regard to work. However, there are strong intra-individual differences in how such experiences play out over the course of one's career. Thus, while on the surface, today's careers may appear to be somewhat haphazard, or even random, they are clearly driven by our unique personal histories, developing skill sets, motivations and interests, and experiences.

While the boundaryless and protean career models focus heavily on the changing career context, the lifespan development career model emphasizes worker skills, career interests, and personal values, as these are the primary building blocks for career entry, successful job performance, creating stability, and advancing in one's career. In addition, the lifespan development model calls attention to the need to examine careers as they unfold over time. Thus, Feldman (2002a) notes that "Careers, then, are neither static nor self-encapsulating in nature. Rather, they evolve over time and are influenced by both past events and future aspirations" (p. 7). The lifespan development model also emphasizes the need to look at both career stage and life stage at the same time. Thus, someone in their 50s who may be beginning a new career may have a very different starting point and future aspirations than someone starting that same career in their 20s. This model also emphasizes the various levels of effects from individual differences in skills, motives, and traits, to family influences, to organizational influences, to broader macro level factors, such as the economy, which may impact the desirability of various career options.

Agenda for Future Research on Mid and Late Careers

Several authors have proposed agendas for future research on careers. For example, Feldman (2002b) proposes the need for more midrange theories with regard to career development. That is, theories that are neither too broad to realistically be testable, nor so population or context specific as to be non-generalizable. Feldman also emphasizes the need to look at both stability and change in individual's careers. For example, he notes the need to examine why some people don't change careers, organizations, or jobs even when rationally it would make sense for them to do so. Also, much more work has been conducted on the career interests that lead to the formation and development of careers, and subsequent person-environment fit, than on the work skills that would lead to successful fit.

Feldman (2002b) also notes several important empirical and research design issues that need to be addressed in future research on careers. For example, issues around sampling bias (e.g., most past research was based on White, middle-class men holding managerial positions) can affect not only the generalizability of obtained results, but also calls into question the legitimacy of the research question being asked or the theory being use. As an example, do blue collar workers think in terms of careers or jobs? Do they think in terms of mentoring or simply having a sympathetic boss? Another empirical issue is the clarification of constructs such as career stage or boundarylessness. Such terms seem to be used in a variety of fashions in various studies.

There is also a need to balance self-report and multi-source data in career research. The vast majority of research is based on self-report data rather than looking at a variety of sources to collect data on individual's careers. Career researchers can also make creative use of archival data to foster more longitudinal research by using it to provide past data on current research subjects, verify current research subjects' past career trajectories, and collect current data on past subjects' career data. In addition, a clear problem exists in career research where a wide variety of internal (e.g., job satisfaction, organizational commitment) and external (e.g., promotions, pay increases) criteria are used to measure career success. While it will be important for future career researchers to look at both objective and subject issues, a bigger concern may well be how the criterion matches up with the theory being used by the researchers.

Finally, Feldman (2002b) also notes the need to look at both one-way and two-way influences in careers. Too often we assume a one-way influence when studying careers, yet it is clear, for example, in the traditional employee fit models that not only do individual characteristics influence person-job or person-organization fit, but that a dual influence process takes place where employees shape the environment they populate. Thus, over time, it becomes a recursive influence of employee and environment. Another cogent example in the career literature is the research on mentoring. Not only does the mentor influence the protégé's career, but the protégé also influences the mentor and work environment. Those who study mentoring research are just beginning to examine these recursive processes (e.g., Olson & Jackson, 2009).

Additionally, Sullivan and Baruch (2009) acknowledge the recent theoretical and empirical work that has been done to move the field of career development beyond the traditional, linear, male-oriented, organizationally based career, to having a greater appreciation for the varying cultural, work, and personal contexts that have emerged in the 21st century. However, they also note the need for common measurement tools to foster future meta-analyses, as well as more investigations of potential gender and cultural differences in how the various models discussed in this chapter play out for individual workers. They also note that most of the research on non-traditional careers has tended to emphasize the positive aspects of this evolution. However, more work is needed on the potential downsides of newer career forms, especially with regard to their potentially differential negative effects for certain individuals.

For example, contingent workers, who make up a growing portion of the workforce, may be stigmatized as "temporary," or more likely to be subject to discrimination or harassment, and less likely to receive the necessary mentoring and/or training to progress in their career. These changing career patterns also have potentially negative effects for employers, who will likely have more difficulty determining appropriate recruitment, socialization, training, and succession planning strategies given the new short-term transactional employee-employer psychological contract. Thus, future research on both the individual and organizational level impact of evolving career patterns is needed.

In addition, Sullivan and Baruch (2009) note that with increased technological abilities, the permeability of borders, where workers from a variety of countries and cultures may be asked to work together, has never been greater. How will employers manage workers from such a wide variety of cultures, with potentially vastly different career motives and needs? Consortium studies with researchers from a wide variety of countries and cultures would be very beneficial to understanding these issues. In addition, we have discussed a wide variety of non-traditional career models in this chapter. However, not everyone is engaging in non-traditional careers. Therefore, we need to continue to consider of a wide variety of potential career options, including traditional career paths, when studying career issues.

Finally, Wang, Adams, Beehr, and Shultz (2009) discuss how bridge employment may be another career stage, beyond late career. Empirical research is needed to investigate if older workers view their engagement in bridge employment as another career stage or simply as a mechanism for making a smoother transition from late career to retirement.

Chapter 3

The Changing Nature of Work, Workers, the Workforce, and Organizations

Research has consistently shown that work is a very important part of people's lives, identity, social relationships, and meaningfulness/contribution to others (Kanungo, 1982). In fact, work is typically rated second only to family in terms of important life-roles (Meaning of Work International Research Team [MOWIRT], 1987). Thus, it is important to understand the nature of work and how it is rapidly changing in the 21st century (Cascio, 2003). In Chapter 2 we discussed the rapid evolution of career theory in recent years, particularly as related to mid and late career. However, more than career theory has changed dramatically in the last several decades. The nature of work, how work is carried out, workers themselves, as well as the workforce as a whole, have all changed radically in the last half century. In addition, the nature and structure of organizations has transformed dramatically in the last few decades. These macro level changes have strong implications for individuals' careers (Gunz, Mayrhofer, & Tolbert, 2011), particularly for those in the mid and late career. Mills et al. (2008) also showed that even broader macro level factors at the societal level are changing career patterns in all countries, but to varying degrees depending on country specific factors such as educational systems, employment related protections (e.g., employment laws), and other welfare related issues. Below we discuss key changes that are occurring at the individual, job, team, and organizational level and their impact on mid and late career workers. In doing so, we set the stage for much of what we will be discussing in the rest of the book with regard to mid and late career issues.

The Changing Nature of Work

Work in the 21st century is increasingly different from what our parents and grand-parents experienced just a generation or two ago. Overall, work has become less physi-cally demanding, but more cognitively and socially demanding. Johnson, Mermin, and Resseger (2007) recently used data from the Occupational Information Network (O*NET) to examine how job demands have changed over more than three and a half decades. As Johnson et al. note,

> O*NET is a comprehensive database of job characteristics produced by the U.S. Department of Labor's Employment and Training Administration and is the only data source on objective job demands. It rates about 800 occupations on more than 200 scales, included required skills, abilities, education and training, knowledge and work styles. O*NET also measures tasks performed and the characteristics of the physical work environment. (p. v)

Johnson et al. (2007) then linked occupational information from the O*NET database with information from the March 1971 and March 2006 Current Population Survey (CPS) in order to describe the current and past distribution of job demands. The CPS collects information on employment, health status, and demographics, including occupa-tion, gender, race, age, and education level from a large, representative sampling of U.S. households. Johnson et al. found that the nature of work has changed dramatically in the last several decades. Jobs have, indeed, become less physically demanding and unsafe working conditions less likely to be unsafe, but jobs are also more cognitively demanding and more psychologically stressful.

Specifically, Johnson et al. (2007) found that (a) Between 1971 and 2006 the share of jobs involving any general physical demands declined from about 57% to 46%; (b) The share of jobs requiring high cognitive abilities and strong interpersonal skills grew from about one-quarter to one-third over the 35-year period (a 35% increase); (c) Surpris-ingly, the shift from physically demanding work to more stressful, cognitively demanding work was actually more pronounced for women than for men; (d) Workers aged 50 and older (those most likely to be in their mid or late career) experienced sharper declines in physically demanding work than did younger people, but steeper increases in stressful, cognitively demanding work; and (e) Occupational job growth trends suggest that the prevalence of job demands are not expected to change dramatically based on projections through 2041.

We laud Johnson et al. (2007) for providing empirical evidence for the often-cited trends that work in the 21st century is indeed becoming less physically demanding and hazardous, but more cognitively and interpersonally demanding, which typically leads to perceptions of higher levels of psychosocial stress. However, it is still unclear at this point *why* the more cognitively and socially demanding work is perceived as more stressful, and, of particular interest to the current discussion, how this may differentially impact those in their mid and late career, compared to workers in their early career.

For example, it could be that those in their mid and late career will need to make more adjustments and show more resiliency as they started their careers in an era when jobs were not as cognitively and socially demanding. As a result, the nature of work today is more stressful to them compared to workers in their early career (Shultz, Wang, Crimmins, & Fisher, 2009). Alternatively, future research may find that it is the fact that those in their mid and late career have worked their way up the career ladder to the point where they are likely to be working on significantly more cognitively and socially complex work and that is what results in differences in perceived stress across career stages.

CASE STUDY

Denise, a women in her early 50s, earned her PhD in business in the mid 1980s and quickly became a successful consultant. In fact, within a few years of taking a job with a prominent management consulting firm, she was offered a partnership role in the firm. At first the extra money and responsibility was exciting and engaging. However, Denise soon realized that her true passion was working with clients. However, her new partnership status required her to take on more interpersonally challenging roles as a supervisor and mentor to her junior colleagues, which she found more stressful and taxing than her consulting duties, even though it often required less time and effort. As a result, she eventually relinquished her role as a partner and ultimately left the company. She continued her consulting career on her own for several years, but found the uncertainty of owning her own business and all the additional demands that came with it, almost as stressful as being a partner in a major consulting firm. So, about five years ago Denise started teaching part time and quickly realized she really enjoyed interacting with students and teaching classes in business. As a result, she applied for a full-time, tenure track teaching position and has been a full-time professor of management ever since. Thus, Denise's mid career experiences are an excellent example of how resiliency and adjustment at mid career can help prolong one's career by reducing the stress one experiences and maximizing one's talents in her areas of strength.

In addition to the changing nature of the mix of job demands, the concept of jobs, as a distinct bundle of tasks, is beginning to become an outdated concept as the nature of work and the workplace continue to rapidly evolve (Cascio, 1995). That is, jobs are much less well defined and entrenched today than they were just a decade or so ago. Instead of each job having its own set of unique competency requirements, meta-competencies such as emotional intelligence, which includes competencies such as flexibility, adaptability, interpersonal communication, self-leadership, and influence skills have become key components to all jobs in the 21st century (Yeatts, Folts, & Knapp, 2000). This also reinforces the need for today's workers, no matter what career stage they may be in, to engage in continuous skill development and improvement.

Each of us pays a very high price, personally and professionally, when we choose (either consciously or non-consciously) to focus on the logical and analytical facets of situations and people to the exclusion of the emotional and intuitive. Emotions provide information, which goes beyond that which is purely rational and analytical. When used effectively, emotions facilitate creativity, problem solving, decision-making, stress management, and relationship building in a wide variety of situations.

Common wisdom has conditioned us to believe that emotions interfere with or disrupt our ability to think rationally. As the old saying goes—"rule your feelings, lest your feelings rule you." From this vantage point, emotions are seen as animalistic, disruptive, and immature. The work of Mayer, Salovey, and Caruso (2008) moves beyond this view of emotions. They define emotional intelligence as the ability to:

1. Accurately perceive, understand and express emotions to promote one's growth emotionally and intellectually;
2. Use emotions to gather relevant information, facilitate creativity and the ability to think through issues, ideas, situations, etc.;
3. Understand and analyze emotions and use emotional knowledge in meaningful ways; and;
4. Consciously control and regulate the expression of emotions, both in oneself and in others.

Research on emotional intelligence reinforces that individuals who are higher in emotional intelligence perform better in a wide range of jobs (e.g., managers, salespeople, consultants) (Goleman, 1998; Hunter, Schmidt, & Judiesch, 1990). Overall, emotional intelligence is more predictive of performance in high emotional labor roles than those jobs that have few emotional labor demands (Joseph & Newman, 2010).

The need to maintain and develop meta-competencies (i.e., emotional intelligence) has become particularly important as the rapid expansion of technology and ever expanding accumulation of knowledge continues to make continuous learning and development a key to remaining successful and productive on one's job in the 21st century. Thus, mid and late career workers of today need to continue to engage in professional development activities that will keep them current on the latest job related technologies and information (this will be discussed in more detail in Chapter 9). However, as we noted in the previous chapter, with the changing nature of careers, the onus will be on the mid and late career workers themselves, not their employers, to seek out ways maintain their level of professional competence.

CASE STUDY

In Chapter 2, we discussed an interview with Clarice, a 59-year-old African American woman who had recently decided to accept an early retirement package from her employer. Clarice continued to develop her computer skills throughout her career. She started as an administrative assistant, but eventually became Help Desk Support Technician due to the technical skills she was able to develop during her career. In addition, Clarice used her technical skills to develop a part-time travel agent business. So, when her employer offered an early retirement package to her, she was comfortable accepting the package, knowing that she could use the skills she developed to grow her part-time business into a full-time one. Thus, Clarice was confident in making this transition in her late career from full-time employed worker to self-employed worker; a phenomenon that is becoming increasingly common and which we discuss later in this chapter.

Moreover, individuals are much more likely to be working as part of a work team in today's world of work. This may include working in on-site teams, as well as virtual teams using technology. As a result, jobs in the 21st century are requiring increased interpersonal and communication skills, as well as coordination and group facilitation skills (Cascio, 2003). For example, on-site work teams will require the need to coordinate work functions and activities in order to accomplish goals. Thus, today's jobs are becoming less about completing specific individualized tasks and more about working together with work team members to accomplish group level goals. Accordingly, a given individual may have to take on additional tasks or roles that are not typically part of his/her job description in order to accomplish the team goals.

For example, an individual in their mid or late career may be assigned to a group project where the group needs to develop an innovative production process. As a result, the group is likely to consist of workers from various departments, including research and development, production, marketing, and engineering. Consequently, everyone involved on the team, including the mid and late career workers, will need to exhibit emotional intelligence (i.e., flexibility and adaptability) in their efforts to complete the project in order to accommodate the group nature of the project.

In addition, virtual work teams may require coordinating work with coworkers in other locations, possibly including other countries. This will require increased technical knowledge and sophistication in order to coordinate work across not only multiple locations, but also across numerous time zones. Thus, a worker in the United States may finish his part of a project and hand it off before leaving work for the day (e.g., via email or a file sharing website) to a coworker in Europe or Asia, only to come back to work the next morning to find that the coworker overseas has completed her part of the project while the U.S. worker was sleeping. This global coordination of work has the potential to result in increased efficiency for employers due to the dramatically reduced downtime that would be experienced if all team members were at a single location.

CASE STUDY

One of the authors, Ken Shultz, who is unmistakably in his mid career, recently edited a special issue of an international research journal with a colleague he had never met in person. When Ken was asked to edit the special issue, he sought out a colleague from Europe to help him. Though Ken had never met his colleague in person, through email, Skype, and telephone conversations, he and his European colleague were able to coordinate the various tasks of the project (e.g., soliciting manuscripts, contacting reviewers, assigning manuscripts to reviewers, reviewing manuscripts, writing an introductory paper) over a six-month period to complete the special issue of the journal on time. This coordination was not always easy with an eight to nine hour time difference, different national holidays and work schedules, in addition to the lack of direct personal contact. However, this serves as an excellent example of how geographically disperse virtual work teams (especially if you include the dozen or so ad hoc manuscript reviewers from more than a half dozen different countries) can function efficiently with the use of technology and extra coordination efforts.

In the same way, the idea that most work occurs between 8 a.m. and 5 p.m. has also been eroding over the last half century. While some jobs (e.g., public safety, health care, some manufacturing) have always required rotating shifts, given the global expansion of work and the need to work with colleagues multiple time zones to the east or west, as well as the shift to a service based economy, more individuals are having to be available outside the traditional Monday through Friday work hours (Shultz & Olson, 2013). Also, the increased use of technology (including smart cell phones, tablets, and lap top computers) with instant access to the Internet has made it possible to work from almost anywhere, 24 hours a day 7 days a week. On the one hand, this can be a good thing for workers in the 21st century, as it allows for maximum flexibility in meeting family and personal demands outside of work. On the other hand, it also means that many workers may feel tethered to their workplace, with no possibility of escaping the constant drumbeat of work.

Work in the 21st century is also becoming more ephemeral. Gone are the days where workers seek out a prominent local employer (e.g., the auto industry in Detroit, the steel industry in Pittsburgh) and look to obtain career long employment with that one employer or industry. Instead, work in the 21st century is much more likely to be contingent (e.g., part-time, temporary, contracted). In addition, organizations are continuing to outsource jobs to temporary agencies and to shift jobs overseas, be they manufacturing or customer service jobs. Thus, as we discussed in the previous chapter, mid and late career workers in the 21st century need to be able to change the way they think about both objective and subjective job and career success (Robson, Hansson, Abalos, & Booth, 2006).

Changing job demands have a number of implications for workers in their mid and late career. First, the sharp decline in physical job demands in the last three decades bodes well for the continued employability of older workers in their mid and late careers. These declines should increase the chances that older workers will be willing and able to remain in the workforce (i.e., they will have increased workability). Conversely, increases in cognitive demands and stressful working conditions may compel older workers to either leave the workforce or to seek job and/or career changes that would allow them to escape their present hectic, stressful, high pressure jobs, as both Denise and Clarice did (Yeatts et al., 2000). In Chapter 4 we go into much more detail about the cognitive and physical changes that occur with age and their implications for continued work in mid and late career.

Job design factors (e.g., opportunities for decision making, skill variety) are also likely to impact mid and late career workers in terms of how they are able to successfully age at work. For example, Sanders and McCready (2010) recently reported that job design factors contributed to 23% of the variance in feelings of generativity and 15.5% of the variance in personal sense of control, two important successful aging factors. Thus, knowing which job design factors (here skill variety and coworker support) are most important in order to maximize the continued career success of mid and late career workers can help prolong work lives for those in their mid and late career.

In addition, the changing nature of work more broadly has implications for mid and late career workers in the 21st century. First, mid and late career workers will need to adjust to the increased use of both on-site and virtual teams in the workplace. After spending much of their career serving as individual contributors, this may be an uncomfortable adjustment. However, this adjustment and flexibility will be critical to continued success in the 21st century workplace (Yeatts et al., 2000). In addition, mid and late career workers will need to continue to develop their technological skills in order to remain competitive in the 21st century workplace. This will be important not only for work in virtual team environments, but increasingly training and developmental opportunities (as we discuss in detail Chapter 9) will most often be available on-line. As a result, workers in their mid and late careers must sustain their motivation to continue learning how to use these tools to facilitate their ability to complete their work and to effectively work in virtual (and global) teams (Deal, 2007).

Additionally, with increased use of virtual work and telecommuting, both workers and managers need to shift their focus in terms of performance management (discussed in detail in Chapter 8) from time on task to results accomplished. This shift will have particular implications for workers in their mid and late career that may have started their career with the notion that the way one moves up in their career is via "face time" and "being seen." With a shift to focusing on results rather than time, mid and late career workers, who consistently say flexibility and autonomy are important characteristics will begin to see the true benefits of how work is being redefined.

The Changing Nature of Workers

Workers in the 21st century are more educated, on average, than ever before (Johnson et al., 2007). However, given the increased cognitive and technical demands of today's work, it is not surprising that today's workers feel the need for near constant professional development and upgrading. This phenomenon is particularly true for workers in their mid and late careers who may have finished their formal education decades ago and are now faced with potentially several additional decades of work before retirement, or increasingly, continued part-time work after they retire from their career jobs (Wang, Adams, Beehr, & Shultz, 2009). However, where they obtain this continuing education and development is also changing, as employers are often reluctant to invest in employees who may not be staying with the company for very long.

Consistent with the protean career perspective discussed in Chapter 2, workers in their mid and late careers need to assume responsibility for their continued professional development and growth. Unlike their parents who may have been able to rely on the munificence of their large corporate employer to dictate their continued professional development, today's workers need to ensure their own professional preparation and continued development by actively seeking out a wide variety of professional growth activities. These may occur within their own organization, or increasingly, outside their employing organization via professional associations and on-line training opportunities. The key is that obsolescence is not an option if one wants to stay employable in a workplace where job security (i.e., having a job with a given employer) has been replaced by employment security (i.e., having a set of marketable skills that some employer is willing to pay for) (Cascio, 2003).

Increased education levels typically mean that today's workers are also likely to enter the workforce later in life than a generation or two ago. However, starting in the mid to late 1980s, we have also seen a reversal of the trend toward earlier retirement for men. This is also associated with increased longevity among both men and women. Thus, the shortening of men's careers that was occurring due to factors at both ends of the age spectrum, may be expanding as education becomes a lifelong process and retirements are pushed off for both professional and personal reasons (we discuss this latter issue in detail in Chapter 11 on the transition to retirement).

In addition, workers in the 21st century have a different psychological contract with their employers than their parents and grandparents had with theirs. That is, the expectations of both workers and employers have changed dramatically in the last several decades. Specifically the implicit psychological contract between workers and organizations has shifted from a longer term relational contract, to a short-term transactional contract. Thus, effort and loyalty on the part of the employee that led to career advancement and job security, which was part of the relational psychological contract, has been replaced by a transactional contract focused on flexibility and a willingness to develop new skills on the part of the employee in exchange for the organization providing an opportunity for professional growth and development (Greenhaus, 2003).

On the worker side, employees have higher expectations regarding greater flexibility in how and when they work. Further, workers in their mid and late careers are more likely to be experiencing work and family balance demands from both ends of the spectrum. That is, they may well be sandwiched between dependent children and grandchildren, and elderly parents (Neal & Hammer, 2007). Thus, workers in mid and late career may have even greater needs for flexibility in scheduling and completing their work than their younger, early career counterparts. In exchange, employers are providing less security and fewer guarantees regarding continued and future employment. As a result, today's workers are increasingly aware of this shift and are changing their own attitudes toward work.

Workers today are also more likely to be in dual career relationships when compared with their parents or grandparents. As a result, their relationship to work will be filtered by increased family related demands for both women and men. Women are also more likely to experience a single parent household with dramatically increased need to juggle both work and family demands. However, even in dual career households, women are more likely to shoulder the lion's share of the child and elder care demands. Thus, with increased longevity and many women delaying child bearing, it is not unusual for women to be sandwiched between the need to care for both school age children and elderly parents or relatives.

CASE STUDY

Priya, a 55-year-old Indian women in Mumbai, recently decided to accept an early retirement incentive package (ERIP) from her employer. She finished her PhD education at age 33, while raising two boys as a stay at home mom. Once she completed her degree, she began working as a professor at a local university. While she still enjoys her job, after a successful 22- year career, she has decided to accept an ERIP due to the increased elder care demands of her in-laws, who now live with her and her husband. Thus, while Priya did have a successful 22-year career, her career undoubtedly could have been longer had she started earlier and was able to continue longer if not for the childcare demands that delayed the onset of her career and the eldercare demands that are now truncating her career.

The changing nature of workers has numerous implications for those in their mid and late career. First, workers in their mid and late career need to fully appreciate that continuous training, as well as skill acquisition and development, will be needed not only to maintain competence in their current jobs/careers, but also in order to stay competitive in today's job market. Empirical work by Simpson, Greller, and Stroh (2002) indicates that older workers have, in fact, been increasingly engaging in continuing education activities, including job and career related courses, thus facilitating the continued maintenance and development of their careers. Also, while mid and late career workers may be less likely to lose their job than younger workers, when they do, they are likely to be without work for much longer periods. However, the more current and relevant their skill sets are, the shorter their new job search should be compared to mid and late career workers who have not continued to develop their talents and skills.

In addition, mid and late career workers need to embrace the newer career models discussed in Chapter 2. Specifically, the protean and boundaryless career models fit well with the changing nature of work and workers, in that these models put the onus squarely on the shoulders of the workers themselves to chart the directions of their careers. In addition, taking a life-span approach to career development would help mid and late career workers to acknowledge their current career stage and thus make decisions regarding their career that are in line with their current situation and future aspirations from their current perspective. The kaleidoscope career model also fits well with where most mid and late career workers are in their career in that it addresses both gender differences in careers and career aspirations, as well as delineating mid and later career workers desires to move beyond traditional career paths. Its focus on the unique combination of factors (particularly authenticity, balance, and challenges—The ABCs of careers) encapsulates much of the changing nature of workers.

Finally, mid and late career workers are likely to be diverse in terms of their circumstances (e.g., health status, shifting goals and aspirations) compared to early career workers (Robson et al., 2006). As a result of this growing variability in key individual differences as we age, mid and late career workers often transition from focusing on extrinsic career success factors (e.g., pay and promotions) to more intrinsic career success factors (e.g., meeting one's own goals and aspirations, or mentoring early career colleagues). Thus, the changing nature of workers themselves has important implications for those in their mid and late careers.

The Changing Nature of the Workforce

Just as the nature of work and workers is changing, so too is the nature of the workforce. Increasing diversity of the workforce is not only evident in surface characteristics (e.g., race, age, sex), but also in deeper level traits and characteristics (Shultz & Olson, 2013). That is, we are seeing increased diversity in the workforce in terms of experiences, cultural background, and education levels. Therefore, when organizations discuss the need to "value diversity," they need to look beyond demographic factors, to other human characteristics that make workers unique.

Additionally, as the population ages, so too does the workforce. As a result, mid and late career workers will make up an increasing portion of the workforce. This trend has several implications, including the fact that older workers are more likely to be working for younger supervisors than in the past. The implications of this role reversal are discussed in Chapter 8. In addition, the larger portion of older workers, relative to younger workers, also has an influence on the nature of mentoring relationships in organizations. That is, on the plus side more mid and late career workers will be available to mentor early career workers. However, there may also be some resentment on the part of early career workers that late career workers in particular are not moving on to retirement as fast as they would like, which would allow early career workers to progress more quickly through the ranks. As a result, the dynamics of the mentoring relationship may be strained by this growing trend of late career workers extending their careers longer than they have in the recent past.

We also discussed in Chapter 2 the fact that late career workers may extend their careers, but take them in a different direction. For example, the fastest growing segment of individuals who are self-employed is those 50 and older (Giandrea, Cahill, & Quinn, 2008). In addition, Giandrea et al. found that workers over 50 were much more likely to switch from wage and salary work to self-employment than the other way around. Thus, as late career workers transition from paid employment working for others to self-employment, this will free up positions within organizations for early career workers, while also allowing late career workers themselves to begin tapping into their pensions, as well have more flexibility, independence, and less stressful continued employment, as we discussed in the case of Clarice earlier in this chapter.

However, people work for many reasons beyond making money. A 2003 AARP study of people between the ages of 50 and 70 reported that they planned to continue working rather than retire in the traditional sense and engage in only leisure activities. The reasons why they chose to continue to work after they "retired" from their previous employment included to: stay mentally active (87%); stay physically active (85%); be productive and useful (77%); do something fun (71%); help other people (59%); be around people (58%); learn new things (50%); and pursue a dream (32%). Thus, even when individuals in late career begin the transition to retirement, they are increasingly likely to continue to stay engaged in the workforce for a wide variety of reasons.

In addition, globalization, as well as increased outsourcing and offshoring of work, will also dramatically affect the makeup for the workforce (Cascio, 2003). Many organizations will create leaner core staff, while outsourcing much of their work to more transitory contingent workers. As a result, the most prominent employers may well be temporary help agencies and consulting firms rather than the large corporate employers. Thus, the dynamics of the workforce will continue to shift and become even more dynamic making it complex for mid and late workers to navigate if they wish to prolong their careers.

The changes to the psychological employment contract that we discussed earlier with regard to the changing nature of workers have implications for the workforce more broadly. For example, mid and late career workers who may have hoped to stay with the same employer until retirement see that possibility increasingly slipping away with the changing psychological contract. However, as we discussed in Chapter 2, mid and late career workers are much more likely to be more fully embedded in their job, organization, or occupation, thus they may have fewer perceived and actual options for changing jobs, organizations, and/or careers. This prolongation of late career workers' career in the same place may force early career workers to shift their focus elsewhere in order to continue to make progress in their careers.

The changing nature of the workforce has several implications for those in their mid and late career. First, mid and late career workers will need to adapt to a much more diverse workplace compared to when they began their career (Yeatts et al., 2000). This includes not only demographic diversity but also diversity in terms of education level, background, and perspectives. In addition, mid and late career workers may for the first time, be working for younger supervisors. This goes against traditional norms where the supervisor is usually older than the subordinate. Thus, mid and late career workers will need to be able to change their mind set in order to benefit the most from having a younger supervisor.

In addition, as more mid and late career workers make the transition from being employed by organizations to being self-employed, they will need to engage in additional training and development to make sure they can survive being self-employed. Many individuals who begin their own businesses don't fully understand the need for capitalization and the numerous additional demands they will need to take on as new business owners. In addition, increased globalization may force both employed and self-employed mid and late career workers to alter their career continuation plans.

Finally, the changing psychological contract between employers and workers has strong implications for mid and late career workers. For example, these workers may well need to rethink their plans for retirement. As a result, the dynamics of the workforce itself are likely to be altered with more older workers extending their careers through various forms of bridge employment including continued employment with their present employer, self-employment, and various forms of continued paid employment with new and different employers. Some may be engaging in second (or third) careers, while others are simply trying to hold on to their current standard of living.

The Changing Nature of Organizations

Organizations are faced with a wide variety of forces, many rapidly evolving, that are impacting how they run their business, as well as how they treat their workers. A primary force that has continued to accelerate for leaders in for-profit organizations is increasing global competition. A half century ago this was primarily in the manufacturing sector, however, today every industry, including the service sector, is increasingly being impacted by global competition. As a result of these external forces, most organizations today appear to be in near constant reorganization and restructuring mode. That is, they need to continually rethink organizational structures and reporting relationships in order to remain competitive in an increasingly global business environment. Such restructuring often includes mergers and acquisitions, as well as downsizings and layoffs of workers. Part of the goal of such restructurings, particularly after mergers and acquisitions, is to realize supposed cost efficiencies by reducing staff and consolidating resources (e.g., closing offices). However, longitudinal research has shown that these "efficiencies" are rarely, if ever realized, but can have dramatic effects on workers (Morris, Cascio, & Young, 1999).

These actions have a major impact on workers' experiences, particularly mid and late career workers. Many professional and managerial workers who were largely immune to layoffs and downsizings in the past are now often the primary targets of such downsizings. As a result, mid and late career workers often need to begin new careers, sometimes in dramatically different career paths, particularly if they are highly embedded in their current geographic location and that location provides few opportunities within their current career path.

In addition, Arthur, Inkson, and Pringle (1999) talked about how the traditional career stage models, where each stage is typically associated with a particular age range, are no longer linear and one way. Instead, mid and late career workers who have been downsized and thus engaged in career transitions, may need to recycle through career stages such as fresh energy, informed direction, and season engagement. These organization-based changes are also necessitating the need for mid and late career workers to develop the career competencies of knowing why, knowing how, and knowing whom (Arthur et al., 1999) in order to maintain and extend their careers.

In addition to unemployment due to layoffs, many individuals in their mid and late careers are likely to experience underemployment in their subsequent job after a layoff (Shultz, Olson, & Wang, 2011), which may lead to higher levels of experienced work stress (Shultz, Wang, & Olson, 2010). Even those who survive the downsizings are likely to face underemployment from the perspective of being plateaued in their current career trajectory (Allen, Russell, Poteet, & Dobbins, 1999). Career plateauing can take one of two forms: structural (i.e., an inability to move up the career ladder) or job content (i.e., increased responsibility on the current job is unlikely) (Greenhaus, 2003). Brown-Wilson and Parry (2009) asked a fundamental question: "How desirable are later life career plateaus and how dependent is this desirability on whether the career plateau is the result of employer action (circumstance) or individual employee decision (choice)?" (p. 76). The focus of career success often shifts from external (e.g., hierarchical career progression) to internal (e.g., achievement of personal goals) as one moves toward late career; the late career employees who become plateaued may not necessarily always be in an undesirable position (Robson et al., 2006). The circumstances behind their plateaued status and their source of career success may actually play a larger role in determining their satisfaction with their plateaued status than the status itself. These are timely concerns, as career plateauing appears to be increasing in both frequency and duration as individuals continue to extend their careers (Brown-Wilson & Parry, 2009).

Organizations are also changing the way they structure work. A relatively cheap and cost efficient benefit to offer workers is a flexible work schedule. While workers often express a desire for more flexibility in when, where, and how they do their work, this can also mean increased total hours worked and increased levels of stress as workers feel that they are constantly tethered to the workplace via smart phones, lap tops, and tablets. In addition, the "benefit" of being able to work from home can result in increased work-family conflict. Thus, work schedule flexibility may often be more attractive in theory than in practice.

Another key aspect of how organizations are changing the structure of work is the use of more contingent workers. For example, in higher education an increasing number of classes are being taught by part-time instructors, instead of full-time, tenure track professors. As a result, career trajectories of those who desire to become college professors are inextricably being altered by this changing way of doing business. Individuals many now need to piece together part-time teaching positions with several employers rather than with just one. In southern California these contingent workers in higher education are referred to "freeway fliers" as they must constantly drive from one campus to another in order to piece together full-time work.

The changing nature of organizations has various implications for mid and late career workers. First, like all workers who experience downsizings, these workers are likely to experience increased stress and decreased job, career, and life satisfaction. However, these experiences are likely to be heightened for mid and late career workers who are likely to have much more invested with a given employer. Thus, for them, it is not only the loss of a job, but the loss of entrenched social networks, tangible pensions, and well-established daily routines. In addition, the "lucky" survivors of downsizings are likely to experience decreased commitment, lower intentions to stay, and a loss of trust with regard to the organization. Consequently, workers' views of hard work, loyalty, and managing one's career have experienced seismic shifts as a result of the changing nature of organizations (Cascio, 2003).

The changes in the way organizations operate reinforces the need for all workers to embrace the protean career model, where the employee drives his own career trajectory. However, mid and late career workers who entered the workplace under a different career model will need to work harder to transition to this new way of thinking about careers. The view that career success equates to linear career growth within a single organization just doesn't fit anymore (Lee, Kossek, Hall, & Latrico, 2011). Instead, mid and late career workers need to embrace the likelihood of multiple careers across several organizations within their lifetime. This will require continuous, lifelong learning as well, in order to maintain and develop one's skills to stay competitive in today's rapid changing corporate landscape, as mobility, rather than stability, is the new norm.

Directions for Future Research

Gunz et al. (2011) recently noted that the vast majority of career research has focused mainly on the careers of individuals and the factors linked to the person and his/her immediate context, but has generally neglected to examine the broader context within which careers are lived. Thus, Gunz et al. provide several recommendations for future research noting that, "research exploring the broad context within which careers are lived helps us understand better the nature of career in an Internet-based, globalized economy and how these careers, in turn influence developments in that context" (p. 1614). For example, empirical research that analyzes the extent to which changes that have resulted from globalization have directly impacted careers can make a significant contribution to the careers literature. In addition, in-depth studies of the changing family structure, and women's increased labor force attachment, and how these have directly impacted both men and women's careers is needed. Gunz et al. also note that "Contributions that elaborate on contextual frameworks, taking into account multi-level factors and demonstrating their descriptive and explanatory potential for career analysis, are strongly needed" (p. 1614).

Future research examining the changing nature of work, workers, the workforce, and organizations will clearly need to be both multidisciplinary and interdisciplinary. That is, many diverse disciplines study these issues including industrial/organizational psychology, organizational behavior, management science, sociology, economics, industrial relations, human factors, anthropology, and many others. Each discipline has something unique and important to contribute to the study of the evolving nature of work. However, it is important that the various disciplines know and cite each other's work, as well as communicate and collaborate in studying these changes. Thus, we need to move beyond simply acknowledging the multidisciplinary nature of this area, to encouraging and facilitating interdisciplinary, collaborative studies that investigate the changing nature of the world of work.

An excellent example of taking an interdisciplinary approach to studying work and the workplace was the Committee on Techniques for the Enhancement of Human Performance (CTEHP; 1999) sponsored by the National Academy of Sciences. Researchers from multiple disciplines worked together to examine how the changing nature of work, workers, the workforce, and organizations are all impacting work in the military in the United States. Such interdisciplinary work is important not only for interpreting the results from various disciplines, but also in framing the questions that should be investigated in future studies in this area. Thus, while the initial impetus for their work was how these changes are impacting the military in the United States, their extensive work is also applicable to both the private and non-military public sector work as well.

In addition, in order to go beyond abstract discussions of changes in these areas, we need to make sure that we examine and detail the direct experiences of workers in rich and extensive detail, as CTEHP (1999) did. This will require a broad and nationally representative sample of workers in various jobs and industries in order to fully capture the diverse nature of the unique features of these various industries and sectors. The CTEHP study captured this well for the military environment, but this needs to be expanded to the civilian sector as well.

Another area of future study is to examine how these changes will impact issues such as designing new jobs, developing effective talent management strategies, and providing timely career counseling to workers who are both entering the workforce for the first time and, most relevant to this volume, to those in mid and late career who may be contemplating a career change. We discuss many of these issues later in this book, providing future research directions specific to those topical areas specifically.

An important question that needs to be addressed in future research is how these multiple factors across multiple levels come together to impact mid and late career workers. That is, we need to view workers in terms of their unique set of circumstances that come together to form how they currently are and how they interact with the environment. This would also include examining how some of these recent changes may serve as barriers to individuals in the mid and late career by creating underemployment, excessive stress, and potentially age discrimination in the workplace.

Future research should also address how these changes may differentially impact voluntary versus involuntary mid and late career changes. That is, the factors that may serve as an impetus, as well as a barrier or facilitator, for mid and late career change are currently unknown. As mid and late career workers continue to make career transitions more frequently than in the past, more research on the nature of these career transitions, particularly the voluntariness of the transition, is needed, particularly as the nature of work, workers, the workforce, and organizations more broadly continue to evolve.

Finally, how workers define career success has also changed with the changing context of careers. Thus, future research needs to address how the various changes in the context of careers have impacted what both subjective and objective career success means to workers at various career stages. This will be particularly important for workers in their mid and late careers who may be experiencing more frequent career transitions than they anticipated when they began their career.

CAREER ISSUES UNIQUE TO MID AND LATE CAREERS

Chapter 4

Career Issues Unique to Mid and Late Careers
Individual Level Factors

In this section of the book, we review the career-related issues that are unique to mid and late career workers. In doing so, we aim at recognizing three types of analytic perspectives that exist in this literature to help us organize this review and synthesize the relevant research findings. First of all, we recognize that career stage differences still exist among early mid career workers, late mid career workers, and late career workers (Shultz & Wang, 2008). For example, early mid career workers will most likely be assessing the career progress they have made and determining whether job or career changes may be necessary to meet their desired goals. In addition, job and career embeddedness factors (i.e., those things that keep us in a particular job or career; Mitchell, Holtom, Lee, Sablynski, & Erez, 2001) such as spousal employment, children's schooling, job satisfaction and attachment, and social relationship at work, are also likely to be different for those in early mid career versus those in late mid career or late career. Further, for late career workers, the unique career challenge they face is to successfully prepare for and transit into their retirement (Wang & Shultz, 2010; Shultz & Wang, 2011). Therefore, in this part of the book, we scrutinize the impact of different factors for workers in different stages of their careers.

Second, we recognize that multiple career-related criteria exist for mid and late career stages. For example, career success can be evaluated in terms of the success of individuals relative to their cohorts at a certain time point, as well as the pace and form of the career progress individuals make relative to their cohorts in a certain period of time (Judge & Hurst, 2008). Further, career success can be evaluated by using both objective and subjective criteria. Objective indicators of career success, i.e., "indicators of career success that can be seen and therefore evaluated objectively by others" (Ng, Eby, Sorensen, & Feldman, 2005, p. 368), may include pay (e.g., O'Reilly & Chatman, 1994) and occupational status (e.g., Ganzeboom & Treiman, 1996). Subjective indicators of career success may include career satisfaction (e.g., Heslin, 2005), career attachment (e.g., Adams &

Beehr, 1998), and job satisfaction (e.g., Judge & Hurst, 2008). However, besides career success, other criteria may be particularly relevant to mid and late career workers. For instance, work-family balance may be an important outcome to consider when one's career is evaluated from the family perspective. Further, career-related decisions, such as career change, relocation, and retirement decisions, have critical implications for one's financial, physical, and psychological well-being, thus are important to consider as well. Therefore, in this part of the book, we pay attention to a broad range of criteria when we evaluate different factors that may impact mid and late careers.

Third, although there are a wide variety of factors that may impact mid and late careers, we recognize that they can largely be organized into three categories: individual-level factors, job-level factors, and organizational-level factors. This categorization helps us to better understand the common theoretical mechanisms behind the effects of these factors. Further, it provides a good taxonomy to summarize research findings, which is consistent with previous literature in mid and late career issues (e.g., Feldman, 1994; Wang, Henkens, & van Solinge, 2011; Wang & Shultz, 2010; Wang, Zhan, Liu, & Shultz, 2008). In this chapter we examine the individual-level factors, while the job-level factors are addressed in Chapter 5 and the organizational-level factors are addressed in Chapter 6.

Here, the individual-level factors we review include both individual dispositions (e.g., cognitive ability and personality) and individual attributes (e.g., health and financial conditions). Although both dispositions and attributes denote individual differences, dispositions are usually viewed as being stable and relatively free from environmental influence (Mischel & Shoda, 1995), whereas attributes may change rather easily over time and across different situations (e.g., Barnes-Farrell, 2003).

Individual Level Factors: Dispositions

Cognitive Ability

Cognitive ability (also called general mental ability or general intelligence) refers to a person's total mental capacity for cognitive operations (e.g., abstract thinking, reasoning, learning, planning, and problem solving; Gardner, 1999). Cognitive ability has long been viewed as an important predictor of individuals' career success. The major causal impact of mental ability on ones' career success has been found to be through the acquisition of job and career knowledge. In other words, the reason that more intelligent people are more likely to achieve career success is that they acquire more job and career knowledge and acquire them in a more rapid manner. In turn, this knowledge of how to perform the job and achieve career development causes individuals to be more likely to succeed in their careers (Schmidt & Hunter, 1998). Given the strong association between cognitive ability and job- and career-related knowledge, it is important to recognize that individuals with higher levels of cognitive ability may also have more career advancement opportunities and career options. In other words, there is more variety in ways for individuals with higher levels of cognitive ability to achieve both subjective and objective career success. Consequently, in terms of career development patterns, individuals with higher levels of cognitive ability may be more likely to purposefully change their career paths even when they are already in their mid or late career stages.

Different theories and models about cognitive ability emphasize different components and/or functions of intelligence. Naglieri and Das (1997) have presented a neuropsychological theory of intelligence that posits three major functional areas of intelligence: planning, attention, and simultaneous or successive information processing. There is no doubt that these three functional areas are closely tied to one's job performance. The question is whether one of these functional areas may be more important than the others when individuals are in different career stages. Given the characteristics of different mid and late career stages, we argue that the planning function may become more and more important along one's career development. This is because when individuals move from the early mid career stage to late mid career stage, their job responsibilities are likely to evolve from tasks that require specific job knowledge, skills, and techniques to tasks that require more leadership and managerial functions, especially in white-collar jobs (Shultz & Wang, 2008). Therefore, they are more likely to experience the need for strategic planning and coordination rather than intensive information processing and concentration of attention when their careers enter the later stages. This functional shift is also consistent with the reductions in cognitive ability that people experience when they grow older (Park, 2000), which we will discuss in more detail later.

Gardner (1999) also proposed a model of cognitive ability, which posits a number of intelligences, including the traditional linguistic, spatial, and mathematical dimensions in addition to interpersonal and intrapersonal dimensions, claiming that different dimensions have been important to people from different cultures at different individual development stages. Gardner's interpersonal and intrapersonal dimensions seem similar to some aspects of emotional intelligence, such as emotion appraisal and regulation of emotion (Mayer, Salovey, & Caruso, 2000). Given that emotional intelligence represents individual differences in ability and capacity to monitor and recognize one's own and others' emotions, and to use this information to regulate one's emotions and actions, it is also conceivable that emotional intelligence may be particularly relevant to leadership and managerial positions where interpersonal concerns are important parts of the job. In addition, as people continue to develop in their mid adulthood, their social networks typically expand rapidly, which require effective management (Super, 1990). Therefore, cognitive ability in interpersonal dimensions becomes essential in dealing with work and non-work related social relationships. To the extent that a person's non-work related social relationships are well maintained, it may allow the person to invest more energy to develop his/her career. Therefore, we argue that when individuals move from the early mid career stage to later career stages, their emotional intelligence may become more relevant to their career success than in earlier career stages.

Cognitive Aging

When people grow older, even though their general knowledge remains stable or even increases, they tend to experience a reduction in cognitive ability (Park, 2000). Specifically, cognitive aging features declines in processing speed, working memory, and inhibition function. For example, Salthouse (1996) pointed out that one of the factors accounting for age-related decline in cognitive performance was a general slowing of processing speed of mental operation with aging. This processing speed slowness could lead to loss of information during the cognitive processing, because the cognitive operation may take a longer time to process the information than it could be retrieved. Similarly, when people grow older, their working memory capacity (defined as the amount of on-line cognitive resources that provide simultaneous storage and processing of information) declines, resulting in older adults performing worse than young adults on those cognitive tasks requiring both processing and storing information (Park, 2000). Hasher and Zacks (1988) also found that, with aging, people have more trouble inhibiting their attention to irrelevant information and concentrating on relevant information, which makes it difficult for older adults to perform tasks that require long periods of mental concentration. Overall, the cognitive aging literature suggests that age-related reduction in cognitive resources may lead to more difficulty for older workers in dealing with high mental load tasks, which require retention of large amounts of information or rapid cognitive processing (Wang & Chen, 2004, 2006). It has also been shown that to maintain the same level of task performance, older workers have to expend greater effort on these types of tasks than younger adults (Bunce & Sisa, 2002).

Given these declines, it may appear that older employees in their late career stages tend to have greater difficulty than younger employees performing tasks that require retention of large amounts of information or that require rapid cognitive processing. This difficulty may be a major reason why people make career path changes in their late career stages. This is especially true for certain occupations. For example, air traffic controllers usually retire from their jobs when they are 45 years old due to the high cognitive demands of the job. However, it should also be recognized that the effect of cognitive reduction may not start to interfere with well-mastered job activities until one reaches 60 or even older age (Abraham & Hansson, 1995; Colonia-Willner, 1998). To deal with the difficulties resulting from cognitive aging, it is important for mid and late career workers to receive training in order to take advantage of new technologies to assist their work. Often time, applications of new technology (e.g., enterprise resource planning systems) relieve workers from excessive information processing by organizing and automating routine productive processes, thereby decreasing the cognitive load imposed on workers. In addition, organizations may also want to provide more breaks for older workers to relieve them from the potential negative effects of performing cognitively intense tasks.

Personality

In this section, we discuss several personality traits that influence people's mid and late careers. Theoretically, personality traits are thought to influence biographical experiences and individual development via their association with emotional appraisals, motivational priorities, and coping strategies (McCrae & Costa, 2008). Prior research has linked personality traits to career interests in early career stages (e.g., DeFruyt & Mervielde, 1999; Tett & Burnett, 2003). However, few studies have examined how personality traits may be relevant to issues people face in their mid and late career stages. As Mischel and Shoda (1995) pointed out, individual differences in personality traits drive people to be systematically different in how they selectively focus on different features of situations, how they categorize and encode them cognitively and emotionally, and how those encodings activate and interact with other cognitions and affects in the personality system. We link personality traits to issues in mid and late careers following this notion of cognitive-affective mediation process.

Core Self-Evaluation

One personality trait that has been recently linked to career development is core self-evaluation. According to Judge and Larsen (2001), core self-evaluations are fundamental trait premises that individuals hold about themselves and their functioning in the world. These evaluations capture the dispositional antecedents of people's appraisals of the external world (Judge, Erez, & Bono, 1998) and their subsequent reactions to those appraisals (e.g., responses to feedback; Bono & Colbert, 2005). In research, **core self-evaluation has** typically **been** operationalized **as the latent** personality **trait that** accounts for the correspondence among **four** lower-order **psychological** traits: **self-esteem, generalized self-efficacy, locus of control, and neuroticism. Despite usually being studied in isolation, these four** lower-order traits **are conceptually similar and empirically** related (Judge, Bono, & Locke, 2000). Self-esteem is the overall value that one places on oneself as a person; generalized self-efficacy is a person's evaluation of how well one can perform across a variety of situations; locus of control is the perceived degree of control of events in one's life; and neuroticism is the tendency to have a negative cognitive/explanatory style and to focus on negative aspects of the self.

Research on the individual core traits from the careers literature has suggested that these lower-order traits influence the quality of early career experiences. Neuroticism has been linked to career self-efficacy and interests (e.g., Hartman & Betz, 2007), while neuroticism, external locus of control, and low self-esteem are associated with career indecision among young adults (e.g., Bacanli, 2006; Lounsbury, Tatum, Chambers, Owen, & Gibson, 1999). The general premise is that when individuals are high on neuroticism, external locus of control, and low on self-esteem and generalized self-efficacy (i.e., having lower levels of core self-evaluations), they are less likely to take actions regarding their careers and will be less happy with their career decisions. This is because individuals with lower levels core self-evaluations are less likely to actively pursue goals that will improve their self-regard. Specifically, according to self-verification theory (Swann, Stain-Seroussi, & Giesler, 1992), individuals with positive self-regard seek situations that offer feedback and information that supports their view, while individuals with negative self-concepts seek situations that justify and reinforce negative self-views. Thus, the information gathered by individuals to make self-appraisals is at least partly determined by their existing self-concepts. Judge et al. (1998) extended self-verification theory into people's perception of the nature of their work. According to Judge and colleagues, individuals with positive core self-evaluations seek and categorize information in their work environments that is likely to lead to positive conclusions about their work experience, while individuals with negative self-evaluations attend to a host of negative aspects of their work environment (i.e., stressful job conditions and annoying co-workers). These assessments may also account for the positive relationship between core self-evaluation and mid-career satisfaction such that individuals with positive self-evaluations are more satisfied with their jobs, because these individuals see more variety, challenge, and intrinsic worth in their work (Judge & Hurst, 2008).

Following the logic of self-verification theory (Swann et al., 1992), it is conceivable that individuals with high core self-evaluations in their early mid careers are more likely to change their jobs or career paths when their work or career environment contradicts with their positive self-appraisal and threatens their self-images. This may be especially true for individuals who entered their careers with relatively little knowledge about them. On the other hand, individuals with high core self-evaluations may be less likely to have job or career changes in their late mid career and late career stages, because they may be more satisfied with their long-term career choices.

Previous research has also demonstrated that individuals with high core self-evaluations often perform better on their jobs (Judge et al., 1998). Specifically, these individuals with positive self-views are more likely to achieve favorable job performance due in part to high levels of motivation and confidence in their abilities to perform. Consistent with this argument, Erez and Judge (2001) found that, in complementary experimental laboratory and field studies, core self-evaluations were linked to goal setting and persistence on a problem solving task, which mediated much of the positive relationship between core self-evaluations and job performance. In addition, Judge et al. (1998) argued that core self-evaluation represents an ability or skill factor that is particularly meaningful for certain job assignments. For example, when confronted with challenging obstacles, those with positive self-evaluations tend to cope more effectively than those with low self-evaluations by remaining persistent and by using effective problem solving strategies. Further, those with positive self-evaluations tend to be particularly effective in positions that require positive interpersonal relations or stress tolerance, such as management positions (Bono & Colbert, 2005). Therefore, it is conceivable that individuals with high core self-evaluations are more likely to attain higher levels of career achievement than those with low core self-evaluations, because the positive effects of core self-evaluations on job complexity, work motivation, goal attainment, and job performance should all lead to greater opportunities to advance one's career (Judge & Hurst, 2008). As such, it provides another explanation to link core self-evaluation to career satisfaction in mid and late career stages, because the higher the career achievement, the more intrinsic and extrinsic rewards should be received by the individual.

As we discussed above, in general, core self-evaluations seem to be beneficial for individuals' career development. A recent study by Judge and Hurst (2008) further suggested that this beneficial effect on one's career exists throughout the life span, facilitating faster career growth. In addition, core self-evaluations seem to affect the likelihood, duration, and health effects of unemployment as well as the success of job changes. For example, people with high core self-evaluations search for jobs more assiduously when unemployed (Wanberg, Glomb, Song, & Sorenson, 2005) and experience sustained good health and life satisfaction during spells of unemployment (McKee-Ryan, Song, Wanberg, & Kinicki, 2005). On the other hand, people with low self-esteem, one of the core traits, are more likely to be unemployed or to hold temporary, rather than permanent, jobs (Salmela-Aro & Nurmi, 2007). Furthermore, men low in emotional stability (i.e., high in neuroticism) are more likely to experience job changes that are shifts downward in socioeconomic status (Gelissen & Graaf, 2006).

Again, the effects of core self-evaluations on employment stability and extrinsic career growth might be due in part to self-verification processes. For example, people with low self-esteem are more likely to remain in jobs with flat wage profiles, while they show signs of waning organizational commitment in jobs where they are treated fairly (Wiesenfeld, Swann, Brockner, & Bartel, 2007). Although research on the role of self-verification in employment contexts is nascent, it already suggests that people with low self-views leave or are less content with job conditions that provide positive feedback and bode well for future success. This may lead to more career plateauing, lateral or downward mobility, and employment instability. People with high core self-evaluations may also be well-equipped psychologically to take increasing amounts of satisfaction and fulfillment from their work. In particular, people with high core self-evaluations might draw greater satisfaction from their extrinsic success. This notion is consistent with the emerging area of positive psychology (Diener & Seligman, 2004), which suggests that some individuals are better able to capitalize on positive experience and, in so doing, experience increments to well-being greater than those derived from the experiences themselves. Recent studies have found that positive self-views enhance the tendency to savor positive experiences and to experience enhanced affect and self-relevant thoughts as a result of doing well (Wood, Heimpel, & Michela, 2003; Wood, Heimpel, Newby-Clark, & Ross, 2005). Thus, it appears that individuals with high core self-evaluations may experience stronger psychic rewards from their career successes, triggering "upward spirals" in their psychological well-being.

Taken as a whole, it seems that individuals with higher core self-evaluations may be quicker in reaching their extrinsic (e.g., pay and occupational status) and intrinsic (e.g., career satisfaction) career success than those with lower core self-evaluations. This is supported by empirical findings derived from a longitudinal panel study using a nationally representative sample (Judge & Hurst, 2008). However, it is still unclear whether this faster career growth may be influential on individuals' experiences in mid and late careers. Specifically, given the faster career growth, individuals with higher core self-evaluations may be able to accumulate enough wealth to retire earlier than their counterparts with lower core self-evaluations. It is also possible that the faster career growth may lead people to reach the top of their careers when they are still relatively young. That may prompt them to consider changing careers or jobs to enrich their experiences (this may be especially true for individuals with high core self-evaluations, as they strive to be challenged and seek intrinsic rewards). It should be noted that it is still unclear whether the effect of core self-evaluation is independent from the effect of cognitive ability, because it is conceivable that people with higher levels of cognitive ability are more likely to experience success in their lives and thus are also more likely to cultivate higher levels of self-regard.

Extraversion, Conscientiousness, and Openness to Experience

Earlier we discussed the potential effect of neuroticism on mid and late careers in the core self-evaluation framework. Here, we focus on discussing effects of several other Big Five personality traits, namely extraversion, conscientiousness, and openness to experience, on mid and late careers. Extraversion refers to individuals' behavioral tendencies in being sociable, gregarious, assertive, talkative, and active (Erdheim, Wang, & Zickar, 2006). Conscientiousness refers to the dependability and volition of a person. The typical behaviors associated with conscientiousness include being hard-working, achievement-oriented, persevering, careful, and responsible. Openness to Experience is related to scientific and artistic creativity, divergent thinking, and political liberalism. The behavioral tendencies typically associated with Openness to Experience include being imaginative, cultured, curious, original, broad-minded, intelligent (Digman, 1990), and having a need for variety, aesthetic sensitivity, and unconventional values (McCrae & John, 1992).

Given that positive emotionality is a hallmark of extraverts (Watson & Clark, 1997), it makes sense that extraverts would have greater confidence about their careers and are more satisfied with their career choices. However, extraverts are more social than introverts, which may help them build substantial social networks that offer them more employment alternatives. Previous research has shown that employees who perceive that they have several viable alternatives will have weaker commitment to their organization than those employees who perceive that they have few alternatives (Erdheim et al., 2006; Meyer & Allen, 1997). Moreover, because extraverts tend to get more of what they want out of social interactions, they may in general perceive more job alternatives than introverts (Watson & Clark, 1997). Therefore, in terms of career and job change patterns, extraverts can be expected to be more likely to change their jobs and careers than introverts in their mid and late career stages.

Conscientious individuals are typically hard-working, achievement-oriented, and more responsible. This greater work-involvement tendency can provide them increased opportunity to obtain formal (e.g., pay, promotion) and informal (e.g., recognition, respect) rewards in their work and careers. To the extent that conscientious employees earn such rewards, they should have heightened levels of satisfaction with their jobs and careers, thus are less likely to change their career paths after they have achieved momentum in mid career. However, conscientious individuals also tend to hold higher levels of moral standards and are more sensitive to injustice (McCrae & John, 1992). Therefore, if all their hard work is not reciprocated with comparable rewards, it is conceivable that conscientious individuals are more likely to change their work environment (e.g., by changing jobs) to reinstate the sense of fairness. Nevertheless, given the high levels of achievement-orientation that conscientious individuals have, it is unlikely for them to change career paths in reaction to unfair treatment at work. Their persistence and dutifulness in goal pursuit are more likely to drive them to prove themselves in the career path that they have chosen. In addition, individuals with high levels of conscientiousness are also more likely to have strong work-role identity, which may make them delay their retirement (Wang & Shultz, 2010).

Since openness to experience can be viewed as an individual's need for "novelty, variety, and complexity and an intrinsic appreciation for experience" (McCrae, 1996, p. 326), we speculate that people who score high on the openness dimension are more exploratory and more willing to pursue job and career alternatives than those who score low on this dimension. In addition, openness to experience may predict the tendency for people to engage in non-traditional forms of employment, such as telecommuting and virtue business, especially when they have to provide care to children or elders in their mid to late careers. It is also conceivable that openness to experience may be related to post-retirement employment patterns as well. Specifically, when deciding to engage in bridge employment, individuals with high levels of openness to experience may be less likely to work in the same career field as they did prior to their retirement, but rather in different career fields.

Resilience

Personality-based resilience concerns relatively stable individual differences in how people respond to potentially stressful events. Resilient individuals are less likely to appraise events as stressful, less likely to have intense negative reactions to stressors, more likely to choose effective coping strategies, and less likely to experience adverse outcomes from stressors. According to Wang, Sinclair, and Deese (2010), resilience traits can be described as cognitively-oriented information processing styles that people have for (a) interpreting demanding events as potentially threatening or potentially rewarding, (b) evaluating their own capacity to respond to demanding events, and (c) constructing positive interpretations of prior experiences. Resilience traits are relevant to mid and late careers because as individuals move forward in their careers, the broadened responsibility and the multiple work and non-work related roles that they have to fulfill are likely to create more stress for them. As such, resilience traits may be particularly important for individuals in their mid and late careers to deal with stress and prevent disruption of their career advancement.

Two frequently studied resilience traits are psychological capital and hardiness. Psychological capital is a relatively new concept from the literature on positive psychology and human strengths. Luthans, Avolio, Avey, and Norman (2007) describe psychological capital as a composite of four such strengths: *hope* (e.g., believing that one can accomplish his/her goals), *optimism* (a positive outlook about the future), *adaptability* (the ability to adapt to challenging events), and *self-efficacy* (the belief that one can successfully complete tasks or goals). A growing body of research has demonstrated that higher levels of psychological capital are associated with higher job satisfaction and better job performance (Luthans et al., 2007).

Hardiness consists of three dimensions: commitment, control, and challenge (Maddi, Kahn, & Maddi, 1998). *Commitment* reflects a general tendency to be engaged by and finding meaning and purpose in one's life. *Control* reflects the belief that one is capable of effectively responding to demanding situations in their lives. Finally, *challenge* includes cognitive flexibility and tolerance for ambiguity, which allow people to easily integrate unexpected or otherwise stressful events and to view them as opportunities for personal growth, rather than as threats. Although hardiness has received less attention in the organizational and vocational psychology literature than in military and health psychology, many studies link hardiness to health outcomes (e.g., Florian, Mikulincer, & Taubman, 1995).

According to McAdams and Pals' (2006) taxonomy, psychological capital and hardiness may be viewed as characteristic adaptations—traits reflecting relatively stable ways people learn to adapt to situations in their lives that may be modified through experience. In general, it is believed that individuals with higher levels of psychological capital and hardiness are more likely to be able to effectively and quickly recover from setbacks and adapt to the changes in the environment. They are also more likely to hold a positive attitude toward the tasks that they are performing and the environment that they are in when experiencing setbacks. As such, these individuals are less likely to view the stressful events in their life as being threatening, but rather as challenges that they need to overcome. In turn, they may be less susceptible to the increased stress and hassles when they advance into mid and late careers stages. In addition, previous research has shown that work-related stress is a prominent factor that "pushes" individuals into retirement (Wang, 2007; Wang et al., 2008). Given the utility for psychological capital and hardiness to buffer the work-related stress, it is conceivable that individuals with higher levels of psychological capital are less likely to retire earlier than they planned.

Individual Level Factors: Attributes

Physical Health and Physical Aging

One important individual attribute that has robust impact on one's career path is physical health. Poor health can make it difficult for individuals to continue work. People's health conditions can also impose limits on the types of careers they are able to pursue. For example, for people with cardiovascular conditions, performing tasks that are physically demanding carries too much risk. Previous research has also shown that health problems are important reasons that "push" older workers to retire. Older workers may simply have to retire, because they are not able to maintain their performance levels due to health issues. This may also create a sense of involuntariness for the retirement decision, further leading to dissatisfaction about the decision as well as the retirement life (Shultz et al., 1998; Wang et al., 2008).

Other than pre-existed physical conditions or environment-elicited physical conditions, physical aging may also impact people's mid and late careers. With aging, there is a gradual loss of muscle mass and muscle strength (McArdle, Vasilaki, & Jackson, 2002). Because of this, maximal exercise capacity declines with age as well (Fielding & Meydani, 1997). Normal aging is also accompanied by the loss of bone tissue throughout the body. Bone loss begins in the late 30s, accelerating in the 50s, and slows by the 70s, which increases the risk for degenerative arthritis, the leading cause of disability among older adults within industrialized countries (Sowers, 2001). It also leads to increased rates of traumatic fractures.

In addition, metabolism generally drops as people grow older. For instance, with increasing age, mitochondria produce less adenosine tri-phosphate (ATP), the body's main metabolic source of energy. There is also an oxidative function reduction in aging livers, which may lead to age-related differences in responding to environmental chemical exposures (Jansen, 2002). This oxidative function reduction may also cause medication to stay in the body longer and to create the potential for toxicity if the medication schedule does not take this into account. Further, research evidence suggests that the total number of lymphocytes in the body probably does not change with aging. Nevertheless, major changes occur in how well lymphocytes work (Aldwin & Gilmer, 1999). For example, older adults' immune systems take longer to build up defenses against specific diseases. As a result, older adults become more prone to serious consequences from illnesses that are easily defeated by young adults. Additionally, various forms of leukemia, which are cancers of the immune cells, increase with age.

Along with physical aging, research has shown a general trend toward decreasing energy, and, as a result, reduced capacity for physically demanding tasks with increasing age. The implication of this, obviously, is that age-related physical changes may make it more difficult for older employees to perform physically demanding tasks. As such, career jobs that require workers to perform very quickly or that require workers to perform physically demanding activities for long periods of time are generally less attractive as mid and late career options.

Further, physical aging may make older employees more vulnerable to occupational hazards, as physical aging is generally intertwined with decreases in the immune system functioning and muscle strength. Typical occupations that may carry higher occupational safety and health risks for older employees include: administrative support (e.g., carpal tunnel syndrome), production/craft/repair occupations, transportation and material moving, farming/forestry/fishing, private household services, and protective services. The risks are primarily in the areas of exposure to chemicals, being struck by heavy objects, exposure to violence, and repetitive motions. As such, these career jobs are also less attractive as mid and late career options.

With physical aging, health care may become an important factor to consider for older workers who make mid and late career decisions. Entering the 21st century, health care costs have been increasing rapidly in the United States, as has the cost for health insurance coverage. People who work for small businesses or who are self-employed usually have to pay more to get the same health benefit enjoyed by government or large corporate employees. Therefore, mid and late career changes may function as a possible pathway to reach good quality, future health care. It should be noted that although the availability and quality of health care have been extensively discussed by general literature as well as popular media as a factor that impacts mid and late career decision making, very few empirical studies in career change decision making literature have examined it. Nevertheless, given its importance to both older workers' physical and financial well-beings, its potential impact for older workers' mid and late career change decisions should not be overlooked.

Experience and Expertise

One thing that we know typically occurs as people age is that they gain experience and often have higher levels of task-related expertise. As one would probably imagine, experience is typically associated with higher levels of work performance. This makes workers in their mid and late careers quite attractive to employers, as hiring them saves considerable training cost and at the same time their performance would be better than new job incumbents, at least initially. This is particularly true for today's workforce. Demographics show that in 2012 nearly 20% of the total U.S. workforce is age 55 or older, up from just under 13% in 2000. With the pending retirement of large numbers of baby boomers, many analysts are predicting growing labor shortages. In fact, according to one report (AARP, 2005), some employers have been facing that problem for several years. In addition to the widely publicized shortages of nurses and other health care professionals, organizations that rely on such specially trained individuals as teachers, engineers, and many other skilled workers are feeling the pressure of labor shortages. In light of the declining proportion of younger workers, older workers who engage in bridge employment can provide some beneficial labor market resources to overcome the growing labor shortages in the United States. Employers are more than ready to better utilize the productive powers and expertise of these experienced older workers.

Experience and expertise are also important when complex tasks are performed at work. Given the age-related cognitive changes described earlier, it would appear that older workers would tend to have greater difficulty than younger employees performing cognitively demanding tasks. While it has been shown that older workers do have more difficulty on such tasks, there have also been studies showing no age-related difference in the performance of such tasks. Scholars have suggested that older employees with higher levels of task-related expertise are able to develop strategies to compensate for their cognitive declines without impairing their task performance. As such, experience and expertise are particularly useful for mid and late career workers to continue their careers without having to make a career path change or exit.

A special type of knowledge that may be relevant to one's career development is called savoir faire (or simply put, "savvy"; Pinder, 2008). For employees in an organization, savoir faire involves knowing how to do things that capitalize one's performance, social, and emotional gains in the organizational environment. For example, a savvy employee would know both the organizational structure and the political power distribution in the organization quite well. She or he would also know from whom information should be sought in different situations. Typically, employees achieve organizational savior faire by accumulating organization-related experience over a long time period. That allows employees to have sufficient opportunities to learn, observe, and acquire the related knowledge. A savvy employee is often the one who climbs the organizational ladder faster than others (Ritti, 1994).

Similarly, for workers in their mid and late careers, the level of career savvy could be an important factor in determining whether they could make further progress in their respective fields. Only knowing how to perform well in one's career field (i.e., having the ability and the skills) is not necessarily enough for one to be successful in that career. The person also needs to know how to build a resourceful social network in his/her career field, how to promote the recognition for his/her career-related achievement, and most importantly, how to influence his/her peers in the same career field. This type of knowledge accumulation could be difficult to achieve when workers switch from one career to another, especially when the time for transition is limited. Previous research has shown that having an experienced mentor could greatly facilitate the process for gaining job, organization, and career related knowledge (e.g., Allen, McManus, & Russell, 1999), suggesting that individuals in their mid or late careers may still benefit greatly from formal or informal mentoring activities. We discuss the issue of mentoring in much more detail in Chapter 9.

Age-Related Motivation

According to the Socioemotional Selectivity Theory (SST), a basic awareness of passage through different life stages is ubiquitous in all cultures and people, and that this awareness will have implications for people's motivations (Carstensen, 1991; Carstensen, Isaacowitz, & Charles, 1999). SST also posits that individuals are typically agentic in that they set goals and behave in ways that are likely to help them achieve those goals (Carstensen et al., 1999). Put together, these two principles indicate that where one is in his or her "life time" (i.e., whether one is relatively young or relatively old) strongly shapes the types of goals an individual will pursue. Specifically, the theory posits that when individuals are younger, they are closer to the beginning of the life cycle, and thus view "time" as time since birth. Thus, their goals are future-oriented: they aim toward knowledge acquisition, career planning, and the development of new social relationships that will pay off in the future (Carstensen, 1991). Older individuals, by contrast, view "time" as time left in life. Thus, they will have more present-oriented goals: they aim toward regulating their emotions to be positive, pursue emotionally gratifying relationships with others, and engage in activities that will benefit them relatively immediately (Carstensen,

1991). Overall, according to SST, older adults focus more on socio-emotional outcomes, while younger adults are more driven by skill, knowledge, and opportunity development and, thus, are more information-oriented.

While little research has examined SST in the workplace, several studies do suggest that age-related differences in goals and motivations do manifest themselves in organizational settings. For instance, research has suggested that older workers are less career-development oriented and often avoid challenges at work, while younger adults tend to have a "learning orientation" and thus use challenges as education and development opportunities (Kanfer & Ackerman, 2004). In addition, research has shown that compared to older employees, younger employees are typically more competitive rather than cooperative (Wong, Gardiner, Lang, & Coulon, 2008). Therefore, it is conceivable that older workers will be less likely to invest more time and energy to seek career advancement than their younger counterparts after they move into their mid and late career stages. Further, research has shown that older adults typically display more affective commitment to their organization while younger employees tend to place more importance on "employability" and opportunity for advancement (D'Amato & Herzfeldt, 2008). Therefore, we will expect less frequent career or job changes among older workers than younger workers, as older workers prefer more stable environment and values their established social network.

Given that older workers may put more value on regulating their emotions to be positive and pursuing emotional gratifying relationships with others, they may respond better to a work or career environment that promotes a more cooperative and less political work climate among employees. Their socio-emotional focus may also lead them to be more likely to succeed in performing service jobs that are not physically demanding. Further, older workers may prefer not to face too many new challenges, especially those of evaluative nature, at work. Accordingly, they may develop a negative attitude toward performance evaluation and formal feedback activities when they move from mid to late career stages. In this sense, the quality of the feedback delivery may become more important to older workers than the content of the feedback.

Future Research Directions

In this chapter, we have reviewed two groups of individual-level factors that may impact mid and late careers. In general, the impact of individual dispositions (e.g., cognitive ability, cognitive aging, and personality) on mid and late careers is studied less often than that of individual attributes (in particular, physical health). This may be due to the fact that individual dispositions are relatively more stable, which makes it difficult to develop corresponding interventions to help solve career issues people face. Therefore, individual dispositions are often treated as the distal predictors of career changes and career success when researchers set up their theoretical models. Nevertheless, we argue that it is important to study individual dispositions, because it helps us to develop a more comprehensive understanding regarding why people are behaving in certain ways or holding certain attitudes when it comes to career-related issues. Only paying attention to proximal factors often blurs the deep-level causes of the phenomena, especially when different proximal factors may share the same dispositional cause. For example, conscientiousness may be the consistent cause for a person to change the job (due to perceived unfairness at work) but not the career (due to persistency in pursuing the career goal) in his/her mid or late career stage. As such, examining individual attributes as mediators (or proximal factors) that link individual dispositions (or distal factors) to mid and late career outcomes may be particularly fruitful.

Another future research direction to consider is the interactive effect between individual dispositions and individual attributes in influencing one's mid and late careers. For example, the interaction between one's cognitive ability and work motivation may influence people in different career stages differently. While cognitive ability and work motivation may have multiplicative beneficial effect in early career stages due to their joint facilitation of skill and knowledge development, such joint effect may become weaker when one moves into mid and late career stages and has accumulated sufficient experience and expertise about his/her career. In addition, it may also be interesting to examine the interactive effect between different individual dispositions, such as cognitive aging and resilience. It is conceivable that resilience may at least be able to partly offset the stress and anxiety brought by cognitive aging in facing daily tasks

It should be noted that although we have addressed age-related motivation from the perspective of SST, it is also important for future research to consider other types of intra-individual value and priority changes over time. For example, when moving from early career stages to mid and late careers, an individual's career salience (i.e., the relative importance of a career in one's total life; Greenhaus, 1971; Super, 1982) may change accordingly. Specifically, it is possible that at one's early career, work and career roles are more salient and central to one's life. This centrality may later be diluted by the additional marital roles and parenting roles. We will further discuss the challenges posed by role overload and conflict for workers over 50 in Chapter 10. However, research has rarely examined how intra-individual value and priority changes over time may impact mid and late careers, which should be a focus for future studies.

Chapter 5

Career Issues Unique to Mid and Late Careers

Job Level Factors

In this chapter, we review the important job-level factors that may impact mid and late careers. When considering one's career, it is natural to pay attention to the particular jobs that form one's career (Greenhaus, 2003). Following Hall's (1976) classic definition of career ("the individually-perceived sequence of attitudes and behaviors associated with work-related experiences and activities over the span of a person's life," p. 4), it is obvious that jobs are the fundamental elements that shape one's work-related experiences and activities. Considering the multiple career-related criteria existing for mid and late career stages that we reviewed in Chapter 4 (e.g., pay, occupational status, career satisfaction, job satisfaction, career change, relocation, and retirement decisions), the extant literature has indeed shown that multiple aspects of one's job are related to these criteria. For example, it is well known that the job requirement plays an important role in determining the pay and occupational status (e.g., Lawler, Ledford, & Chang, 1993; Ledford, 1995). In addition, career and job satisfaction are at least partly influenced by job characteristics (Loher, Noe, Moeler, & Fitzgerald, 1985), as well as other aspects of jobs, such as work schedule, shift, and number of hours (Holtom, Lee, & Tidd, 2002). Finally, various job demands and work stress induced by them are important determinants for career withdrawal, career change, and retirement decisions (Cartwright & Cooper, 1997; Wang & Takeuchi, 2007; Wang, Zhan, Liu, & Shultz, 2008).

In this chapter, we apply two perspectives to organizing our discussion regarding job-level factors that may impact mid and late careers. The first focuses on examining how job patterns influence one's mid and late careers. In other words, we are interested in understanding whether features of job patterns, such as the frequency of employment, the duration of employment, and the types of employment, would influence one's mid and late career. Therefore, the first perspective largely deals with the effect of cumulated job history a person has on his/her mid and late careers. To facilitate this analysis, we use the notion of "job cycles" that are analogues to "career cycles" advanced by Hall (2002) to characterize one's job history. In particular, we analyze different types and features of job cycles and illustrate how they may influence mid and late careers, as well as how these cycles may themselves manifest in one's mid and late career stages.

The second perspective we rely on to discuss job-level factors that may impact mid and late careers is based on theories of job design (Morgeson & Campion, 2003). Here, we will mainly focus on delineating the job factors specified by job characteristics theory (Hackman & Oldham, 1980), the sociotechnical systems theory (Trist, 1981), as well as the contextual factors at the job-level (Morgeson & Humphrey, 2006). Our discussion of this perspective will also explore the implication of the recent advancements in relational job design (Grant, 2007) to the mid and later career stages.

Job Cycles

Definition

To facilitate the discussion of the effect of cumulated job history on one's mid and late career, we first define job cycle as a key construct to understand job history. This construct is inspired by the term "career cycles" discussed by Hall (1976) to describe the series of career changes people may experience during their life long career pursuit. According to Hall (2002), a new career cycle is started when a person begins *exploring* some sort of change—a new way of working, developing new skills, developing new relationships and connections, or pursuing some new job opportunities. Then, the person engages in some *trial* activity, perhaps doing some part-time "moonlighting" work in a new area or taking on a new project at work that requires learning new skills or concepts. If this trial activity is rewarding and successful, the person might go more deeply into the new area, make a commitment to it, and become *established* in it. This would lead to *mastery* and continued work in this career. Eventually, the cycle ends when the person exits one career and joins another one. Given that people could be exploring and engaging in trial activity in one career path while establishing or mastering another career path, it is important to note that different career cycles could overlap with each other in time.

Similar to career cycle, we define job cycle as the cycle that starts with entering a job and ends with job exit. Therefore, two job cycles could overlap with each other as well. However, job cycle differs from career cycle in terms of several key features. First, a job cycle's scope is typically smaller than a career cycle. A career cycle often consists of more than one job cycle. A person could go through several job cycles before he or she establishes and masters a particular career. As such, consecutive job cycles may capture an adjustment and adaption process to a particular career path (Dawis & Lofquist, 1984). Second, each job cycle is characterized by the specific environment (e.g., social and physical environment; Morgeson & Humphrey, 2006) within which the job is embedded. This notion of environmental factors is often absent in the consideration of career cycles, as the notion of career focuses more on the general work activities rather than specific context of a particular job (Hall, 1976; Peterson et al., 2001). Third, a job cycle also has more important and direct implications on a person's financial well-being than career cycle. A person's employment offers an important source of income. In addition, employment is associated with other financial benefits as well (e.g., health care and retirement pension). Therefore, while people may not experience significant financial hardship in-between career cycles (as they may still hold jobs), the likelihood for experiencing such hardship is great when they are in-between job cycles. Finally, while career cycles are typically used to emphasize the dynamic protean career process, which is largely internally driven, guided by the person's values and results in ongoing self-reinvention (Hall, 2002), job cycles emphasize less on the motivation and idiosyncrasy of the person in influencing the entering or exiting a particular job cycle. Instead, the notion of job cycle emphasizes more on the impact of external force on job-related dynamics, such as downsizing induced employment termination that is associated with the macro economic climate.

Features of Job Cycles in Early Careers That May Impact Mid and Late Careers

Following the definition laid out above, in this section, we discuss the features of job cycles in early careers that may impact mid and late careers. These features include the number of job cycles one had, the average length of job cycles, the various types of jobs one held, the financial resources accrued over job cycles, as well as the ways one moved from one job cycle to another in one's early career. It should be noted that we do not see it to be necessary to specify a distinct age to separate early careers from mid and late careers (see our discussion in Chapter 2). Instead, we rely on the relative time order to facilitate the discussion here.

The Number of Job Cycles

The number of job cycles can be captured by considering the total number of jobs a person held in a given period of time. As we noted earlier, each job cycle offers a specific social and physical environment. Therefore, the more job cycles one goes through, the more experience one will accumulate in dealing with different social and physical environments. As noted by the attraction-selection-attrition (ASA; Schneider, Goldstein, & Smith, 1995) model, this experience often serves to facilitate a sense of self-awareness that helps people to understand what types of job environment fit them the best. This is particularly relevant for early career stages, because in these stages people typically try out different career options and attempt to select the best one that matches their abilities and serves their interest (Mirvis & Hall, 1994). Therefore, it is conceivable that the more job cycles one goes through in an early career, the more likely one will be satisfied with his or her career decisions and situations in mid and late careers.

The Various Types of Job Tasks

Following the above argument, experiencing job cycles that are characterized by various types of job tasks in early career stage will also be beneficial for development in mid and late career stages. Specifically, the more job tasks a person experiences in the early career stage, the more likely the person will develop a large variety of competencies that will be useful for him/her to further mid and late career development. In addition, the experience of various job tasks can also facilitate the self-awareness regarding one's own expertise and unique abilities, as well as offer opportunity to foster strong self-efficacy regarding job adaptation (see discussion regarding the utility of efficacy and core self-evaluation in

Chapter 4). Finally, the experience on various job tasks could also increase the number of career options when a person enters mid and late career stages.

The Average Length of Job Cycles

Given that it typically takes a while for a newcomer to fully adjust and adapt to a new job and its environment (Kammeyer-Mueller, 2007; Wang, Zhan, McCune, & Truxillo, 2011), it is important to also pay attention to the average length of job cycles during a person's early career. We expect the average length of job cycles in one's early career will have a negative relationship with later development in mid and late career stages. Specifically, the shorter time a person spends in each job cycle, the less likely the person is able to fully master the skills and knowledge associated with that job position. According to the cumulative advantage/disadvantage theory (DiPrete & Eirich, 2006), the cumulative disadvantage process is capable of magnifying small differences over time and makes it difficult for an individual who is behind in resource development at a point in time to catch up (DiPrete & Eirich, 2006). One type of resource that is associated with a job cycle is the opportunity for training and employee development. In a long run, people who have shorter tenure on each job they hold will be at disadvantage when entering mid and late career stages, because they will have had fewer opportunities to develop their job-related skills and knowledge compared to their counterparts who spent more time in each job cycle. Thus, it is less likely for those people to enjoy the benefits from job-related training and development. Consequently, they will have fewer career options when entering mid and late career stages.

It should be noted that when considering average length of job cycles together with the number of job cycles and types of jobs a person experiences in the early career stage, there may exist an optimal point where a person has a sufficient amount of job environment and task exposure, but also spends enough time on each job to master it. In other words, given that the average length of job cycles may be highly negatively related to the number of job cycles and the types of jobs one goes through, a combination that maximizes a person's experience in and adaptability to multiple types of job tasks and job environment will be most beneficial.

The Financial Resources Accrued Over Job Cycles

Following the cumulative advantage/disadvantage theory (DiPrete & Eirich, 2006), another type of resource associated with job cycles and is subject to the jeopardy of cumulative disadvantage is financial. Specifically, we expect that if a person is able to accrue a good amount of financial resources over job cycles in his early career, the person will be more likely to engage in intrinsically motivating career activities in mid and late careers. This is because with sufficient financial resources accrued in early career, the importance of the job as the income source may become secondary, and the person may have more freedom to choose the career arenas that they are interested in. On the other hand, people who did not accrue sufficient financial resources in early careers, may still have to follow career paths that would offer them financial security, which may limit their later career options. Supporting this notion, Wrzesniewski, McCauley, Rozin, and Schwartz (1997) found that those people who held low paying jobs when entering late career stages were likely to see work as a means of gaining financial resources rather than to see work as a stepping stone to advance in one's career pursuit. However, this view of work was not adopted by people with high paying jobs.

The Ways Individuals Move from One Job Cycle to Another

Finally, it is important to discuss the potential effect of the ways individuals move from one job cycle to another. In particular, we argue that the voluntariness of such movement has important implications for one's mid and late career pursuit. Specifically, according to the unfolding model of turnover (Lee, Mitchell, Holtom, McDaniel, & Hill, 1999), when people exit their jobs voluntarily, they often have had enough time to both socioemotionally and financially prepare for the exit. In fact, often times, people voluntarily leave their jobs because they have already located alternative jobs (Lee et al., 1999). Therefore, when people voluntarily exit one job cycle, their subsequent job cycles are less likely to be adversely influenced due to inadequate preparation and they will spend less time in-between job cycles which essentially should increase the average length of their job cycles.

To contrast, when people exit one job cycle involuntarily, they will often spend a longer time locating a new job, and the search for a new job is likely to be influenced by the level of financial pressure they experience (Wanberg, Glomb, Song, & Sorenson, 2005). Therefore, they may enter the next job cycle without particularly being satisfied with the job conditions, which may prompt them to leave the job soon again and shorten their time spent in the new job cycle. As such, their self-efficacy for adapting to new job tasks and job environment may also be undermined. Taken together, we argue that, in the long run, exiting job cycles involuntarily will be detrimental for one's development in mid and late careers due to the disruption this type of job cycle exit creates to one's life as well as job-related skill and knowledge development.

Job Cycles in Mid and Late Careers

Having discussed the potential impact that features of job cycles in one's early career may have on mid and late careers, it is important to note that job cycles may also have unique manifestation patterns in mid and late career stages as well. Here, we discuss four potential kinds of job cycle patterns. These patterns underscore the fact that people in their later career stages can be more selective and reflective about the process that they go through, as well as be more effective in utilizing the self-awareness accumulated in early career stages to aid their career-related decision making.

One Job One Cycle

The pattern of one job one cycle is a common form of job cycle among older workers in their late career stages. Research in older worker employment has shown that people often retire from a job that they hold for a significantly long period of time (e.g., greater than six years). Researchers have suggested that this is mainly due to the traditional defined benefit pension structure, which encourages long-term employment in one organization as the length of employment typically factors into the calculation of pension benefit (Greenhaus, 2003; Wang, Adams, Beehr, & Shultz, 2009). However, given that more organizations are shifting toward the pension structure of defined contribution (Wang et al., 2009), we expect that fewer people will stick to this one job one cycle pattern in the future.

Job Cycles that Share Similar Job Tasks

This pattern of job cycles is often seen among workers who are well-trained and enjoyed their professional identity (e.g., accountants, engineers, academics). In their mid and late careers, due to the salient professional identity, further developing and maintaining their profession-related skills and knowledge becomes the central job-related need (Hall, 2002). In addition, these knowledge workers are more likely to be targeted by recruitment efforts due to the unique expertise they have (Greenhaus, 2003). Therefore, they are more likely to experience more than one job cycle in their mid and late careers, but the job tasks that characterize these job cycles are likely to be similar.

Job Cycles that Share Similar Job Environment

After going through early career stages, some workers may be purposefully searching for a particular type of job environment that they deem to fit themselves better. For example, the self-awareness facilitated by the early career experience may lead introverted workers to seek a job environment that entails fewer interpersonal interactions. For some of these workers, jobs may be merely viewed as a means of gaining financial resources to support the life style they prefer; it is the socioemotional experience embedded in the job environment that means more to them. Further, according to the socioemotional selectivity theory reviewed in Chapter 4, workers in their mid and late career stages often focus less on getting ahead with their status pursuit, but more on maintaining a stable social and physical environment (Kanfer & Ackerman, 2004). As such, although workers in mid and late career stages may still move in and out of job cycles for financial reasons, at least some of them would prefer to have a similar job environment across job cycles.

Simultaneous Job Cycles

Simultaneous job cycles form a pattern in which workers experience more than one job cycle at the same time. Two very different types of workers may exhibit this pattern of job cycles in later career stages. First, workers who have accrued substantial financial resources through early and mid career stages are more likely to spend their late career stages maximizing their job experiences to fulfill intrinsic needs, such as trying out a job that they may have always wanted to do and go through a totally new job training process. Given that workers in their late career stages may feel a sense of urgency, as they typically are aware of the years left before they exit the workforce (Bidwell, Griffin, & Hesketh, 2006), they may engage in multiple job cycles at the same time to maximize their experience. The second type of worker is one who is under significant financial pressure. That worker may simply have to take on multiple jobs at the same time to fulfill financial needs in his or her later career stages.

It should be noted that among the four kinds of job cycle patterns described above, only the one-job-one-cycle pattern may not exhibit at the same time with other patterns. The remaining three patterns are not mutually exclusive. For example, people who engage in job cycles that share similar job tasks may also engage in job cycles that share similar job environment. Further, people who engage in job cycles that share similar job tasks may also engage in those job cycles simultaneously. The key to understanding different combinations of job cycle patterns is to consider both internal and external forces that drive individuals to exhibit a certain pattern of job cycles in their late career stages. In Chapter 4, we have already provided a detailed discussion regarding the internal forces that drive individuals' career-related choices and behaviors. Below, we discuss those external forces in the forms of job characteristics to gauge their effects on one's mid and late career.

Job Design Theories and Job Characteristics

We now review job characteristics that may influence mid and late careers. We do so by following major theories of job design, which provide us a comprehensive list of job characteristics, such as task characteristics, knowledge characteristics, social characteristics, and contextual characteristics (Morgeson & Humphrey, 2006). It is evident that the scope of these job characteristics is larger than the traditional motivational job characteristics discussed in the job characteristics theory. Nevertheless, we will start with reviewing the job characteristics theory to provide a foundation for discussing how those traditional motivational job characteristics may influence mid and late careers.

Job Characteristics Theory

Hackman and Oldham (1976, 1980) proposed the job characteristics theory to suggest that five job characteristics produce critical psychological states in the job holder, and ultimately result in a set of positive work-related outcomes. These five job characteristics are skill variety, task identity, task significance, autonomy, and feedback. First, *skill variety* involves the use of a wide variety of the worker's skills and abilities. Second, *task identity* involves the extent to which the worker feels he or she is responsible for a meaningful and whole part of the work. Third, *task significance* involves the impact the job has on the lives of others. Together, these three job characteristics are presumed to increase the meaningfulness of work. Fourth, *autonomy* involves the amount of freedom and independence an individual has in terms of carrying out his or her work assignment. This was expected to increase experienced responsibility for work outcomes. Fifth, *feedback* concerns the extent to which the job duties provide knowledge of the results of the job incumbent's actions. This was expected to provide knowledge concerning the results of work activities.

These five job characteristics in Hackman and Oldham's model are presumed to influence three critical psychological states of the workers. Specifically, skill variety, task identity, and task significance are all posited to influence the experienced meaningfulness of the work, while autonomy is expected to relate to experienced responsibility for outcomes of the work and feedback is expected to relate to knowledge of results. These critical psychological states in turn influence workers' motivation to perform their jobs and lead to positive work-related outcomes (e.g., work effectiveness and satisfaction).

For workers in their mid and late career stages, experiencing meaningfulness of the work and taking responsibility for outcomes of the work may be the two most important psychological states. This is because both these psychological states are important for maintaining a person's work-related identity. According to Super (1980, 1990), people typically have already developed stable work-related identity when they enter mid and late career stages. As such, from a motivational standpoint, it is important to keep the congruence between their job tasks and the work-related identity they cherish. Specifically, workers in their mid and late career stages will appreciate the opportunity to practice various skills they learned throughout their career. In addition, as they typically have matured in terms of work experience and task knowledge (i.e., different from their counterparts who are in early career stages that focus on learning), jobs which offer task identity, task significance, and autonomy will be most congruent with their professional image. Consequently, these job characteristics will be most appealing to workers in their mid and late career stages.

On the other hand, a job that offers too much external feedback (e.g., feedback from supervisors or coworkers) may be demotivating for these workers, because the external feedback could be interpreted as threatening their professional image, especially considering that they are not in the learning stages of their careers any more. Following this theorizing, these workers may be more motivated to perform jobs where feedback is internally embedded. In other words, when feedback can come from the job task itself (e.g., when the task is carried out in the trial-error manner; Hackman & Lawler, 1971), it will be easier for workers in mid and late career stages to accept the feedback and utilize it to further improve their work.

Sociotechnical Systems Theory

Although job characteristic theory has received some support in the empirical literature (e.g., Fried & Ferris, 1987; Loher et al., 1985), it only focuses on task characteristics, while ignoring other types of job characteristics, such as the social characteristics and knowledge characteristics. To facilitate the discussion of these two types of job characteristics in relation to mid and late careers, we next review the sociotechnical systems theory.

The sociotechnical systems approach was originally based on work conducted by Trist and Bamforth (1951) that focused on the use of autonomous groups to accomplish work. This perspective suggested that forms of work are composed of people interacting with each other and a technical system to produce products or services. Following this conceptualization, this soicotechnical interaction had a reciprocal and dynamic influence on the operation and appropriateness of the technology as well as on the behavior of the people who operate it. Given the interdependence between human and technical systems, sociotechnical systems theory suggested that productivity and satisfaction could be maximized via joint optimization. In other words, optimal job functioning would occur only if the social and technical systems were designed to fit each other (Trist, 1981).

The advantage for applying the sociotechnical systems theory to understanding job characteristics lies in the fact that it considers both the social environment of the job (i.e., interaction between workers) and the knowledge required to perform the job (i.e., the technical aspect of the job). In fact, an extension of this theory by Cummings (1978) suggested that even within a single job, the various job tasks need to be well differentiated by clarifying different knowledge characteristics that are required to perform the job. He further pointed out that the social environment for performing the job largely determines whether the technology side of the job functioning can go smoothly. Based on these notions, we analyze knowledge and social aspects of jobs and inspect how they may influence workers' mid and late careers. Specifically, knowledge characteristics reflect the kinds of broad technical demands (e.g., abilities, skills, and declarative and procedural knowledge; Morgeson & Campion, 2003) that are placed on an individual as a function of what is done on the job. We pay attention to four kinds of such knowledge characteristics here.

Job Complexity

Job complexity refers to the extent to which the tasks on a job are complex and difficult to perform (Campion, 1988). Although originally conceptualized as an aspect of mechanistic job design, Edwards, Scully, and Brtek (2000) found that complexity is a distinct factor. Because work that involves complex tasks requires the use of numerous high-level skills and is more mentally demanding and challenging, it is likely to have positive motivational outcomes for workers performing it. However, for workers entering mid and late careers, job complexity's effect may be well associated with their use of strategies of selection, optimization, and compensation (SOC; Freund & Baltes, 1998). Specifically, when dealing with complex jobs, they may optimize their learning experiences by selecting the skills and tasks that compensate for their weaknesses and emphasize their strengths. These workers are typically in a better position in utilizing SOC strategies than their counterparts who are in early career stages, because they have accumulated more knowledge and skills over their career and probably have a more comprehensive perspective when facing complex jobs. Therefore, for those who can successfully apply SOC strategies, high levels of job complexity may prove to be motivating. However, for those who cannot efficiently use SOC strategies, high levels of job complexity may turn out to be overwhelming and may diminish one's self-efficacy for performing such jobs.

Information Processing

The amount of information processing needed at work reflects the degree to which a job requires attending to and processing data or other information. Some jobs require higher levels of monitoring and active information processing than others, such as air traffic controller (Wall & Jackson, 1995). Similar to job complexity, high levels of information processing requirement may be motivating, as successfully accomplishing them signals possession of higher levels of job-related abilities and skills. However, workers in mid and late careers may be at a disadvantage when facing high levels of information processing requirements, because usually their cognitive abilities are not at developmental peak any more due to the normal aging process (see our review in Chapter 4). Therefore, for older workers in jobs characterized by high information processing demands, they are in particular need of using technological aids to help them process the information to perform the job. It should be noted that compared to technological aids, SOC strategies may be less effective to use in dealing with jobs that have high information processing demands. This is because information processing often requires both processing speed and capacity, which is difficult to strategize and optimize in real-time (Martin & Wall, 1989).

Problem Solving

Problem solving reflects the degree to which a job requires unique ideas or solutions and reflects the more active cognitive processing requirements of a job (Jackson, Wall,

Martin, & Davids, 1993). Problem solving involves generating unique or innovative ideas or solutions, diagnosing and solving nonroutine problems, and preventing or recovering from errors. As such, it is conceptually related to the creativity demands of work and is a natural extension to the information demands of a job (Shalley, Gilson, & Blum, 2000). On the one hand, workers in their mid and late career may have accumulated sufficient experience and knowledge that could guide them quickly to solutions for problems encountered in their jobs. On the other hand, if problem solving imposes high demands of information processing, then this type of job will be more challenging for older workers than their counterparts who are in early career stages. As we discussed in Chapter 4, older workers' success in these types of jobs is likely to depend on the extent to which their experience can compensate for the need for information processing. In other words, if older workers could quickly locate several prominent solutions based on their experience, then the need to go through all possible solutions becomes less relevant.

Specialization

Specialization reflects the extent to which a job involves performing specialized tasks or possessing specialized knowledge and skill. This notion of specialization was first identified by Campion (1988) and later clarified by Edwards, Scully, and Brtek (1999). Specifically, as opposed to the breadth of activities and skills inherent in task and skill variety, specialization reflects a depth of knowledge and skill in a particular area. Compared to younger counterparts who are in early career stages, older workers in mid and late careers typically enjoy knowledge advantages in dealing with highly specialized jobs. In addition, to maintain satisfactory performance on highly specialized jobs, a life-long learning orientation is a must. As such, older workers who are open to learning and new experiences are most suitable for these type of jobs.

Before we dive into the discussion of social characteristics of jobs, it is important to recognize that these characteristics are rooted from the social information processing model of Salancik and Pfeffer (1978). Specifically, this model argues that social information processing embedded in one's job plays an important role in shaping the person's job experience. For example, Weiss and Shaw (1979) conducted a study in the lab setting to demonstrate that social information could impact task perceptions and task satisfaction. O'Reilly and Caldwell (1979) also showed that social cues were important for affective outcomes in the workplace. To date, findings in the literature support this model, and suggest that (a) task perceptions and attitudes are influenced by social information; (b) workers do actively compare their jobs and situations to those of others; (c) the influence of social information appears to be strongest for attitudes, whereas objective task characteristics impact both attitudes and behavior. With these findings in mind, we discuss three kinds of social characteristics of jobs.

Social Support

Social support reflects the degree to which a job provides opportunities for advice and assistance from others. This includes the notion of supervisor and coworker social support (e.g., Karasek et al., 1998) and the construct of friendship opportunities at work posited by Sims, Szilagyi, and Keller (1976). Although not traditionally studied in job design contexts, research from other domains suggests that social support is critical for well-being (Ryan & Deci, 2001; Wrzesniewski, Dutton, & Debebe, 2003), particularly for jobs that are stressful or lack many motivational work characteristics. According to the socioemotional selectivity theory reviewed in Chapter 4, older workers in their mid and late career stages often put more values on regulating their emotions to be positive and pursuing emotionally gratifying relationships with others. Therefore, whether a job environment offers easily accessed social support may be particularly important for their job and career related evaluations and decisions. If they are not satisfied with the social support they receive from their job environment, they are probably going to be more reactive than their younger counterparts.

Interdependence

Interdependence reflects the degree to which the job depends on others and others depend on it to complete the work (Kiggundu, 1981). As such, interdependence reflects the "connectedness" of jobs to each other. Integral to this definition are two distinct forms of interdependence: (a) the extent to which work flows from one job to other jobs (initiated interdependence), and (b) the extent to which a job is affected by work from other jobs (received interdependence) (Kiggundu, 1981). Both forms of interdependence carry implications for the extent to which the job can be accomplished under sole control of a worker. The higher the initiated and received interdependence, the less likely a person can accomplish the job without interacting with other parties at work. Following the socioemotional selectivity theory, it is conceivable that older workers who are in their mid and late career stages are more likely to enjoy the social contact at work for the reason of positive emotional gain.

Interaction Outside the Organization

Interaction outside the organization reflects the extent to which the job requires employees to interact and communicate with individuals external to the organization. This interaction could take place with suppliers, customers, or any other external entity. The "dealing with others" construct (Sims et al., 1976) is similar, although we focus solely on interactions with individuals beyond the organization's boundaries. Following the socioemotional selectivity theory, we would probably expect that social contact is generally preferred by older workers as they are more emotionally oriented, but, after considering the nature of interaction outside the organization, we actually derive an opposite prediction. Specifically, when older workers interact with organization outsiders, they are likely dealing with people who they are not very familiar with and the nature of the interaction is probably more evaluative and job-specific. As such, this interaction may evoke stressful feelings such as uncertainty and anxiety, but not positive emotional experiences. Consequently, we expect that older workers will be less satisfied with jobs that require high levels of interaction outside the organization. On the other hand, younger workers who are in their early career stages may view interaction with individuals external to the organization as opportunities to develop new social relationships that may facilitate their future career development (Carstensen, 1991). As such, they may be more satisfied with jobs that require more interaction outside the organization.

Contextual Characteristics

So far we have reviewed motivational characteristics, knowledge characteristics, and social characteristics that may be embedded in a job. It should be noted that the contextual aspect of a job is also important to consider, as it typically determines the job's physical boundaries (Morgeson & Humphrey, 2006). We review three such contextual characteristics here.

Ergonomics

Ergonomics reflects the degree to which a job allows correct or appropriate posture and movement. The importance of this aspect of work design can be found in the extensive ergonomics literature as well as job design research (Campion & Thayer, 1985; Edwards et al., 1999). For older workers, ergonomic concerns are very important. This is because ergonomics are not only related to the physical comfort workers experience at work, but also serve as protective factors for one's physical health. As we reviewed in Chapter 4, with normal aging, people experience decline in muscle-skeleton functions and are less efficient in recovering from physical injuries. As such, it is critical for older workers to pay attention to the ergonomic features in their job to avoid loss of productivity due to injury or chronic diseases.

Physical Demands

Physical demands reflect the level of physical activity or effort required in the job. Specifically, we focus on the physical strength, endurance, effort, and activity aspects of the job. These aspects of the job all impose physical stress on one's body. Therefore, older workers have to pay special attention on these job aspects to assess whether their physical conditions can meet the requirement of these physical demands. Further, the physical demands carried by a job also have implications for the need of a comprehensive health care package. For older workers, such health insurance related concern is more salient, because the adverse health effect induced by these physical demands may not surface right away, but rather through accumulation of physical stress.

Work Conditions

Work conditions reflect the physical environment within which a job is performed. It includes the presence of health hazards (Stone & Gueutal, 1985) and noise, temperature, and cleanliness of the working environment (Edwards et al., 1999). In Chapter 4, we reviewed the aging-related effects on people's sensation and immune system. It is obvious that if these work conditions are outside of the safety boundaries, older workers are more likely to be vulnerable to the adverse effects than younger workers.

Relational Job Characteristics

Recently, Grant (2007, 2008) has developed the notion of relational architectures in understanding relational job characteristics that affect employees' interpersonal interactions and connections, as well as shaping their employment experiences. Specifically, the relational architecture of jobs refers to the structural properties of work that shape employees' opportunities to connect and interact with other people. In particular, relational architecture of jobs connects employees to the impact of their actions on other people (i.e., beneficiaries). For example, firefighting jobs typically involve enriched relational architectures (e.g., Thompson & Bono, 1993). They provide frequent opportunities to make a lasting difference in the lives of many beneficiaries (i.e., the community that firefighters serve), as well as meaningful contact with these beneficiaries through physically and emotionally close interactions that occur in the performance of fire rescues, delivery of emergency medical services, and instruction of community fire safety courses.

Grant (2007) introduced two sets of relational job characteristics (i.e., relational architectures of jobs) that structures opportunities for employees to have impact on, and form connections with, beneficiaries. The first set of relational job characteristics allows job impact on beneficiaries, which includes whether the job enables employees to make a lasting difference or an ephemeral difference in beneficiaries' lives, affect many or few beneficiaries, impact beneficiaries daily or occasionally, and prevent harm or promote gains to beneficiaries. In general, these job characteristics provide good indictors of the prosocial nature of the job. It is conceivable that when the job allows the worker to effectively exert positive impact on beneficiaries, the worker is more likely to experience positive emotional gain as a result of performing the job. Therefore, following the socioemotional selectivity theory, older workers in their mid and late career stages will be more motivated by jobs that offers these relational job characteristics, as they put more value on pursuing emotionally gratifying relationships with others than their younger counterparts.

The second set of relational job characteristics refers to job features that help workers to form connections with beneficiaries. These job characteristics include the frequency of contact, the duration of contact, the physical proximity of contact, the depth of contact, and the breadth of the contact. Specifically, the frequency of contact refers to how often the job provides opportunities to interact with beneficiaries. The duration of contact refers to the length of time for interactions with beneficiaries that the job provides. The physical proximity of contact refers to the degree of geographic and interpersonal space in the interaction that the job provides. The depth of contact refers to the degree to which the job enables the mutual expression of cognitions, emotions, and identities. Finally, the breadth of contact refers to the range of different groups of beneficiaries the job places in communication with the employee. As argued by Grant (2007), all these five relational job characteristics indicate experienced meaning of the contact. In other words, the more frequent, extended, physically proximate, expressive, and broad the contact with beneficiaries, the more meaningful the contact is to employees. As such, employees on jobs with these relational job characteristics are more likely to develop affective commitment to the beneficiaries of their jobs. Again, as socioemotional selectivity theory suggests that older workers put more emphasis on nurturing existing social relationships, we expect that when they are on jobs that greatly facilitate forming connections with job beneficiaries, they will be more committed to their job beneficiaries and more motivated to carry out prosocial actions to their job beneficiaries.

Future Research Directions

There are several possible directions for research and theory in the area of job level factors and their relationship and impact on mid and late career workers. For example, more research is needed that explicitly examines the independent and joint impact of various job cycle factors on mid and late career workers. That is, how does the average length of the job cycles one experiences at various career stages interact with other job cycle factors such as type, number, nature of job tasks, and voluntariness of the job cycles one has experienced over their career? In addition, the influence of early job cycles on later (mid and late career) job cycles is still unknown. In addition, we know that financial factors have a prominent influence on retirement decisions. Thus, the financial capital accrued over the job cycles individuals experience will likely have a critical influence on the decision to prolong one's late career or to potentially encourage early retirement. How, such factors interact with the other characteristics of job cycles noted above is still unclear. Thus, longitudinal research that is able to look at job and career trajectories over time would be essential to fully understanding these issues.

Another area for future research is the need to look at the various job characteristics models and how their stated components work together to influence workers in the mid and late career. For example, how do task, knowledge, social, and contextual characteristics independently and jointly influence mid and late career workers' experience of work? For example, looking specifically at the knowledge characteristics, how do increasing job complexity, information processing and problem solving demands, as well as increasing specialization all come together to shape mid and late careers? In addition, how might sociotechnical systems theory build on the classic job characteristics model in terms of explaining mid and late career worker's unique experiences at work?

In this chapter, as we did in several others, we discussed the SOC model and how workers in mid and later career may implement the model to stay employable and to progress in their career. However, at present, it is unclear how these SOC strategies may best be implemented in terms of the job cycles and job characteristics models we discussed earlier in this chapter. For example, would workers in mid career be more likely to engage optimization strategies (i.e., building on strengths), where as those in their late career, who may be experiencing more physical and cognitive declines, be more likely to focus on selection (i.e., narrowing down the tasks they focus on) and compensation (i.e., pulling in more resources to compensate for declining skills)?

Finally, with the increased use of work teams (as discussed in Chapter 3), are relational and social job characteristics likely to become more salient for workers in their mid and late career? We hypothesized earlier that when dealing with intra-organizational colleagues, social job characteristics would likely be a welcome addition for mid and late career workers. However, we also hypothesized that when dealing with inter-organizational colleagues, increased social job characteristics may actually be seen as stressful and demanding, so as a result be unappealing to mid and late career workers. Are these differences likely to play out and, if so, what additional moderators may help to explain the differing relationships between the two types of colleagues?

Chapter 6

Career Issues Unique
to Mid and Late Careers
Organizational Level Factors

In this chapter, we review the important organizational level factors that may impact mid and late careers. Most people's career experiences are linked to one or multiple organizations. In fact, organizations may be one of the most important social contexts for individuals who enter their adulthood and remain so until they fully exit from the workforce (Hulin, 2002). Research has consistently shown that organizations play important roles in shaping people's knowledge and skills (e.g., Goldstein & Ford, 2002), values and motivations (e.g., James & James, 1989), emotional experiences (e.g., James et al., 2008), daily activities and time structures (e.g., Wang, Liao, Zhan, & Shi, 2011), and social relationships (e.g., Ferrin, Dirks, & Shah, 2006).

We apply two perspectives to organizing our discussion regarding organizational level factors that may impact mid and late careers. The first perspective is built upon the notion of employee-organization relationship (EOR). Given that workers in mid and late careers may expect different types of obligations from the organization compared to workers in their early careers and may use their perception of EOR to inform mid and late career-related decisions (e.g., turnover, early retirement, or bridge employment), incorporating an EOR perspective to understand the organizational-level factors that may impact mid and late careers is extremely important. To do so, we first discuss the general theoretical framework of EOR. We then discuss the details regarding how EOR may be linked to important mid and late career-related decisions. Specifically, we discuss empirical evidence that links two EOR indicators, perceived organizational support (POS) and organizational commitment, to career-related decisions.

The second perspective we rely on to identify organizational level factors that may impact mid and late careers is the strategic perspective of human resource management (HRM). Given that an organization's HR practice often entails financial and motivational consequences for its employees and is likely to trigger the sense making process for its employees, it is important to understand the impact of organization's HRM strategy on workers who are in their mid and late careers. Specifically, we first review the concept and relevance of strategic HRM to mid and late career workers. We then discuss how different HR practices may influence mid and late career workers' financial situation, knowledge transferring activities, motivation and performance, and eventually their retention and recruitment.

The Employee-Organization Relationship

Theoretical Framework for EOR

The EOR literature has drawn upon social exchange theory (Blau, 1964) and the norm of reciprocity (Gouldner, 1960), as well as the inducements-contributions model (March & Simon, 1958) to provide the theoretical basis for understanding the employee and employer exchange relationship. Although the exact focus of these theories may vary, a common theme that emerges in these theories is that EOR can be conceptualized as a resource exchange between the organization and the employee. Specifically, social exchange theory specifies that when the organization hires an employee, a sequence of beneficial exchanges initiates between the organization and the employee. These beneficial exchanges evolve to create feelings of mutual obligation between the organization and the employee and lead the exchange partners to develop trust that beneficial treatment will continue to be reciprocated by the exchange partner (Cropanzano & Mitchell, 2005). Trust is important because there is some inherent risk that the benefits provided may not be returned as the nature and timing of benefits are not specified. The typical benefits employees may receive from their organizations include, but are not limited to, economic/material benefits, informational benefits, time benefits, and social-emotional benefits. The typical benefits organizations may receive from their employees include, but are not limited to, productivity, organizational citizenship behaviors, and loyalty (Cropanzano & Mitchell, 2005; Tsui, Pearce, Porter, & Tripoli, 1997).

Moreover, the EOR literature has established the importance of the norm of reciprocity as a key mechanism that governs the social exchange between the organization and the employee. The norm of reciprocity refers that in social exchange relationships, the bestowing of a benefit creates a normative obligation to reciprocate (Gouldner, 1960). Therefore, employees generally feel obligated to respond equitably to treatments they received from their organizations and also expect their organizations to reciprocate to their contributions to the organization. Based on the norm of reciprocity, two psychological constructs are important to consider for understanding EOR: psychological contracts and perceived organizational support (POS).

Rousseau (1989) defined psychological contracts as "individual beliefs in a reciprocal obligation between the individual and the organization" (p. 121). Essentially, she argues that the explicit deals between companies and their workers on resource exchanges are complemented by implicit ones holding considerable organizational implications. Subsequent research has supported her argument, linking psychological contract breaches and fulfillment to outcomes such as job satisfaction, organizational commitment, turnover intentions, in-role performance, and organizational citizenship behavior (Rousseau, 1995). POS, on the other hand, is defined as employees' "global beliefs concerning the extent to which the organization values their contributions and cares about their well-being" (Eisenberger, Huntington, Hutchison, & Sowa, 1986, p. 501). POS develops when employees perceive that the favorable treatments they receive from their organization are based on discretionary choice rather than circumstances beyond the organization's control. Such voluntary aid is welcomed as an indication that the organization genuinely values and respects the employee. Governed by the norm of reciprocity, POS produces a felt obligation for employees to care about the organization's welfare and to help the organization reach its objectives, which in turn lead to employees' reciprocation to the organization in the forms of increased commitment to the organization and heightened productivity (Rhoades & Eisenberger, 2002; Takeuchi, Wang, Marinova, & Yao, 2009).

Similar to social exchange theory, the inducements-contributions model (March & Simon, 1958) views the employment exchange as one where the organization offers inducements in return for employee contributions. Individuals are satisfied when there is a balance between inducements provided and contributions given. Therefore, again, the key for the employment exchange is whether the benefit provided by the organization is valued by the employee subjectively (e.g., part of the psychological contract) and is perceived as being based on discretionary choice by the organization (e.g., help forming POS). If employees are satisfied with what the organizations provided, they are more likely to reciprocate with attitudes and behaviors that are valued by the organization.

After reviewing these theoretical frameworks, it is evident that each employee's perception of EOR is largely determined by the organizational treatment that he or she receives. However, depending on the unique things that may be valued by different employees, same organizational treatment may lead to different perceptions of EOR for different employees. Further, these different EOR perceptions may prompt workers in their mid and late careers to reciprocate differently to their respective organizations. Next, we consider workers' career-related decisions in their mid and late careers as a unique type of reciprocation triggered by their perceptions of EOR.

EOR and Career-Related Decisions in Mid and Late Careers

Literature has shown that EOR may impact individuals' job-related decision-making processes (Coyle-Shapiro & Shore, 2007). For workers in their mid careers, poor perceived EOR may lead them to quit their organization and search for alternative employers that could potentially improve the organizational treatment they receive. For workers in their late career stages, one of the most important career decisions they have to make relates to retirement (Adams & Beehr, 1998). As a type of work withdrawal behavior, retirement will occur in different forms sooner or later in one's career life (Shultz & Wang, 2011). As such, workers' decisions regarding when to retire and how to retire could be impacted by EOR. In this section, we discuss the linkage between EOR and these employment-related decisions made by workers in their mid and late careers.

Before we start our discussion, we would like to clarify that job search and turnover decisions may differ from retirement decisions in nature in terms of their respective career implications. Specifically, job search and turnover decisions are usually led by the withdrawal intention from the workers to exit the organization, but do not necessarily mean that they would change their career paths. To contrast, retirement can be viewed as a mutual withdrawal of workers and their organizations (Adams, Prescher, Beehr, &

Lepisto, 2002) and typically triggers the process for individuals to exit the workforce eventually (Shultz & Wang, 2011; Wang & Shultz, 2010). Depending on the specific decision-making scenario, EOR-related organizational factors (e.g., perceived organizational support and organizational commitment) compose an important set of variables that influence employees' career-related intention and actual decisions.

In general, positive perception of EOR may prevent employees from conducting job search, decrease the intention to turnover, and postpone employees' retirement due to three possible reasons. First, social exchange theory suggests that employees who perceive a high level of EOR may feel obligated to reciprocate their organizations by increasing their work input (Coyle-Shapiro & Conway, 2004; Cropanzano & Mitchell, 2005), which may be translated into higher levels of engagement to their job, stronger sense of loyalty to the organization, and longer working life for workers approaching their retirement age. By contrast, negative perception of EOR may lead to more job search activities and stronger intention of turnover or retirement. Once workers in their mid and late careers perceive their organizations to be less supportive, less willing to provide discretionary benefits to them, and even discriminating against older workers, they will be more likely to withdraw from the organizations as reciprocating to organizations' withdrawing resources from them.

Second, workers who perceive high levels of EOR may expect better treatment from organizations when they approach certain career stages. For example, workers in their mid career stages who experience or expect to experience career plateau are more in need of organizational support in job enrichment and skills update. Workers who perceive high levels of EOR are more likely to be sure that they will receive this support from their organizations. Therefore, there is less motivation for them to proactively plan for switching employers as a means to fulfill these needs. Similarly, workers who are approaching retirement age tend to compare their working status with their expected post-retirement life. On the one hand, they value their work role identity; on the other hand, they expect less demands and more personal time during retirement. Compared to older workers with unpleasant relationship with their organizations, workers with higher levels of EOR are more likely to expect a better supportive system from their organizations, such as flexible work schedule and respect for older workers. Therefore, positive EOR may encourage older workers to continue working in their organizations by satisfying the older workers' expectation of reduced work commitment without losing their work role identity.

Third, positive EOR may allow employees to enjoy their work environment more. Workers may have lower levels of intention to search for jobs, leave the organization, or retire, simply because they enjoy working in their organizations. With a higher level of emotional attachment to and identification with the organization created by the high-quality social exchange entailed in positive EOR, workers are likely to be willing to stay in their organization for a longer time. Below, we present empirical evidence for the relationship between two EOR indicators, perceived organizational support and organizational commitment, and workers' job search, turnover, as well as their retirement intention and decision.

Perceived Organizational Support (POS)

For employees, theire organization serves as an important resource of tangible benefits such as wages and medical benefits, as well as socioemotional support such as respect and caring. Employees who form a positive perception concerning the organizational support would feel attached to their organization and obligated to help the organization reach its goals. In turn, they would expect improved performance to be rewarded (Eisenberger, Huntington, Hutchinson, & Sowa, 1986; Rhoades & Eisenberger, 2002).

POS has been shown to be negatively related to job search behaviors (Rhoades & Eisenberger, 2002) and turnover (Baranik, Roling, & Eby, 2010) across workers at different ages and in different industries. However, there is a lack of empirical work directly examining the effect of POS in impacting workers' retirement intention. Nevertheless, different literatures have paid attention to organizational factors that may impact workers' retirement through studying perceived socioemotional support from organizations. For example, in some organizations, older workers may encounter age-related discriminations from their supervisors because of stereotype-induced bias in possible decline in work capability (Posthuma & Campion, 2009). Experiences of being discriminated and the lack of action from the organization to intervene could significantly lower the perceived quality of EOR from the employees' perspective. Supporting this notion, Zappala, Depolo, Fraccaroli, Guglielmi, and Sarchielli (2008) showed that older workers tended to retire late if the management team in their company displayed special attention to maintain the employability of elderly employees and the supervisors took into account their age, health, and capacity when assigning tasks and conducting evaluations. The positive effect of these management and supervisory treatments may be explained by a heightened level of POS. Accordingly, respect and consideration by management teams and supervisors may effectively increase older workers' perceive support.

Organizational Commitment

Organizational commitment is closely related to POS, which can be viewed as individual perception of organization's commitment to an employee (Cropanzano & Mitchell, 2005). According to social exchange theory, employees are prone to exchange their commitment for an employer's support (Eisenberger et al., 1986). Many empirical studies have been conducted to examine the relationship between organizational commitment and employee withdrawal from the organization (Erdheim, Wang, & Zickar, 2006; Mathieu & Zajac, 1990) and most of them revealed negative relationships between organizational commitment and job search behaviors as well as turnover. In other words, employees who have higher levels of organizational commitment are less likely to search for alternative jobs and turnover.

Empirical studies have also examined organizational commitment on retirement-related outcomes, such as early retirement intention (e.g., Gaillard & Desmette, 2009), retirement intention (e.g., Adams & Beehr, 1998; Adams et al., 2002), and planned retirement age (e.g., Taylor & Shore, 1995). The effect size of organizational commitment is small to moderate, but organizational commitment is usually a significant predictor of retirement after controlling for individual characteristic variables such as age, personal finances, and health (Wang & Shultz, 2010). Furthermore, organizational commitment has been shown to predict retirees' bridge employment intentions. According to a recent empirical study (Jones & McIntosh, 2010), although organizational and occupational commitment both predicted retirement intention, a stronger predictive effect was found for organizational commitment than occupational commitment in predicting bridge employment in the same organization.

Among the studies mentioned above, the commitment construct is typically operationalized by measuring older workers' affective organizational commitment. Because of the specification of organizational commitment, researchers have begun to explore the potential differences between specific forms of commitment in impacting retirement decision (e.g., Jones & McIntosh, 2010; Luchak, Pohler, & Gellatly, 2008). For example, Luchak et al. (2008) examined the relationship between two forms of organizational commitment (i.e., affective commitment and continuous commitment) and planned age of retirement under defined-benefit pension plan. According to commitment theory, individuals' motivation to stay is experienced as a mind-set that varies depending on the perceived reasons of stay. Specifically, working is a personal choice due to enjoyment for employees with higher levels of affective organizational commitment, while working is a necessity to avoid social and economic adversity for employees with higher levels of continuous organizational commitment. Their results showed that affective commitment was positively associated with planned age of retirement, whereas a curvilinear relationship was found between continuous commitment and planned retirement age such that employees had higher levels of continuous commitment tended to retire at the age when their pension benefit reached maximum. As such, the positive effect of affective organizational commitment reflects the emotional reason of stay versus retirement, and the curvilinear effect of continuous organizational commitment reflects the cognitive benefit-cost calculation in retirement decision-making process.

It is necessary to point out that the relationship between EOR and retirement intention and decision is not exclusively negative. Although most of the empirical studies have found inconsistent associations between EOR and work withdrawal are focusing on turnover as the key withdrawal indicator, we expect the impact of EOR on retirement intention/decision may also vary due to the different strategic goals of organizations. In particular, positive EOR may lead to an increased rather than decreased tendency to retire if organizations strategically encourage employees' retirement. With a higher level of EOR, older workers may also tend to expect a satisfying retirement package from their organizations. Therefore, we expect a pleasant retirement process for those leaving organizations with which they have positive EOR. Below, we switch to the strategic perspective of HRM to continue our discussion on the organizational-level factors that may impact mid and late careers.

Strategic HRM and Mid and Late Career Issues

Strategic Human Resource Management

Strategic management researchers have argued that HR practices must be designed to align with the particular firm strategy and environmental constraints faced by a particular organization (Boxall & Purcell, 2008; Schuler & Jackson, 1987; Wood, 1999). Recently, researchers have begun to acknowledge that a firm's practices need to not only meet the strategy and environment constraints, but also to do so in a way that meets the needs of different groups of employees (Lepak & Snell, 2002; Tsui et al., 1997). For example, employees in their early career stages will have different needs compared to employees in their mid and late career stages. Therefore, differentiated systems of HR practices are needed to address both the needs of various constituents within the organization and the contingencies posed by the organization's strategy and environment.

Given these distinctions, a different attitude toward employees who are in their mid and late careers could be expected by virtue of the organization's strategy and supporting culture of human resources management. For example, according to Porter's (1985) categorization of business strategies, under an innovation/differentiation strategy (i.e., basing the business growth on high levels of employee creativity, long-term focus, greater willingness to take risk, and high tolerance for ambiguity and unpredictability), the organization may wish to design HR practices that will retain the knowledgeable employees to the organization for longer periods of time and take advantage of their willingness to take risks. Under a cost leadership strategy (i.e., basing the business growth on managing predictable and repetitive behaviors of employees), the organization's culture of stability and low risk-taking might best be supported by HR practices that minimizes risk of turnover for mid career workers while encouraging an earlier retirement date for late career workers to limit the cost. Meanwhile, under a quality enhancement strategy (i.e., basing the business growth on constantly improving precision and quality in reaching the organization's goals), the employer might want to design HR practices that could maintain the high-level performers while at the same time push out those who cannot contribute to the quality enhancement.

When matching HR practices to any of the above mentioned business strategies, it is important for an organization to conduct a retirement eligibility analysis (via survey or examination of HR records) to examine its current labor force, auditing how many employees plan to retire in the near future and identifying who among these employees the organization would like to retain. In addition, it is also important for the organization to conduct a strategic job analysis to understand anticipated human capital (e.g., skills and knowledge) needed relative to future corporate objectives and anticipatory changes in the business environment (Sackett & Laczo, 2003). This analysis can be done by using the group discussion technique (Sanchez & Levine, 1999). Specifically, the organization can bring together a group of subject-matter experts (e.g., incumbents, managers, strategy analysts) and brainstorming about the expected task and ability requirement for future jobs. The experts may also identify possible organizational or environmental conditions that could affect future jobs (e.g., changing labor markets, technology, demographics, political or economic trends), consider what aspects of jobs are the most likely to change and what skills or attributes are important to those aspects (Pearlman & Barney, 2000), or visualize how future tasks might be performed given the possible technological changes and business emphasis (Sanchez & Levine, 1999). The results of strategic job analysis can help the organization to clarify its workforce planning goals, thus making sure that their HR practices match the future growing anticipations of the company well. Below, we discuss specific HR practices that are most relevant to workers who are in their mid and late careers.

Employee Benefits

Organizations typically offer benefits to their employees for three purposes: (a) to meet their goals for corporate social responsibility, (b) to attract and retain workers, and (c) to increase productivity and foster positive work-related attitudes among employees. As such, practices concerning employee benefits are important ways for an organization to carry out its HR strategy. It should be noted that employee benefits are expensive for organizations. According to U.S. Bureau of Labor Statistics (2010), employers spend about 34.5% of their total compensation budgets on employee benefits. Given this high expense, organizations must be concerned about costs and cost containment as they develop and administer the types of benefit programs that will help them meet their strategic goals.

From the standpoint of mid and late career workers, the two most important categories of employee benefits are likely to be *health care benefit* and *retirement benefit*. As we mentioned in Chapter 4, with physical aging, health care is an important factor to consider for older workers who make mid and late career decisions. Mid and late career changes may function as a possible pathway to reach good quality future health care. This concern is particularly salient when it is considered with the recent rapid increase in the health care cost. However, employers are not required by law to provide health insurance coverage for their employees or their retirees. In fact, the proportion of large employers offering health insurance in the United States has steadily declined over the last 20 years (Strumpf, 2009). The same trend is observed among the large employers who offer health benefits for their retirees. The share of employers with at least 200 employees offering any type of retiree health benefits dropped from 66% in 1988 to 35% in 2006 (TIAA-CREF Institute, 2006).

The decision by an employer to offer health care benefits, and the manner in which they are offered, should be based on a number of strategic goal-related factors. At the most basic level, employers provide benefits to align employee behaviors and attitudes with organizational strategy before they retire (e.g., in their mid and late careers) and, to a certain degree, offset the financial burden of the health care cost incurred by the employees, and sometimes their families (especially for those single-earner families with children). Employers may also provide health care benefits to their employees after they retire to offer some security and continuance, which is also beneficial for maintaining the tie between the retirees and the company. Of course, all these benefits should be offered with a concern for costs as the bottom line.

However, these goals for providing health care benefits do not always coincide with one another. For example, an organization may want to foster long-term relationships with their mid and late career employees by demonstrating legitimate concerns for their long-term welfare even after retirement. Retiree health benefits would seem to be one mechanism to accomplish this strategic goal. However, these types of benefits are costly, and the research suggests that older employees are as much as 21% more likely to retire if they have access to retiree health benefits (Robinson & Clark, 2010). The same is true for the case of early retirement. For example, Strumpf (2009) showed that a retiree health insurance offer may increase the probability of early retirement by over one-third for both men and women. In addition, Fronstin, Salisbury, and VanDerhei (2008) found that about one-quarter of early retirees have employer-sponsored retiree health benefits. Thus, rather than encouraging longer tenure, this benefit might be used to encourage employees to retire if its costs can be justified for that purpose. In this case, the organization might be better off considering other benefits that signal organizational support. This example illustrates the need for careful consideration of the utility of different health benefits within the package, as well as the way they will interact in affecting employee attitudes and behaviors.

Another type of employee benefit that is important to mid and late career workers is retirement benefits. From an individual standpoint, retirement is a process that begins long before, and continues well after, one retires (Shultz & Wang, 2011). The key task in the years leading up to the point when a worker officially retires is retirement preparation. Retirement preparation involves planning and taking those actions needed before retirement to help ensure that one has a satisfying lifestyle after retirement. The main way in which organizations help workers with their retirement preparation is through the provision of retirement-related financial benefits.

Traditionally, retirement income has come from three main sources, social security programs, employer-provided retirement benefit programs, and personal savings (Wang & Shultz, 2010). Employer-provided retirement income benefit programs have been the main way in which organizations have helped employees fund their retirement years. Retirement income benefit programs are fairly common in the United States with 71% of private sector workers having access to such programs and 80% of those taking part in them (U.S. Bureau of Labor Statistics, 2009). While there are a variety of specific types of retirement income benefit programs, they are generally divided into two broad categories (a) defined benefit (DB) plans and (b) defined contribution (DC) plans. Each of these two types of programs has features to consider in the context of an organization's strategy.

The DB plans specify a particular benefit pay-out level (typically in the form of lifetime installments) once the employee retires. The payout level is determined by a formula, which most commonly includes the employee's length of service and earning history with the employer. In most situations, employees must work for a specified period of time before becoming eligible (vested) for a payout at retirement. DB plans are not portable. They cannot be transferred from one employer to another. As a result of these rules the largest payouts accrue to those who have remained with a single employer for a long period of time and have their highest earnings with that employer. The funds used to generate the payout are not under the control of the employees, and the employees do not direct how those funds are invested. In DB plans the organization makes a long-term cost commitment and assumes the market risk (fluctuations in the investment markets). Thus there is considerable uncertainty for the organization. The employee assumes the "service" risk. That is, that they will continue working for the same employer over a long period of time. It is also the case, that these plans "penalize" work with that same employer beyond a certain point. This is because the additional benefit amount provided for additional years of work rarely approaches the amount of benefit lost by forfeiting a year of payout. This feature makes it easier to predict when people will retire. For mid and late career workers, if their organizations offer DB plans, it will most likely to translate into high retention rates among the mid career workers, while pushing late career workers to consider retirement when they are eligible for Social Security payment. The latter is particularly likely to be the case if the sum of the Social Security income and the income from the DB plans is close to or equal to the salary income from full-time employment.

In DC plans the amount of payout upon retirement is not specified but an amount of investment contribution is. That is, the employer agrees to contribute a certain amount (usually a percentage of salary) to a retirement investment account such as a 401(k) or 403(b) account. Oftentimes, both the organization and employee make contributions. The payout at retirement is based on how well the investment account has performed. DC plans are "owned" by the employee, and the employee directs how the contributions are invested across a set of funds (e.g., mutual funds). DC plans are portable. If employees leave an organization, they may transfer their account into other retirement accounts. In this type of plan the organization has much greater certainty surrounding the costs of the plan. The amount of contribution is generally known from year to year. Because they are portable, employees do not assume the service risk; however, because they are employee-directed, employees assume the market risk related to the investment. For mid and late career workers who enrolled in the DC plans, they will be less mindful about their retirement benefits when they consider alternative jobs. However, due to the market risk, workers may have to postpone their retirement in adverse economic situations due to loses in retirement investment in DC plans and workers in their late careers may have to continue working longer, as it is difficult to be sure whether there will be market stability in their retirement years so that their investment in the DC plans can provide them sustainable streams of income.

At one time DB plans were the more common of the two types of plans. However, over the past 20 years there has been a considerable shift from DB to DC plans, and currently more private sector workers are covered by DC (56%) than DB plans (31%) (U.S. Bureau of Labor Statistics, 2009). Research suggests that this shift has been driven by several factors including: (a) regulatory changes that make defined benefit plans more difficult and costly to administer; (b) as work has shifted from traditional manufacturing, unionized industries to service (nonunionized) industries, defined benefit plans have disappeared along with union contracts; and (c) the changing nature of the workforce itself (e.g., increased number of women, dual career couples, education levels, etc.) has made for an increasingly mobile workforce that needs retirement plans that can "move" with them (e.g., Aaronson & Coronado, 2005; Broadbent, Palumbo, & Woodman, 2006).

In addition, Westerman and Sundali (2005) argued that DB plans tend to signal relational psychological contracts between employee and employer, whereas DC plans tend to signal transactional psychological contracts between employee and employer. Therefore, they suggest that the shift from DB to DC plans is just one part of a broader movement toward more transactional employment relationships generally. Considering these factors, the shift from DB to DC plans at the aggregate level can be viewed as organizations responding in a strategic manner to align their retirement income benefit offerings to the realities of their production processes and labor markets under a given set of constraints (government regulations and costs).

At the level of the individual organization, these same factors call for designing a retirement benefit plan that is aligned with the overall strategy of the organization (internal alignment) and the characteristics of labor market (external alignment). Some organizational strategies, such as those that seek to gain competitive advantage through employees who must acquire and use organizational specific knowledge or customer relationships developed over a long period of time, can be enhanced by benefit strategies that promote long-term relationships between employer and employees. Some organizational strategies can benefit from the predictable exit of employees owing to those their preferences or concerns about productivity at older ages (e.g., as might be seen in physically demanding manual labor positions). These types of strategies likely benefit from some of the features of DB plans. On the other hand, some organizational strategies such as those that seek to leverage technological and other types of innovation among employees may find that long-term employment relationships do not enhance the organization's ability to compete nor are they necessarily preferred by a labor market that has grown increasingly concerned with mobility. In these types of scenarios organizations are likely to benefit from the features of DC plans.

HR Practice to Promote Knowledge Transfer

Although organizations may provide support to employees in the forms of employee benefits, they also face the issue regarding the management of the aging workforce. Demographic projections have shown that by 2040, about 30% of the total U.S. workforce will be age 55 or older, up from just under 13% in 2000, leading to a sizable increase in the number of people who will transition into retirement in the coming decades (Toossi, 2006). This reflects the fact that the population as a whole is getting older due to several factors, including the aging of the large Baby Boom Generation, lower birth rates, and longer life expectancies (Alley & Crimmins, 2007). On the one hand, with the baby boomers reaching their retirement ages, many analysts are predicting growing labor shortages in tomorrow's workforce. In fact, according to a recent research report provided by the AARP (2005), in addition to the widely publicized shortages of nurses and other health care professionals, organizations that rely on such specially trained individuals as teachers, engineers, and many other skilled workers are also starting to face significant skill shortages.

One issue that comes with the projected labor shortage is the potential loss of accumulated knowledge when employees leave their organizations due to the turnover or retirement of mid and late career workers (DeLong, 2004). In one recent survey, 71% of employers reported being concerned about the loss of knowledge resulting from the retirement of older employees (MetLife, 2009). Although the sum amount and value of lost knowledge are difficult to quantify, anecdotal evidence suggests they are considerable (DeLong, 2004). In order to retain the accumulated knowledge of its retiring employees, organizations need a knowledge management process that is able to identify and transfer valuable knowledge so that it can be used by others to achieve organizational objectives (Argote & Ingram, 2000; Slagter, 2007; Wang & Noe, 2010).

The HR manager plays a key role in the knowledge management process. To begin, the HR manager must work with senior managers to determine the size and scope of the knowledge management effort based on an assessment of the organization's strategy, resources, and knowledge base, as well as employee demographics and capabilities. These will allow the organization to develop the knowledge management approach most suited to its needs. An important part of this process is being able to locate and identify the type and value of the knowledge to be retained. Once this process is underway the organization can begin developing the knowledge transfer process.

Key elements of the knowledge transfer process aimed at workers in their mid and late careers include facilitating an organizational culture that supports knowledge transfer and developing and deploying specific tools needed to achieve knowledge transfer. This culture may be manifested by: (a) valuing employees nearing retirement for what they know, (b) creating mutual respect and trust among the parties to the process, and (c) an emphasis on learning and development (Slagter, 2007). Human resources management practices such as reward and recognition programs can facilitate the development of such a culture. The importance of these cultural elements is supported by recent research in the general knowledge management literature linking knowledge management practices to organizational performance (Zack, McKeen, & Singh, 2009). They are especially important in the context of knowledge transfer from mid and late career workers given that, in most cases these employees will transfer their knowledge to a younger generation of workers (Stevens, 2010).

In terms of developing and deploying specific knowledge transfer tools, the organization has a wide range of options, mainly in two broad overlapping categories: (a) documenting processes and (b) interpersonal processes. Documenting processes focus on knowledge transfer in written (most often in electronic) form to create repositories of knowledge. The tools used to create these involve task-based and cognitive job analysis methods, the development of procedure manuals, expert-system and knowledge-based support tools, and training programs. Interpersonal processes focus on knowledge transfer via interactions with those who have the knowledge. Traditional tools for accomplishing this include succession planning, structured on the job training and apprentice programs, job shadowing and developmental job assignments, and coaching/mentoring. Other methods include critical incident and after action review sessions, communities of practice, story-telling sessions, and internal help desk and consulting teams.

The tools and approaches to knowledge transfer for any particular organization necessarily involves a consideration of all of the issues described above. They must match tools and approaches to strategy and types of knowledge. They must also consider the learning preferences of the knowledge transfer parties (older and younger workers) and tailor their methods accordingly. The key is to establish a culture that encourages and values knowledge-seeking on the part of the younger workers and knowledge-sharing on the part of older workers who are in their mid and late careers. In addition, this culture could also facilitate the fulfillment of the generative motivation for older workers and make them feel valued by the organization and their younger colleagues. In turn, older workers may be willing to remain in the organization longer and find their work to be more meaningful and significant, or once retired, more willing to return to their organization to serve in a mentoring role (Madvig & Shultz, 2008). It should be noted that the mutual awareness of the intergroup stereotyping processes could interfere with clear communication between older and younger workers, thus hindering the knowledge transfer.

Motivation and Performance Management for Older Workers

Another significant challenge for managing an aging workforce is maintaining motivation and work performance. While there is little empirical evidence to suggest that motivation (e.g., Kanfer & Ackerman, 2004) and performance necessarily decline with age (e.g., McEvoy & Cascio, 1989; Ng & Feldman, 2010), there is growing evidence that there is something unique about motivating older workers. Techniques that work on younger workers may not be effective on older workers nearing retirement. For example, Warr (1997, 2001) suggested that expectancy theory might be useful to understand older worker motivation but focused primarily on the fact that older workers are motivated by different job characteristics. He argued that older workers' preferences are more likely to include things such as security (physical, job, financial) and opportunities to utilize their skills rather than high job demands, job variety, and feedback. Thus, as workers age, organizations may find that they are not motivated by the same things as in the past. This suggests that, as an organization's workforce ages, the reward structure may need to be realigned with worker needs and desires.

Claes and Heymans (2008) further conducted focus group sessions with HR managers and identified three sources of motivation that might be applied to enhance work motivation of older workers. First, HR managers indicated that older workers attached more importance to having contact with their superiors, a relationship with the owner, and having opportunities to take on responsibility and, consequently, were more motivated when these conditions were met. Second, older workers were more motivated when they were given clear goals that were challenging and time-related. Third, the HR managers observed that older workers were highly motivated by the opportunities to mentor others, pass along their knowledge, and receive recognition for their efforts.

Given that few empirical studies have been conducted in evaluating effective HR practices that are designed in particular to manage older workers' motivation, it is still difficult to make concrete recommendations. Nevertheless, to match motivation practices with the organization's strategy, it is important for HR manager to understand the source of low motivation among older workers. Further, we can draw some guidance for HR practices with the understanding that the key question is whether the organization wishes to encourage older workers to retire or wishes to extend older workers' value in the workplace. As with other policies discussed earlier, a company concerned about cost containment may wish to encourage retirement of older, more expensive workers. These organizations could adopt more age-based policies and practices that establish an implied retirement age and climate. They may want to offer early retirement, create benefits for retired employees, or designate an age for phased retirement eligibility.

On the other hand, an organization that is focused on quality of service, product, or processes may wish to extend the work life of older, knowledgeable workers for as long as possible. HR policies and practices that accommodate older workers' changing physical and cognitive challenges (e.g., job redesign, ergonomic changes, job reassignment, and career development) should increase work motivation for older workers. Accommodating older workers' changing preferences for leisure and work may also encourage them to stay in the workplace longer, albeit with reduced hours but perhaps with sustained motivation.

Retention and Recruitment

One key HR issue regarding the internal labor force of an organization is retention. Retention efforts can be aimed at retaining workers in the organization on a full-time basis or part-time basis. Customizing the types of employment (i.e., full-time vs. part-time) is important, because retention often is not a one-size-fits-all case. Different workers may have the intention of leaving the organizations for different reasons. Identifying these reasons and providing solutions that could address the workers' concerns are important challenges to an organization's HR system in terms of its flexibility and its adherence to the organization's business strategy. For example, an employee who is in his/her mid career may decide to leave the organization due to elder care needs. In that case, accommodating the employee with flexible work schedules may successfully address the problem without significantly losing productivity (Matz-Costa & Pitts-Catsouphes, 2010). On the other hand, an employee who is approaching retirement may be retained to work on a part-time basis. This may involve the use of phased retirement (i.e., the continuing employment of current employees at a reduced workload until full retirement) and contingent work arrangements. Formal phased retirement programs offered to all employees tend to be relatively less common than informal programs. Studies estimate between 6% and 22% of employing organizations use formal programs and approximately 50% and 65% offer informal phased retirement on a case by case basis (Bond, Galinsky, Kim, & Brownfield, 2005; Hutchens & Grace-Martin, 2006). Contingent work arrangements include approaches such as rehiring retired workers as independent contractors and as "temporary" workers through staffing effort (Shultz, 2003).

For workers who are in their late careers, decision to delay retirement and/or pursue post-retirement employment with one's current employer is based on a complex set of factors that include individual differences, contextual factors, and work-related variables (e.g., Wang, Adams, Beehr, & Shultz, 2009; Wang, Zhan, Liu, & Shultz, 2008). Many of the individual differences such as demographic characteristics and work-related preferences, as well as contextual factors such as the state of the larger economy are beyond the control of any particular organization. Work-related variables such as working conditions, pay, and benefits are more directly influenced by the organization. These work-related variables can be used to persuade employees who would otherwise retire to continue working for their current employer. As already discussed, workers who have greater accumulated income and reached pension eligibility are more likely to retire. Thus, the types of benefit plans offered can have the effect of encouraging continued work with one's current employer.

In addition, workers with positive attitudes about work are more likely to retire later than those with negative attitudes (Adams & Beehr, 1998; Luchak et al., 2008; Taylor & Shore, 1995). An organization wanting to retain older workers would need to develop HR practices and policies that contribute to such positive attitudes among that group. For example, one recent study found that HR practices such as training and development targeting older workers was positively related to perceptions of organizational support, which was, in turn, related to intention to remain with one's employer (Armstrong-Stassen & Ursel, 2009).

When considering finding the talent from the external labor force that is accessible to an organization, the key HR issue is recruitment. Recruitment is the process of attracting potential employees to apply for open positions in an organization. In one national study of 578 organizations, approximately 62% had taken steps to recruit an age diverse workforce (Pitts-Catsouphes, Smyer, Matz-Costa, & Kane, 2007). Much of the research on applicant attraction suggests that it is based on objective and subjective characteristics of the job (e.g., pay, type of work, etc.) and the organization (e.g., organizational image), the applicants' perceptions of the fit between these characteristics and their own preferences, as well as the competence and credibility of the recruiter (Chapman, Uggerslev, Carroll, Piasentin, & Jones, 2005; Highhouse, Brooks, & Gregarus, 2009).

An organization wishing to engage in the targeted recruitment of workers in their mid and late careers can use a number of approaches to attract them. One approach would be to attempt to match the characteristics of the job and organization to those that are generally preferred by those workers. For instance, research shows that there are several main HR practices that are often used to recruit workers who are in their mid careers. Specifically, for male employees, these often include more opportunities for career growth, more managerial responsibilities, and larger job scopes. For female employees, these often include flexible work schedules, less business travel required, and greater job stability and security. These differences in HR practice patterns are likely due to the gender differences in life-goal priorities when people enter their middle adulthood. Specifically, men in their mid careers may experience more salient motivation for career advancement, while women may feel that they have proved themselves at work already and want to allocate more attention to their family life and caregiver roles. Of course, when organizations attempt to use targeted recruitment, they should find out their targeted persons' exact values and priorities rather than over generalize on certain characteristics (e.g., gender) that can lead to stereotyping.

There are also several typical HR practices used to recruit retirees returning to work. These practices include: (a) flexible work options; (b) training and development opportunities, (c) new, challenging, and meaningful work assignments; (d) improved compensation; (e) unbiased feedback and performance evaluation; and (f) giving recognition and respect (Armstrong-Stassen, 2008a,b). Further, in order to be effective in recruitment, these types of practices have to be communicated in a manner that signals to retirees that the organization values their contributions (Rau & Adams, 2005).

Like the choice to engage in any other HR activities, the choice to engage in targeted efforts to retain and recruit mid and late career workers is based on the business strategy of the organization. It should be recognized that retention and recruitment are only one set of options for ensuring the work of the organization gets accomplished. There are alternatives that might better fit a particular organization (e.g., job redesign and redistribution, outsourcing, off-shoring) that can be considered. Organizations choose between retention, recruitment, or some mix of the two based on their advantages and disadvantages. Retention strategies can have the advantages of facilitating knowledge transfer, signaling a long-term commitment to employees, and reduced costs for on-boarding training. The disadvantages of retention strategies can include a lack of new ideas and approaches, difficulty meeting affirmative action goals, and blocked mobility channels for younger workers. Recruitment strategies are just the opposite. They have the advantages of being able to bring in new ideas, helping meet diversity and affirmative action goals, and opening mobility channels, but also the disadvantages that they can be more costly to implement and they create costs for on-boarding new employees.

Both retention and recruitment can be challenging to implement for organizational reasons as well as legal and regulatory reasons. Many of the suggestions for both retention and recruiting rely on the notion of creating part-time work (reduced responsibility, fewer hours per day, fewer days per week, seasonal employment) and creating contingent work arrangements. While these are attractive to workers in their late career stages, part-time work is not the most optimal configuration for all jobs. In addition, organizations might have legitimate concerns about the job performance of some of its employees. In this case, certain retirements, like other types of turnover, may be very functional.

It is also true that some efforts aimed at retaining older workers can have the opposite effect. That is, rather than retaining workers who would have retired, they may encourage workers who otherwise would have continued working full-time to retire in favor of part-time work (Greller & Stroh, 2003). Indeed, phased-retirement and offering contingent work arrangements have been used as early retirement incentives as opposed to incentives for continued work (Feldman, 2003). As such, retirement counseling or planning programs (e.g., Shuey, 2004) could be offered to employees to guide their use of phased-retirement program or contingent work arrangements. These programs not only help clarify the criteria and content of relevant HR practices, but also help employees better evaluate their status and plan for retirement. Therefore, offering these programs can help better align retirees' retirement transition goals with the organization's retention and recruitment goals. Finally, it should be noted that there are also legal barriers to phased retirement programs. For example, the Pension Protection Act of 2006 relaxed some restrictions on in-service distributions from defined benefit plans while continuing to work for the plan sponsor (e.g., for those 62 and older or who have reached the plans normal retirement age). However, there is still little guidance about how to administer these distributions and some have raised concerns about the legality of targeting older employees for part-time work if that part-time work is at a reduced pay and benefits.

Considering the advantages, disadvantages, challenges to implementation, and costs, organizations attempt to choose the mix of retention and recruitment activities that are best aligned with their strategy. Clearly, organizations that are not experiencing or expecting to experience vacancies and those that may be in retrenchment are not likely to be interested in retention or recruitment to any great extent. Organizations adopting a cost leadership strategy with a focus on routine and standardized work processes and/ or a workforce concentrated in jobs that require skills that are widely available in the labor market can benefit from broad recruiting approaches (i.e., seek to attract large numbers of applicants). In this case, recruiting workers in their mid and late careers may only be a small part of their broader approach. An organization adopting an innovation strategy where new ideas and approaches are important might be better served by recruitment strategies more than retention strategies. An organization adopting a differentiation strategy, which relies on firm-specific knowledge and relationships, or requires specialized skills not generally available in the labor market, is likely to benefit from retention strategies and narrowly targeted recruitment efforts.

Future Research Directions

In this chapter, we have reviewed organizational-level factors that may influence mid and late careers from the EOR perspective and strategic HRM perspective. In general, few empirical studies have been done to investigate the influence of organizational-level factors suggested by these two perspectives on workers in their mid and late careers. This may be due to the fact that career researchers do not often study constructs at the organizational level, especially those in the strategic management arena. Nevertheless, we argue that it is important to shift our attention to those factors, because organization is important in the context of one's career—the organization hosts the resources people need for career development and provides the social environment that shapes a worker's career experience.

One methodological issue that needs to be considered when studying the organizational level factors is the nested data structure. Employees are nested within their respective organizations. Therefore, the data needs to be analyzed in a multilevel analysis framework. Otherwise, it is likely to yield inaccurate standard errors for parameter estimates, leading to the overestimation or underestimation of the relationships of interest

(Snijders & Bosker, 1999). Therefore, as we earlier called for more research to examine organizational level factors, we recommend multilevel modeling technique to be used to warrant achieving accurate estimates of the effects.

Based on the current review, it is also important for future researchers to consider a mediation model to connect the EOR perspective and strategic HRM perspective. For example, it is conceivable that desirable retirement-related HR practices and policies are likely to increase the perceived quality of the EOR, which, in turn, will align employees' retirement decision with organizations' strategic goals for the workforce. Specifically, for older workers, their perception of organizations' resources, practices, and policies provides them information to evaluate organizations' concern and commitment to older workers. Reciprocating to organizations' favorable treatment and expecting more benefit in the future, older workers may increase their work effort by postponing retirement or engaging in bridge employment. For organizations, they design HR practices that are consistent with organizational strategic goals and deliver these practices to employees, which may contribute to the formation of a shared positive perception regarding EORs such that the employer is considerate and supportive. Consequently, a positive EOR increases employees' work well-being and helps organizations to achieve their staffing or downsizing goals.

Another future research direction is to consider the development of EORs in a bottom-up process in which employees observe and communicate with each other to infer and attribute the organizations' commitment to their relationship with employees. Employees' perceptions of EORs are not independent of each other for those working in the same organization or work unit; neither is the retirement decision. For example, the retirement decision of a coworker could prompt others to retire or think about retirement. Observing or hearing about a coworker's unpleasant interaction with the organization may negatively impact the EOR quality for others. Consequently, employees may be less confident in the mutual exchange relationship with the organization. If the EOR perception developed by employees working in the same organization varies across a wide range, it is less likely that the organization will achieve its strategic goal by actively managing its relationship with employees. Therefore, future research should explicitly consider the role that coworkers play in shaping the EORs.

Future researchers may also want to consider societal culture as an important boundary condition to examine effects of EORs and HRM practices among older workers. In different societal cultures, older workers may develop different needs and value different things. For example, in Eastern societies heavily influenced by Confucianism, such as Chinese and Japanese societies, older age is typically associated with seniority and higher social hierarchies (Li, Tsui, & Weldon, 2000). Therefore, older workers in those societies may be more sensitive to whether the organization's HRM practices demonstrate sufficient respect to them. Such respect may not only be associated with the materialized support they receive from the organization, but also the "good faces" (i.e., positive views from others) they gain from the organization's practice. For example, older workers in those societies may particularly value the opportunity for them to participate in company policy making, even though such practice is only a formality (Li et al., 2000). To our best knowledge, no empirical studies have examined the potential joint effect of culture and age on effects of EORs and HRM practices.

It should be noted that another perspective rooted from the organizational climate literature may also be useful to identify organizational level factors that may influence workers' mid and late careers. Organizational climate refers to employees' shared perception about the organizational practice (Ostroff, Kinicki, & Tamkins, 2003). Although we reviewed the various potential influences of strategic HR practices on one's mid and late career, those practices are mainly rooted in an organization's formal HR policies. Alternatively, organizational climate may be formed through informal practices that emerge among the organizational members. Often, it is not the formal organizational policies, but those informal ones that have more direct and stronger impact on workers' experience and behaviors (Ostroff et al., 2003). James and James (1989; also see James et al., 2008) suggested that organizational climate may include employees' shared perception regarding organizational practices such as leader support and facilitation, role stress and lack of harmony, job challenge and autonomy, and cooperation and friendliness. James et al. (2008) argue that these components of organizational climate are results of the shared value systems of an organization's employees, which may influence the behaviors and cognitive appraisals of employees as a group. For example, the organizational climate provides implicit standards against which one's organizational behaviors are evaluated. The extent to which a worker is unhappy with the organizational climate he or she experiences could have important consequences on that person's career-related decisions.

TOPICAL ISSUES RELATED TO MID AND LATE CAREERS

Chapter 7

Mid and Late Career Renewal
Opportunities and Challenges

As each individual's life unfolds, goals evolve, needs change. For some, economic issues and challenges are still of paramount importance in their mid careers and, as a result, make a strong impact on the type of job options those individuals will consider. The combination of earlier career choices and harsh economic climate may have had a negative impact on their career progression and current level of pay and benefits. Others may have been able to successfully climb the ladder and now seek career options that allow them to work in roles in which they find meaning and personal engagement.

In this chapter, we summarize research and practices related to the options, issues, and challenges of career renewal that individuals in their mid and later career face. Much of the work and research that has been conducted on career changes focuses on achieving upward mobility throughout one's career (Rosen, 1972; Shaw, 1987; Sicherman & Galor, 1990). This line of research is based on the underlying assumption that people change jobs and occupations in order to increase their pay and achieve higher levels of responsibility. In this chapter, we will further explore this assumption and more directly integrate the significance of working in roles that give individuals in their mid and late career stages a sense of meaningfulness and allow them to fully utilize their talents. To place the research on career renewal in perspective, we also interviewed several mid and late career workers and included their reflections and experiences about career renewal in this chapter.

Forging a Career Path: The Search for Alignment

Often when individuals make their initial career choices, they focus on where they can make the most money and/or rely on the guidance of their parents and caregivers to help them select the right career based on their skills and talents. For individuals in their mid and late careers today, it is highly likely that they would have followed in the footsteps of their parents when making career choices and considering job options upon graduation

(Bennis & Thomas, 2002; Macky, Gardner, & Forsyth, 2008). For example, in Michigan, a traditional career path for multiple generations of family members was to work in one of the automotive companies or automotive suppliers. For those who grew up in Michigan, it was not unusual, and often assumed, that upon graduation from high school they would take a position at GM, Ford, or Chrysler following in the footsteps of their parents (and often their grandparents). This career path was considered to be the optimal choice since the automotive industry offered high paying jobs (for individuals with a high school education) and financial security for life. With the erosion in the U.S. auto industry and the economic downturns over the past two decades, this is no longer the case. Given the current state of the U.S. auto industry and what it needs to do to ensure its ongoing survival and competitiveness in the global market, this is one example of how a traditional career path with guaranteed lifetime employment is no longer a viable option.

Similarly in the professions, children who had parents who were doctors, lawyers, teachers, etc., often followed in their parents/grandparents footsteps. Parents who had careers in medicine or law, for example, would often encourage their children at a very early age to pursue courses and interests that would prepare them to be accepted into selective undergraduate programs that would optimize their chances of being admitted to the top tier professional schools to earn their degrees and thereby position themselves to be hired by exclusive firms or start their own practices/businesses. Whether in traditional /blue collar or professional positions, individuals often make choices about their career path based on a variety of other factors that often have little to do with their talents or interests (Buckingham & Clifton, 2001; Clifton & Hartner, 2003; Critchley, 2002).

CASE STUDY

Henry, a physician in his late 40s, shared his story and how his career path was virtually set from the time he was born. His father and mother were both physicians, and from an early age he "knew" that he would be a doctor when he grew up. The career path was reinforced by such actions as his parents giving him a real stethoscope for Christmas when he was 10 years old. By the time he graduated from high school, he had all the needed equipment to be a physician and had won more science and math awards than he could count. He always worked hard to get good grades, be the best at whatever he did, and those traits carried over into his practice as a physician. He has been a successful pediatric surgeon for over two decades now. But Henry never felt like he was living his dream and doing what he loved to do. Instead, he was living his parents dream. Now, as he was about to turn 50, both of his parents had died and he had the opportunity to look closely at his decisions and choices. Henry knew that while he was a great doctor and had helped untold numbers of children and their families, it was not where his passion and interests lie. While initially overwhelmed by how much time he felt he had "wasted" in his life, he knew that he had to make a new set of choices to begin using his talents fully. So, despite the huge investment of time and money to gain his medical degree and be the expert he had become, he knew that just continuing down the same path until he retired, was not an option.

The options that are available for those in mid career often allow individuals to choose again to find work that more fully utilizes their talents and gives them a sense of meaningfulness (Beehr & Bowling, 2002; Feldman, 2002c).

Career Renewal: Transitions and Changes

The optimal outcome for individuals in their mid and late careers is to find options that will allow them to renew their careers and not merely maintain the status quo until they are ready to retire from work completely. Power (2009) defines career renewal as "the achievement on the part of individuals in midcareer of greater positive involvement in their work and/or feelings of greater subjective career success (i.e., intrinsic outcomes) as the result of some career or personal transition." (p. 108)

In the past, staying with one organization throughout one's career was the norm and was seen as an act of loyalty and commitment to the company. Individuals were rewarded for this loyalty by the company that "promised" financial security in retirement (pension and medical coverage for life) and the possibility of a satisfying career. However, externally imposed changes (e.g.. technology, globalization) have significantly impacted the available career and job options for workers (Worthing & Buck, 2008). As summarized in Chapter 2, the majority of people do not work for one organization for their entire career (Sullivan & Baruch, 2009).

Increasingly individuals are making choices to move to different organizations to achieve specific career goals as well as in response to downsizing and other organizational changes which "force" them to look for new career paths; many of these individuals hold mid level management positions. Individuals in middle management roles are most frequently targeted to be eliminated as leaders seek to streamline their organizations and reduce costs (Sterns & Subich, 2002). As cited in Chapter 2, for a variety of reasons individuals are taking responsibility for their own career progression (protean careers) and are not relying on organizations to provide them with lifetime employment or financial security.

To develop a more detailed understanding about the impact of job changes on workers over 40, the Health and Retirement Study (Johnson, Kawacki, & Lewis, 2009) gathered data from over 9,000 individuals between the years of 1992 and 2006. The results of this study showed that workers over 50 who changed jobs tended to make less money and were less likely to have pension and health benefits. However, the same individuals reported that their new positions offered more flexible work hours and they experienced less stress than they did in their previous positions. Individuals in their mid and late careers who made the decision to change careers, tended to move out of managerial jobs and move into sales and operations positions (which are less stressful than managerial roles and offer more flexible work hours). The HRS showed that the majority of individuals who downshifted reported that even though their new jobs were less prestigious and had a lower social standing, they enjoyed their new jobs more than their previous jobs (Johnson, Kawachi, & Lewis, 2009).

Johnson et al. (2009) also found that men were more likely than women to continue working if they left their positions when they were in their 50s. Also, for individuals who held advanced degrees (PhD, MA) or professional degrees (MD, JD) were least likely to change jobs and careers. This is more than likely due to the large investment of time and money they made in their career initially. The specialized training and experience they have may be less transferable to other jobs or different occupations (Johnson et al., 2009).

Workers from all occupational groups make decisions to change careers and jobs in their 50s, 60s, and beyond. However, Johnson et al. (2009) found that Hispanics, women, and individuals who did not complete high school tended to move into new jobs significantly less often than their counterparts. Farber (2008) found that the number of males working for private sector organizations for 10 years or more declined from 50% in 1973 to 35% in 2006. Similarly, Mainiero and Sullivan (2006) found that in the same time frame there was an increase in the number of women who chose to move in and out of the workforce at several points during the course of their careers to meet personal and family related needs.

Personal Characteristics Impact Career Renewal

Factors related to personality as well as health and wealth have a significant impact on individuals' motivation and willingness to change jobs and careers after age 50. For individuals who are suffering from deficits in physical stamina/abilities or experiencing cognitive deficits that impact their job performance, they may be pressured to seek new jobs and careers (Feldman, 2007). Personal factors such as poor health and declining mental functioning may necessitate that individuals in their mid or late careers find other jobs that match their current skill and ability levels. Also, external factors (e.g., being fired or laid off) can force individuals to seek out other job options. Both internal and external factors that impact the choices individuals make to change their job can negatively impact their self-esteem and confidence. When these factors make a negative impact on individuals, it undermines their ability to open new doors and convince others (e.g., the hiring manager) that they are fit for the job and have the necessary skills, knowledge, and talents that will contribute to job performance.

Also, some stable personality characteristics can directly impact individual's willingness to seek other jobs as well as make career changes after age 50. The Big Five personality framework is a well-established and researched model and describes the impact of different personality dimensions on work outcomes and success. The five personality dimensions on the Big 5 include: conscientiousness, extraversion, agreeableness, emotional stability, and openness to experience (Hurtz & Donovan, 2000; Salgado, 1997). Of these five personality dimensions, emotional stability and openness to experience may be most closely related to the willingness to seek out other job options in one's mid or later career (Feldman, 2007).

Emotional stability is defined as an individual's feelings of positive self-regard and freedom from worrying about changes. Individuals in mid and late career who are emotionally stable and relatively free of neuroticism will have realistic and positive self-regard and may be more adept at accurately assessing if their talents will allow them to be successful in a new position or career as compared to individuals who have higher levels of neuroticism. As a result, they would be more able to judge the consequences and payoffs associated with specific job changes and if they would find the work to be meaningful. For individuals who are open to experience (as measured on the Big Five), they would be more likely in their mid and late careers to make changes that they believed would give them a sense of accomplishment and feelings of career success. Individuals who are over 50 and are more open to experiences would have been more likely to have made changes earlier in their lives and successfully handled the consequences of their choices. Individuals who are more open to experiences will also tend to make more balanced assessments of the potential rewards and likely hazards, rather than overemphasize the risks when compared to the rewards (or vice versa).

Being successful in setting career goals and achieving successful outcomes through moving to new positions has a direct impact on the willingness of individuals in their mid and late careers to accept the risks involved when making changes. Sterns and Patchett (1984) found that individuals who moved into new positions early in their careers were most open to seeking out career development opportunities and new positions as they entered their mid career. Moving into different organizations and continuing to market oneself through the process of applying for new positions over the course of one's career can positively impact confidence and self-esteem (Sterns & Subich, 2002). For those individuals who have stayed in the same organization for the majority of their career, that choice can reinforce the feelings of specialization and obsolescence that can contribute to the self-perception that "I am not as marketable now" (Veiga, 1983).

There can also be economic costs associated with moving to a new organization or seeking a new position. For individuals who have worked with one organization for an extended period of time and have accumulated a significant pension and/or other benefits, they may perceive these as too valuable to risk losing by changing jobs solely because they are dissatisfied, bored, or see no options for growth or continued learning in their current job (Sterns & Subich, 2002). These individuals may assess the risks as too high and believe that it is "worth it" to just hang on to what they have in their current role. Choosing to remain in a job and holding on until retirement, however, can take a toll on one's feeling of success and effectiveness. Lower levels of self-confidence and optimism will directly impact individuals' willingness to take risks, which, in turn, reduces the options that they see as viable. Viewing oneself as old and obsolete will pose a significant internal barrier to taking action to explore career options in mid and late career, as well as make a negative impact on overall self-confidence and feelings of success in life (Seligman, 2002).

Changing Organizational Demands: Developing Skills to Facilitate Renewal

In an attempt to streamline costs, organizations are using virtual teams and more complex technologies to keep individuals in touch with each other (and their customers). This change to working with others virtually underscores the need to continue to update one's technology skills and the ability to build relationships with individuals who may never meet face to face (Charness & Boot, 2009; Noe, Hollenbeck, Gerhart, & Wright, 2009). Individuals in their mid and late careers who have remained up to date with the newest technologies and maintained their "knowledge expertise" will have the greatest number of available options to choose from and the most flexibility in terms of when and how they do their work. Reinforcing the importance of keeping up to date technology skills, a recent National Public Radio report stated: "Job search experts say the biggest hurdle for older workers is often technology. Applying online is a lot different from going door to door with a resume" (Largey, 2011). The internal motivation to learn and continue to develop and refine their skills would directly contribute to the success of individuals in their mid and late career (Shultz & Wang, 2011).

The importance of keeping up to date with technology and continuing to build positive relationships with others in mid and late career was strongly emphasized in the interviews we conducted. These mid and late career workers we interviewed talked about the importance of continual learning and development regarding how to use technologies and social media to achieve organizational and personal goals.

CASE STUDY

Phyllis, a woman in her 60s, emphasized the importance of being flexible and responsive in one's reactions to both people and how to integrate technology to build relationships when team members are spread across the United States. Phyllis noted that early in her career, she emphasized her technical expertise and sought out projects that would help her use and hone her technical skills. As she progressed in her career and took on more managerial roles, she saw the importance of emotional and social intelligence. Phyllis was recently given several large projects that required the input and ownership of leaders and technical experts from around the country. She needed to integrate best practices and to ensure that the options developed reflected cutting edge research and were fully owned and supported by the individuals in each region who would be implementing the new systems. The complexity of these projects required that Phyllis be able to build relationships with people she only knew "electronically" as she would not have the opportunity to fly across the country on a weekly basis (which would significantly drive up the costs of the project) to meet with key people on the team. While Phyllis was always able to develop strong working relationships with her peers, managers, and direct reports in her region, she found that she had to be very conscious about how to use her emotional and social intelligence to build relationships in the virtual world. Her openness to learning and getting coaching and help from others on how to use the technologies made the difference in the success of the project and the leadership that she brought to everyone on the virtual team.

In addition to the desire to learn and continue to integrate one's talents, many individuals in their mid and late careers have also been internally motivated to seek out new jobs and, in many cases, new career paths to find greater meaning in their work and make a contribution that goes beyond economic benefit. Many individuals in their mid and late careers begin to realize that they are no longer living their dreams or their dreams have changed in significant ways that no longer fit the person they have become in their 50s and 60s. Johnson et al. (2009) note that many older workers are shifting jobs and careers to find work (and open their own businesses) that is less financially lucrative but is more personally fulfilling than their previous work.

Several of the individuals in their 60s we interviewed did exactly that; they consciously chose positions in which they made significantly less money than they had in the past. However, in the interviews each one stated that "they are happier now they than they were in their 20s and 30s." The measures of success that they used to assess their happiness in the present were very different (money and status vs. meaning and autonomy) than those used previously. They stated that now their focus was on the quality of the relationships that they had with their colleagues, their ability to use their talents daily, their love of learning new concepts and tools (e.g., technology to deliver online classes), and their ability to work autonomously and creatively on a regular basis. The transitions made by each of the mid career individuals gave them more confidence and, as a result, they felt they were being more of "who they are" rather than who others wanted them to be. Earlier in their careers, they focused on demonstrating their technical skills and problem-solving abilities (in the discipline of their degrees), now they felt that their accumulated wisdom and ability to work with others allowed them to not only continue to achieve results for the organization, but also feel that they were contributing to something larger than themselves (rather than focusing on the next pay raise or promotion). So, in the process of changing careers and jobs, those mid and late career workers were renewed. They were much more involved in their work and ongoing learning as well as giving more to others and to the communities they served. The steps taken to change their role and career allowed them to focus more on their subjective measures of success and to completely redefine what success meant to them. As Sara, a woman in her 60s said: "Working on fun projects that allow me to develop new skills and help others learn is more important to me now than working on projects that make money for the company and would earn a bonus for me, but was meaningless overall, I couldn't do that any more, I had to make a change."

Know Yourself: Be True to Yourself

Traditionally, when individuals are considering a career change, they engage in a plan and implement approach. This process involves a series of programmed steps that often begin with having individuals reflect on their experiences, skills, educational background, interests, etc., and then identify the types of jobs that would be consistent with them. Once they have identified a range of jobs, individuals begin to network with friends, family, professional colleagues, etc., who can provide them with additional information about where those types of positions are available. However, Ibarra (2004) states that this approach often results in minimal change for the individual and is a low risk process which does not create renewal or optimize the use of one's talents. Taking this approach reinforces individuals' prior decisions and often assumes that they are searching for their true selves and ways to optimize who they are (Cross & Markus, 1994). Ibarra (2004) states that individuals have multiple identities, interests, and talents that evolve over time as careers unfold. As a result, identifying a broader range of options and taking more creative approaches to investigate alternative careers can yield a wider range of roles that are a better fit for individuals in their mid and late careers who are looking for ways to utilize their talents (Buckingham & Clifton, 2001).

Ibarra (2004) contends that the traditional approaches used to help individuals change jobs more often than not reinforce staying put on the career path and in the type of job that individuals are looking to change. So, the challenge for mid career workers is to draw on methods that facilitate making the big changes to optimize the use of their talents and finding career satisfaction rather than using approaches that do not help create the optimal changes. Since many have not been able to make the desired changes in their careers, these individuals are often labeled as resistant to change, or are not ready to make the needed sacrifices to achieve their career goals. But the true culprit, according to Ibarra (2004) may be the methods used to find a new career and not the motives of the individuals who are seeking new options. "Am I doing what is right for me, or should I change direction" (p. 49) is one of the most critical questions a person in mid career need ask himself or herself. There is a clear difference between individuals who are making significant changes in their mid careers in order to continue to grow and learn, and those who choose to stay in unfulfilling positions because of fear of change or financial concerns about the impact that such a change will cost them.

Sterns and Patchett (1984) observed that, for individuals in mid career, making decisions to change jobs, careers, or to continue to engage in career development are usually a combination of changes that occur within the person along with changes that have occurred within the environment (e.g., the industry they have worked in for a duration of time). This model assumes that individuals make multiple changes over the course of their development. For individuals who have sought out and successfully created changes, taking action to do so in one's 60s and beyond is merely an extension of behaviors that have been developed and nurtured throughout one's previous development.

To create a meaningful career change, using the more aggressive test and learn method can make a more dramatic shift in career trajectory (Ibarra, 2004). Since all individuals have multiple identities and interests that evolve over time, individuals need to explore how to create new work and opportunities to integrate them. The process that Ibarra suggests is to "reinvent your working identity" (p. 47). Doing this would include taking steps to try out new professional roles (e.g., doing pro bono work, freelance assignments) and requesting sabbaticals or extended vacations to engage in the type of work that individuals are considering as the next step in their career. This process also includes the expansion of one's network to reach out to people they do not know in order to ask for advice, ideas, and alternatives. Strangers can often provide a different and very valuable perspective that individuals would not have seen nor considered for themselves; nor would their current network of friends, who have known them in their current careers have considered. Strangers have no preconceived notions about an individual's past experiences and degrees. As a result, they are more likely to offer very different suggestions of jobs, positions, organizations, and people who could help facilitate genuine career change.

Finding strangers to network with now is very easy by using Internet social networking sites that can give access to people across the county or across the world who share similar interests and ideas. Joining sites like Linked In and other online sites within a professional area of interest (they exist for every nuance of interest), even Facebook, can provide individuals with access to ideas and people whom they would have never been able to access in the past.

Essential Factors in Career Changes: Money, Motivation, and Meaning

While the career choices made by young adults have been widely examined and researched, understanding the antecedents and consequences of making career and job changes for individuals in their mid and late careers has been neglected (Feldman, 2007; Morrison,

2002). Studies conducted on career mobility for older workers have tended to focus on executive and CEO movement and succession (Ward, Sonnenfeld, & Kimberly, 1995) and retirement and bridge employment (Kim & Feldman, 2000; Zhan, Wang, Lui, & Shultz, 2009). Lifespan research that has been conducted demonstrates that older workers' attitudes about work and career goals evolve and change over time (Barnes-Farrell, 2003; Johnson et al., 2009). Erdogan Bauer, Peiro, & Truxillo (2011) stated that workers in their mid and late careers are motivated by different aspects of work when compared to their younger counterparts. Often, workers in their mid and late careers seek out careers and organizations that hold values that are congruent with theirs, but also allow older workers to use their talents and provide them with opportunities to continue to learn and grow (Deal, 2007).

Clearly, economic stability of individuals in their mid and late careers will impact the career choices they make and the options they pursue. For example, for those individuals who are financially established, they can *afford* to change jobs or careers and work for less money in order to fulfill their dreams and find more meaning in their work. Individuals who are financially established may seek out jobs that allow them to work in a positive social climate making new friends as well as giving them more meaning in their work and a clear sense of purpose (Adams & Beehr, 1998; Pogson, Cober, Doverspike, & Rogers, 2003; Taylor & Shore, 1995). The climate of the organization, the flexibility and autonomy, and the meaningfulness of the work often tend to be a more powerful measure of success than traditional objective career success measures (Dutton & Heaphy, 2003).

The emphasis on the importance of the work climate, having autonomy, and finding meaning in one's work was reinforced through the interviews we conducted with mid and late career workers. Each of these individuals had made a conscious choice to move out of lucrative positions and take roles that paid significantly less. Throughout their 20s, 30s, and early 40's, all had made significant investments, both in time and their personal energy, working to achieve financial success and move up the ladder in their chosen careers. Each of these individuals had achieved the goals they had targeted for themselves in their careers. Despite the objective measures of success, their work lacked meaning to them personally. It was the search for meaning and the desire to do something more that motivated them to change careers and move in a very different direction than they would have even considered when they were in their early 20s. Each of the individuals we interviewed are now in their 60s, 70s, and 80s and they expressed that they love their work and find meaning in the contributions they make on a regular basis. If they had not been motivated to search for something different and take action to create other options, each would have been successful by all external measures (pay and job titles) but dissatisfied because of the lack of meaning in the work they were doing.

Changes in jobs and careers often require the individual to obtain additional training and invest both time and money to build the needed skills and earn additional formal degrees and certificates. For those individuals who have an established financial base, they have less economic risks to manage as they make changes in their mid and late careers when compared to individuals who do not have the money or time to invest in the necessary retraining that would give them such skills or earn an additional degree (Feldman, 1994).

CASE STUDY

We interviewed Sara, who left her corporate position in her 50s to pursue her PhD in order to position herself to become a professor. She was motivated to invest the time and energy to do this since to be considered for a tenure track position in most universities, one must have a PhD. Before making this very large investment of time and money, however, she taught classes at the university level on a part-time basis to find out if what she was searching for was fulfilled through teaching. She found that not only did she love the process of teaching, but that she used new talents and enjoyed the learning process so much that she was more than willing to pursue her PhD full-time. The engagement of her talents and her desire to learn were essential factors fueling the decision to completely change career paths and complete her doctoral work.

Engagement and embeddness in one's work and career contribute to satisfaction with work and life (Crabtree, 2011; Feldman, 2007). Gallup gathered data from more than 47,000 employed respondents worldwide (Crabtree, 2011). Results showed that, regardless of country or region, employee engagement was linked to personal well-being and one's overall life satisfaction. These are powerful data to consider when reflecting on the career and job choices that all individuals, but specifically those in their mid and late career make.

When identifying the positions that will be the optimal fit, individuals in their mid and late careers need to be clear on the talents and experiences that will contribute to their effectiveness in the position and how engaged they will be in the activities that need to be performed in their role. This is particularly important when they appear to be overqualified for the position that they are applying for (Erdogan et al., 2011: Shultz, Olson, & Wang, 2011). Individuals who are recruiting for open positions may be apprehensive about hiring someone who may be trying to get a foot in the door. Therefore, it is essential to be clear about one's motivation and desire to find meaning in the work and describe how prior experiences will help them be effective in the role and allow them to contribute to achieving goals for the organization. Clearly stating one's goals and talents and how those will contribute to organizational performance in the interview process will be important especially since it is likely that mid and late career workers will be interviewed by someone who is younger. Being self-reflective and sharing what was learned in prior jobs and how that will contribute to their effectiveness in the position they are applying for can help facilitate the process and increase the likelihood of being a viable candidate. Not appearing desperate or talking down past experiences to give the impression of fit—but being honest and forthright can facilitate the process for both the individuals and the leaders in the organization who are considering hiring the candidate.

Organizational Culture and Relationships: The Impact on Career Renewal

Significant changes have occurred not only in how work is completed, but also in what people expect from work. In light of these changing expectations, organizational leaders have had to identify ways to adapt the organizational culture and human resource practices to accommodate and support these new expectations to attract and retain employees (Noe et al., 2009). For example, creating and nurturing an organizational culture that supports work/life balance, lifelong learning, and flexible scheduling to accommodate workers' personal needs and preferences are more important than ever to attract and retain top performers, particularly those in their mid and late careers (Hodgetts, Luthans, & Lee, 1994; O'Reilly & Pfeffer, 2000). Through the interviews we conducted, the need for autonomy and ability to work on projects that fully engaged their talents was essential for workers in mid and late career.

CASE STUDY

Phyllis reinforced the importance of organizational leaders taking the time to really understand each employee's talents (regardless of age) and then assigning them tasks and projects that engaged those talents. Phyllis emphasized that workers in their mid and late careers often have wisdom and implicit knowledge that those with less experience do not yet have because they do not have the years of experience to draw upon. She emphasized that age does not necessarily mean that you have such wisdom (some workers are just putting in their time and indeed are not interested in learning more, but are focused only taking home a regular pay check), but many workers in their 50s and beyond do have that wisdom. Therefore, the climate that the leader creates needs to be optimized so that talents can be used for employees of all ages.

This example also reinforces the importance leaders facilitating working relationships among people from diverse backgrounds (e.g., different ages and generational perspectives). Organizational leaders have to take a more complex approach to managing diversity in order to effectively achieve important business goals. The focus on diversity and how to integrate individuals who have divergent values, beliefs, traditions, and experiences has been paramount (House, Javidan, & Dorfman, 2001; Shaw, 1987). To address these challenges, organizational leaders need to continue to develop and set performance goals and measures to facilitate the ability of workers of different ages and with different working styles to build relationships so that they can work together to achieve organizational goals (Molleman, 2005). When organizational leaders focus on diversity, they often are referring to surface-level factors that are typically clearly observable, for example, race, age, gender, ethnicity, and physical abilities (Richards, 2000). The evolution in the workplace however, has taken this to a deeper level to include diversity in terms of geographic location, behavioral style, parental status, educational level, religion, first language, and life experiences (van Knippenberg, De Dreu, & Homan, 2004). All of these factors impact how individuals perceive problems, make decisions, and communicate with others, as well as their beliefs and attitudes about what is right and wrong. Of course, as individuals' age and gain experience and build relationships with others through mid and late career, organizational leaders need to be more savvy in their approaches to integrating people into teams and encouraging them to work together to optimize each other's talents.

CASE STUDY

Anne, a senior leader in her 60s, had a mid level manager in her organization who was in her 30s. This particular mid level manager believed that "older employees" couldn't possibly have the technical skills needed to make changes in the processes to upgrade current systems. Therefore, she systematically "moved" all those employees who now reported to her that were older than she was and hired people who were younger. Her expressed belief was that the up to date technology skills and understanding of the processes that the younger employees learned recently in their MBA programs would allow the organization to raise the performance bar and achieve higher level results. The opposite occurred. Because these younger/new employees did not have relationships with people in different departments that would allow them to influence others and gain buy in and support, their "new programs" failed because of lack of acceptance from these key people in other departments who had to implement the new programs. Those older workers, those "moved" off of the team, were the ones with the relationships across the organization. Consequently, they could engage others to sell the new programs and work side by side with their counterparts in other areas to smoothly implement the new approaches and software.

This is a clear (and often repeated) example of how those in their mid and late careers could optimize outcomes for the organization by working in partnership with younger workers whose technology skills could be integrated with their network of relationships to facilitate changes.

The practical implication of these examples underscores the importance of developing and maintaining positive working relationships with others. Individuals who have positive working relationships with their supervisor can also have greater access to training and development opportunities. Developing new skills and/or refining existing skills can be highly motivating for those individuals who seek out lifelong learning opportunities (Van der Heijden & Van der Heijden, 2006). As the workforce is becoming older on average, age diversity will invariably increase, and older workers will continue to bring a wider variety of experiences, personal characteristics, and talents to organizations. Working in an organizational culture in which individuals are valued even as they reach their retirement years, will contribute to feelings of career success (Taylor, Shultz, & Doverspike, 2005).

Not Just Work: Meaningful Work

Work satisfies a range of needs: economic stability, financial security, skill development, social status, a sense of belonging to a group, recognition for superior work, and the ability to develop one's talents. While all of these elements are important, there is a growing expectation that work will provide value beyond financial and social, by giving workers meaning and a sense of purpose that permeates their lives. Research conducted on the meaning of work over the past 50 years has shown that the vast majority of people (up to 95%) report that they would continue to engage in work activities even if they did not need to do so for economic reasons (Harpaz & Fu, 2002). These results are consistent regardless of culture, age group, occupation, or gender of the participants. The meaning individuals experience through their work could emanate from the importance of the work being completed, or to the engagement of the individual's talents through their work, or to the feeling that one's work contributes to the greater good. Pratt and Ashforth (2003) state that one of the most consistent findings is that those who find meaning in their work are more satisfied with their jobs.

As individuals move through their careers, their definition of what is meaningful can change and evolve (Baltes, Rudolph, & Bal, 2012). Meaning does not come from the *kind* of work one is doing, but from the *relationship* one has with the work being done. Wrzesniewski (2003) argues that meaningful work can be created and enhanced through the process she defines as job recrafting. The actual process of recrafting one's work could take several forms: (a) individuals can change the way they approach the tasks that need to be completed in their work, (b) decrease the type and/or number of tasks that they need to complete, or (c) change the number of interactions they have with others in the process of completing their work. Creating a culture in which individuals have freedom to decide which tasks to emphasize and how to complete those tasks, allows the individual to make choices about how to use their talents to complete their work in the best way for them. Also, for individuals who are performing the same tasks, they can collectively determine the optimal way to complete those tasks, thereby creating meaning for each individual and optimizing performance for the organization (Gaillard & Desmette, 2010; Wrzesniewski, 2003).

Meaningful work, by definition, would engage the energy and focus of the individuals performing the work tasks and activities. Buckingham and Clifton (2001) have discussed in detail the importance of engaging one's talents at work and the experience that creates for individuals. Individuals who are using their talents at work are naturally energized and engaged when learning information that draws on their talents and facilitates their ability to achieve higher levels of performance. Creating and changing the accountabilities in specific jobs in a way that allows individuals to use their talents and giving them the freedom to make their own decisions about what steps need to be taken to achieve those results will optimize the results accomplished. For example, formal job descriptions can undermine the ability of the individual workers to use their talents and find meaning in the work for which they are responsible. Instead, organization leaders can determine what *must be* done in a specific way for safety or other legal reasons, and then define what approaches are "recommended" to achieve results. This approach will encourage people to find meaning in their work and optimize their creativity and engagement in the process (Buckingham & Clifton, 2001; Peterson & Seligman, 2003).

In the interviews we conducted, the definition of success evolved from when they were in their 20s to when they were in their 60s.

CASE STUDY

Sara stated that when she was fresh out of college she focused on using the technical skills that she had diligently honed and developed in college and she actively sought out projects to prove herself as well as further develop her technical skills. Then, as she moved into her 30s, she realized that working with others on teams was also important. To be effective when working on teams, she had to gain credibility by genuinely listening to others and finding ways to integrate their talents into the team solutions (she did not need to be the smartest one with all the right answers). As a result of teaming effectively, she found she was able to get more exposure, and higher raises, and promotions.

For all the individuals that we interviewed, they reached a point of having done many successful projects and contributed to the growth of an organization's bottom line. The problem was that they were no longer really using their talents, learning and growing, and having fun. The number of hours (often more than 60 per week) was not being spent doing meaningful work, but to make the organization more profitable. The definition of success that they articulated in their 60s was now focused on making a contribution to something meaningful and helping others actualize their talents.

Creating Choices and Options for Renewal

Each individual makes specific decisions that impact how his or her career unfolds and job opportunities become reality. Choices are directly impacted by the actions the mid and late career workers make to: (a) continue networking with a wide array of people; (b) continue to expand their technical and technology related skills; (c) build on and expand their interpersonal abilities and communication skills; and (d) stay current on changes and innovations in their work, field, or industry. The options and choices that individuals have available are directly related to the energy invested in one's mid and late career. Making the choice to stay in one's current role and continue working hard/long hours to optimize the ability to achieve important career goals is a clear choice that will allow mid and late career employees to build on the previous "investments" in their technical skills and relationships (along with sustaining whatever pension plan exists in their organization). Another option is to downshift to create more time so that the mid and late career worker has the energy to pursue family and nonwork activities. One could also choose to retire from full-time work and find other pursuits—including part-time, bridge employment that will give one a feeling of satisfaction. To create the options that are most valued by the individual, it is essential to understand one's personal goals and values. Individuals need to be clear and specific about what they need financially, socially, and developmentally in their mid/late career to remain engaged, find meaning, and give back to others.

The days of full job security and "guaranteed lifetime employment" are long gone. Individuals need to be conscious of their own needs and clear about how their choices impact their ability to meet those needs at each of their stages of development (Critchley, 2002).

When identifying on the options available in mid and late career, it is essential that individuals carefully reflect on their definition of success. For the individuals we interviewed, the definition of success had changed considerably from when they began working in their 20s. There are many ways to measure the success of the choices and changes made in their career or job. Traditional indicators such as money and promotion opportunities may no longer be relevant and may cause frustration and depression if they are not seriously re-evaluated. For mid and late career workers, it is essential to be clear on their financial needs and determine if there is indeed a minimum amount of pay that they need to be financially viable and secure (however, that is defined for each person). Johnson et al. (2009) report that older workers do indeed often take a pay cut and relinquish benefits when they make the choice to downshift. For some mid and late career workers, they prefer to walk away from the 9–5 grind and have more flexible schedules, less stress, and more meaning in their lives even if they have to take a significant pay cut.

Future Research Directions

As we continue to refine our understanding of the importance of career renewal strategies for individuals in their mid and late careers, we need to expand our understanding of the following areas. As we continue to conduct research on effective career strategies and actions that renew mid and late career workers, we need to remember that while there are patterns, each person's choices reflect their own personal needs, values, expectations, and desired outcomes.

- *Learning and developing.* For many individuals in their mid and late careers, the desire to learn and continue to develop and refine new skills and abilities is essential. To optimize their learning, individuals need to be very clear on what talents they possess and want to continue to hone. It is very stimulating and exciting to learn new skills and approaches that help individuals improve their talents and bring themselves to the next level of effectiveness. Jobs and roles that encourage ongoing learning to be effective and achieve the targeted results will make a difference for people who enjoy learning and stretching themselves. Future research in this area can help us identify: What approaches can mid and late career employees use to understand their talents and the types of jobs, tasks, and projects that will draw on those talents? What strategies can they use to find roles to optimize the use of their talents? Are there different job search strategies that work more effectively for early career versus late career workers?
- *Sense of purpose and meaning.* Contributing to others can be very motivating and engaging for people in their mid and late careers. Having a clear sense of purpose in their daily activities can also help individuals be persistent when working toward achieving goals. The meaning of the work and the interactions with others can keep individuals motivated to move forward. Research questions could include: How do individuals integrate the importance of finding meaning and "giving back" in the work roles they pursue as they make job choices in their mid and late careers? Are there differences in the importance of meaningful work based on type of work (professional, labor) and level of education achieved?
- *Engagement and flow for mid and late career workers.* Mid and late career workers are often looking for work that engages them fully and allows them to have fun yet remain flexible in what they do and when they do it. Part-time and temporary work can often provide the flexibility and alternatives to fit the daily schedule that individuals in their mid and late careers prefer. This goes beyond the desire to golf every day (which can become draining and no longer fun after 6 months or so). It is best defined by the fact that when one is involved in activities, there is a sense of timelessness and flow (Csikszentmihalyi, 1990). This sense of flow indicates complete engagement and emersion in the tasks that the individual is doing. Research in this area could focus on how individuals in their mid and late careers find flow in their work.

Chapter 8

Performance Management
Issues and Challenges

This chapter focuses on the significance of using performance management processes to optimize the effectiveness and ongoing development of employees in their mid and late careers. When well designed and implemented, performance management systems create the context for individuals in their mid and late careers to use their talents in a manner that facilitates their continued growth and ability to contribute to organizational results. We will also discuss why it is important for these individuals to focus on developing their talents as part of an effective performance management system. Ongoing development of mid and late career workers' talents will optimize their ability to fully use their accumulated experiences and contribute to the organization's key objectives and strategic goals. We will use the concepts of talents as developed by Buckingham and Clifton (2001) to emphasize the importance of ongoing development for employees in their mid and late careers. It is also essential to link performance management systems to training and development processes to ensure that mid and late career employees are developing and expanding their skills and talents (Deal, 2007; Maurer, 2007). The training and development processes will be discussed in detail in Chapter 9.

Performance Management Systems

Performance management is a strategically significant process that organizational leaders use to clarify the relationship between each individual's performance goals and the overall goals of the organization (Langeland, Jones, & Mawhinney, 1998; Noe, Hollenbeck, Gerhart, & Wright, 2009; Pulakos & O'Leary, 2011; Tapinos, Dyson, & Meadows, 2005). When performance management systems are effectively designed and implemented, each employee clearly understands the link between his/her individual performance goals and the organizations' mission, values, and strategic goals (Becker & Klimoski, 1989). Clearly articulating this linkage is essential for effective individual and team performance regardless of the position the individual holds within the organization (Hillgren & Cheatham,

2000). As an example of the importance of this linkage, sales people need to understand how their sales targets contribute to the overall sales goals for the organization. In the context of performance management, the sales people need to understand the quantitative goal (e.g., increase sales of product X by 3% over last year) but also the qualitative goals of the organization (e.g., building partnerships with customers who value sustainability and their impact on the environment). Specifically, if the organization has as part of its mission specific goals focused on environmental sustainability, the sales people need to also build partnerships with the "types" of customers that have values that are congruent with the organizations' mission, values, and goals focused on sustainability. In this example, if sales people are encouraged to sell to customers whose organizations do not support environmental sustainability (i.e., based on the carbon footprint of their customers' organization), the performance management system would be perceived as focused solely on reaching the targeted number of sales (quantitative measure of performance) and not on organizational mission and values focused on sustainability (qualitative measure of performance). This lack of congruence between words and actions needs to be addressed, otherwise the linkage between the organizations stated mission and values and the individual's sales goals would cause people to question the organization's true commitment to sustainability initiatives. On a macro level, for the performance management system to be credible, there should be congruence between the mission, values and goals of the organization and the specific goals set for each individual (Schneier, Shaw, & Beatty, 1991).

At the individual level, the information included on the performance appraisal form is a key part of the feedback that individuals' receive about their performance and the value that they contribute to the organization. Managers also use the information that is written on the performance appraisal to make key human resource decisions about who to promote, transfer, layoff, and give raises to at the end of each performance year (Cascio, 2006; Pritchard, Jones, Roth, Stuebing, & Ekeberg, 1989). Thus, effective performance management processes facilitate the accuracy of human capital decisions. When the system is used effectively, people are transferred and promoted into positions that optimize their performance and their ability to use their talents.

In most organizations, however, individuals do not look forward to engaging in the performance management discussion (most frequently associated with the dreaded annual performance appraisal). For most individuals and managers, the performance management process is perceived as a task that needs to be endured "because HR requires it." Most organizations have some form of performance management process, which they use to make decisions about employee performance and salary adjustments (Latham & Wexley, 1981; Noe et al., 2009). However, less than 25% of organizations report that they use their performance management process for talent management and making decisions on training and development needs (Freedman, 2006). However, research designed to assess the impact of fostering the development of individuals' talents on a diverse array of outcomes (e.g., classroom training, employee commitment, leadership development, organizational profitability), have demonstrated that building talents, rather than the more typical approach focused on improving weaknesses, makes a significant impact on results achieved by the individual (Clifton & Harter, 2003; Seligman, 2002). Effective design and implementation will reduce the negative perceptions of performance management systems and translate it into a meaningful process for individuals and leaders at all stages of their careers.

CASE STUDY

In our interview with Sara, she emphasized the importance of managers' under-standing the talents and past experiences of each of their direct reports. Sara felt that, regardless of the age of the employee, managers needed to optimize the performance of each of their direct reports by assigning projects that allowed them to fully use their talents and draw upon their past experiences. In terms of managing performance, Sara identified the importance of working for managers who are able to understand the different talents of each direct report and then assign them to projects giving them full autonomy to make decisions and find creative solutions to meet the organizations goals. Over the course of her career, Sara found that, in general, younger employees needed more performance guid-ance and coaching when they were given projects. Sara believed that this was due to their limited experience and that they did not have the accumulated "tacit knowledge" to understand the linkages among all the people and the decisions that need to be made so that their projects were successful. Due to the network of relationships Sara had with people across the organization, her performance was often at a higher level than that of her younger counterparts who had not been in the organization or the industry as long as she had. The larger network allowed the mid and late career worker to get things done more quickly and efficiently. Related to this, Sara found that she had a better understanding of the talents that her colleagues had and she knew the best way to involve others in projects to facilitate successful results. Sara's experience showed her that as she got older, she had a clearer understanding of what she could do well and where she needed help (and who had the talents she did not have). She became more confident as a result in her ability to produce results. In her experience, Sara also saw that as people aged in their careers, they developed more emotional intelligence and were better able to understand their own reactions/emotions and others reactions. This understanding helped them to build more effective relationships which also helped them get the work done more effectively (and help others get their work done as well).

Organizations that seek to sustain a competitive advantage through optimizing the effectiveness of their people will place them in positions that allow them to use their talents so that they can maximize their contribution to the organization (Buckingham & Clifton, 2001; Motowidlo, Borman, & Schmitt, 1997). When effectively designed and implemented, performance management systems also clarify the training and develop-ment needs for each individual in the upcoming year. In the performance review, employ-ees and their managers should identify the areas that need improvement in the upcoming year as well as the opportunities for new projects and assignments that will build on the successes of employees in the previous year (Becker & Klimoski, 1989). Effective performance management processes are also directly linked to the career development and succession planning systems of an organization (Rothwell, 2001). An integrated per-formance management system assists individuals, teams, and organizational leaders in identifying development needs, career paths, and promotion opportunities for individuals who possess the talents related to leading projects, people, and departments. This holds true for people at all career stages (Sterns & Miklos, 1995).

Employees in their mid and late careers have experienced many iterations of the performance appraisal process. As such, they understand that while performance management and training opportunities theoretically have the ability to make an impact on their job performance and clarify their goals for the upcoming year; in practice this does not consistently occur (Cawley, Keeping, & Levy, 1998; Sterns & Miklos, 1995). In many organizations, the performance appraisal process is perceived as filled with bias (Bernardin, Buckley, Tyler, & Wiese; 2000), rating errors (Pulakos, 1984) and is perceived as a bureaucratic "necessity" (Noe et al., 2009). Negative bias and stereotypes held against older workers who are in their mid and late careers can have a direct impact on the performance ratings given by their supervisors (Perry, Kulick, & Bourhis, 1996). Specifically, younger supervisors have been found to give lower ratings of performance to older workers (Ferris, 1991; Finkelstein & Burke, 1998). The process can be further distorted by political dynamics that can have a negative impact on interpersonal relationships between an individual and his/her manager (Rosen, Levy, & Hall, 2006).

Biases and Stereotyping: The Impact of Age on Performance and Performance Ratings

We are experiencing a growing dilemma caused by the fact that people are living longer. Longevity for some older workers allows them to continue to engage in work that they truly value and allows them to engage their talents. For other individuals, they must continue to work for financial reasons. The bottom line however is that individuals are working longer. Given this, it is important to understand the age related stereotypes that impact older workers (Posthuma & Campion, 2009). Organizational leaders may hold negative biases about mid and late career employees because they see them as either: (a) not having the necessary skills and most current technical knowledge, or (b) they do not perceive that these older workers are willing/able to learn new skills that are required to complete their work and perform at the same level as their younger counterparts (Cappelli & Novelli, 2010). These biases against older workers are often linked to a lack of understanding of the talents that mid and late career workers bring to their work roles coupled with management/human resource practices that reinforce these biases (i.e., giving training opportunities predominantly to younger workers so that we invest in our future, older people will retire sooner and we will not receive a pay back on the training investment). While it may be true that some older workers do not want to work the same number of hours, and they may not have the same goals and aspirations as they did earlier in their careers, there are also many younger workers who do want to work longer hours and do not aspire to higher level positions either.

Research designed to identify the relationship between job performance and age has yielded inconsistent results (Shultz & Adams, 2007). In 1986, Waldman and Avolio conducted the first meta-analysis on the relationship between age and job performance to identify the strength and nature of the relationship between these two factors. Their results showed that age was positively related to objective measures of job performance and productivity (i.e. older workers produced at a higher level when compared to their younger counterparts). However, Waldman and Avolio's results also showed that there was a negative relationship between the supervisor's ratings of job performance and the age of the employee. Interestingly, their results also revealed a positive relationship between peer ratings of performance and the age of the individual being rated. Taken together, these results support the conclusion that there are biases against older workers given that objective measures of performance show they are higher performers than their younger counterparts, but the subjective ratings given by supervisors of the performance of older workers are lower when compared to the job performance ratings given to younger workers by the same supervisors.

The results of Waldman and Avolio (1986) showed that the relationship between supervisor ratings of job performance and the age of the employee was stronger for those in nonprofessional positions than for those in professional positions. This finding could be related to the physical demands of nonprofessional jobs, yet the fact that the ratings of older workers in professional (knowledge based) positions were still lower than their younger counterparts is an indication of potential age bias reflected by the rater (the supervisor). Supporting this finding of rater bias, Perry, Kulick, and Bourhis (1996) found that some individuals are indeed predisposed to rely on negative stereotypes of older workers and evaluate the performance of older workers more negatively as a result.

In 1989, McEvoy and Cascio conducted a meta-analysis on a wider range of studies (65 studies containing 96 samples), and the results showed that there was no relationship between age and job performance. In addition, they found no moderating effect on the relationship between age and performance based on the ratings given by supervisors. In 2003, Sturman conducted a meta-analysis and found there was an inverted-U shaped relationship between age and performance. That is, at younger ages employees received higher ratings of performance. But at around age 40, the relationship between age and job performance became negative (i.e., the job performance of older workers was rated lower).

Ng and Feldman (2008) recently conducted a meta-analysis to understand why the results of prior meta-analyses yielded such widely disparate and inconsistent results. Ng and Feldman assert that one possible explanation for the mixed results of prior meta-analyses was related to the fact that "performance" was measured by core task activities (i.e., job accountabilities and activities). They developed a framework that expands the traditional definition of job performance to include 10 factors that are related to employee actions and behaviors, all of which impact the context in which work is performed and therefore, how performance is measured. The performance factors included by Ng and Feldman were core task performance, creativity, performance in training programs, organizational citizenship behaviors, safety performance, general counterproductive work behavior, self-rated workplace aggression, self-rated on-the-job substance use, tardiness, and absenteeism. Ng and Feldman (2008) found that age was unrelated to performance on core task performance, creativity, and performance in training programs.

While performance on core tasks was not related to age, Ng and Feldman (2008) found that there was a positive relationship between age and organizational citizenship behaviors (OCBs). These citizenship behaviors included actions such as actively upholding organizational norms, helping out coworkers who needed assistance, and not engaging in negative behaviors such as spreading gossip and complaining. Mid and late career workers exhibited more behaviors that supported the organization in general and contributed to a positive organizational culture. These organizational citizenship behaviors have a positive impact on the organizational culture and climate, and directly contribute to more positive working relationships among employees, which in turn contribute to people working together more effectively and performing at a higher level on job assignments and projects (Motowidlo & Van Scotter, 1994). Podsakoff, MacKenzie, Paine, and Bachrach (2000) found that positive organizational citizenship behaviors contributed to productivity at the group, department, and organizational level of analysis. This indicates that mid and late career workers, who demonstrate more positive organizational citizenship behaviors (OCBs), make a positive contribution to group and organizational performance (Borman, 2004).

CASE STUDY

In our interview with Phyllis, she also identified that older workers do indeed contribute significantly to positive working relationships and the ability to complete difficult assignments. In her experience, she found that performance was more directly related to how engaged the person was, not how old s/he was. Phyllis believed it was her role as a manager to keep all her employees, regardless of age, fully engaged by giving them assignments that allowed them to use their talents and feel a sense of accomplishment and contribution to the team and the organization overall.

One of the reasons for the differences in outcomes of studies designed to measure the relationship between age and job performance is the challenge created by the lack of agreement on how to measure the concept of age. Specifically, Cleveland and Lim (2007) discuss multiple ways of defining age beyond simple chronological age. These include *person-based measures of age* such as subjective, personal, or perceived age (i.e., how old or young individuals perceive themselves to be), as well as functional or biological age. In addition, within organizations there are a number of *context-based age measures* that include psycho-social (e.g., self-perceived or other perceived age) and organizational (e.g., self-perceived or other perceived age in relation to other work group members) measures. Thus, how one defines the concept of age can have a dramatic impact on how it relates to the concepts of performance management, training, and leadership.

Research and experience show that individuals do experience physical and psychological changes as they age. This is a natural part of the development process that each individual experiences as a result of changes and experiences that impact what they learn and how they develop. Overall, as individuals' age, there may be some general slowing in functioning, reduced attention capability, and greater limitations in working memory. However, it has not been found that these changes have a negative (or positive) impact on actual job performance in older adults (Charness & Czaja, 2006; Craik & McDowd, 1987; Gutherie & Schwoere, 1996; Jex, Wang, & Zarubin, 2007; Kubeck, Delp, Haslett, & McDaniel, 1996).

Research has also shown that the concept of declining performance associated with age may be more salient for individuals in physically demanding jobs than for workers in professional and service sector positions (Rothwell, Sterns, Spokus, & Reaser, 2008). For example, research shows that individuals in white collar and professional jobs do not experience the performance peak in their 40s like those workers who are in more physically demanding roles do (Rothwell et al., 2008).

CASE STUDY

In our interview with Mack, he reflected on the relationship between age and performance. Mack has consistently been in professional and managerial roles throughout his career. Now in his 80s, he notes that while his physical stamina has decreased over the years, his cognitive abilities are as sharp as ever. Through his personal experiences, as well as working with colleagues over the past several decades, he has seen that when individuals continue to hone their talents and remain actively involved in their work, they show continued success in solving problems and making decisions that have a positive impact on their ability to do their work in a high quality and effective manner.

In practice, however, biases and outright discrimination against older individuals does occur in organizations. Often, declines in performance are quickly attributed to age rather than considering other aspects of the work or the work environment that may have a negative impact on workers' performance levels (Cappelli & Novelli, 2010; Cuddy & Fiske, 2002; Wilson, 1997). The negative biases are often linked to the beliefs that older workers have lower physical or cognitive abilities or that they are less facil at handling the stresses they face in their work environment and as a result their performance declines (Duncan, 2001; Kite, Stockdale, Whitley, & Johnson, 2005; Rosen & Jerdee, 1976). In an extensive review of 117 publications that were focused on research on age stereotypes, Posthuma and Campion (2009) found that there is actually little evidence that performance declines with age. Conversely, this review demonstrated that job performance actually improves with age, that when declines in performance were found, they were quite small. In fact, Posthuma and Campion's (2009) review shows that health status and individual skill levels are more predictive of performance than age.

Effective Performance Management for Mid and Late Career Workers

The characteristics of an effective performance management process are the same regardless of the age or career stage of the individual employees (Hedge, Borman, & Lammlein, 2006; Latham, Almost, Mann, & Moore, 2005; Noe et al., 2009). It is the *use* of the system that has potentially negative effects on people in their mid and late careers. Performance management systems need to be desinged and implemented to ensure that all individuals have clear goals, coaching and training to assist them in meeting those goals and their performance needs to be evaluated in a fair and equitable manner (Cascio, 2006; Pritchard et al., 1989; Sterns & Miklos, 1995). To be effective, all employees and managers who use the system need to receive training so that they understand the process and develop skills that help others use their talents and perform at an optimal level (Becker & Klimoski, 1989; Cawley et al., 1998). Without training (or training that is effective), managers and employees often merely go through the motions to complete the forms, have their annual appraisal meeting, and then do not discuss performance again until they are *required to do so.*

Performance management systems that are effectively implemented ensure that everyone who uses it understands what to do and why it is important (Bennis, Goleman, & O'Toole, 2008). Both managers and employees need to be willing to invest the time to use the process to facilitate performance improvement and engage the talents of each individual when setting goals and providing coaching and training. An effective performance management system focuses on the goals that need to be accomplished and the resources employees need to achieve those goals. When measurable and specific goals are set, then performance can be monitored by managers and employees. The performance monitoring process helps to ensure that those who are achieving the targeted results can be identified and those who are falling short can receive additional coaching and support, regardless of age. This allows managers to make equitable and informed decisions about who will be promoted, laid off, and receive raises based on performance data rather than subjective criteria that can be negatively impacted by biases or the preferences of the manager (Cascio, 2006; Cawley et al., 1998).

Using an effectively implemented and well-integrated performance management system is not only more equitable for all employees, the ADEA (Age Discrimination in Employment Act) by law requires that organizations eliminate policies, processes, or systems that allow systematic discrimination against employees based on age (Hedge et al., 2006; Noe et al., 2009; Werner & Bolino, 1997). Human resource decisions that are job related, objective, and clearly articulated for all employees and managers ensure that the organization's actions are legally defensible. However, organizations that have policies and practices that systematically discriminate against older workers leave themselves open to legal action (Sterns & Miklos, 1995).

Optimizing the Relationship Between the Manager and Older Worker

Daniels (2000) found that the effectiveness of the performance management process was directly related to the quality of relationship that the manager had with his/her direct reports. The design of the appraisal form and the training used in performance management was less important than facilitating effective communications and a strong relationship between the manager and each employee (Peterson & Hicks, 1996; Pulakos & Wexley, 1983). This underscores the importance of designing interventions to facilitate a strong working relationship between managers and their direct reports as an essential part of the implementation of the performance management process. Research has shown that there are specific manager behaviors that positively impact employee performance (Corporate Leadership Council, 2002). These manager behaviors include:

1. helping individuals understand specifically what they are expected to do and how their performance will be measured;
2. facilitating individuals' success by helping them solve problems and gain access to important resources to complete their work;
3. understanding their employees' talents and assigning them work that draw upon these talents so that they will be successful;

4. providing balanced feedback that focuses on what they are doing well and additional approaches they can use to improve their performance, and;
5. talking to their employees regularly and providing feedback that is perceived as accurate, meaningful and helps the employee do their job better.

To effectively use of the performance management system, training and development that assists managers to exhibit all five of these behaviors should be delivered to facilitate effective relationships between managers and their mid and late career workers. In the interviews we conducted with older workers, they also emphasized the importance of the relationship between the manager and the older employees who report to him/her.

CASE STUDY

Anne emphasized the importance of managers being able to effectively adjust their communication approach to ensure mutual understanding of performance goals. Anne stated that mutual understanding was essential for all employees, not just those in their mid and late careers. With older workers and those who have extensive experience, however, Anne noted that managers need to avoid using pedantic words or coming across as preaching to them. For managers who are younger than their direct reports, they need to identify ways to build on the experiences of the older workers and ask for their advice on how best to achieve important goals. Managers also need to be open to asking their older workers questions about their talents and what types of projects they believe they could contribute to the most. Anne stated that too often younger managers who have older direct reports seem to be concerned that they have to prove that they are the boss. A more powerful and important approach would be to have the manager ask more questions and facilitate a discussion so that the best of everyone's ideas are integrated and contribute to achieving the goals of the organization. Anne emphasized that showing mutual respect is important to building a strong relationship and making sure that people (regardless of their age) receive feedback and are given opportunities to meet the goals that they are assigned.

Older workers also have to be willing to openly share ideas and provide feedback to their managers. They need to be willing to initiate performance discussions when they have encountered roadblocks that their younger managers did not anticipate (Pulakos & O'Leary, 2011). Similarly, older workers also need to be open to feedback and ideas from others and not assume that their years of experience automatically will lead them to the right answer. New ideas can be exchanged with their manager and mid and late career workers need to be open to alternatives that they may not have considered. Without open, two-way feedback between the manager and the older worker, the performance management process will be undermined because there is not sufficient trust in the relationship to make it work effectively (Pulakos & O'Leary, 2011). While there are many ways to build trust in the relationship, Peterson and Hicks (1996) identified the importance of setting realistic goals, following up on commitments, fully sharing information, showing support and providing resources to assist older workers in achieving the targeted results.

Beyond this, managers also need to show interest in the "whole" individual, what is happening both at work and in their nonwork lives.

As individuals continue to work longer, the likelihood of older workers having younger supervisors will continue to increase (Cappelli & Novelli, 2010). To understand the dynamics of this relationship, Van der Heijden and Van der Heijden (2006) examined the impact of age differences between supervisors and employees on performance ratings. The results of their research indicated that having a high quality working relationship between the supervisor and the employee had a positive impact on perceptions of performance when there was a significant age difference between the supervisor and the employee.

There is some research evidence that younger managers interact with their direct reports who are older in a different manner. Perry, Kulick, and Zhou (1999) found that when older workers and their younger supervisors worked together to achieve results, the older workers were able to outperform their younger supervisors. In a follow up study, Perry et al. (1999) set up the experiment so that the younger supervisors were not working in the same room but were physically separated from their workers. In this situation, their results showed that older workers looked for ways to complete their work so that they would have more control and influence over the results they accomplished. Perry et al. (1999) interpreted that the differences in results between the two studies were related to status differences (between the role of supervisor and the role of worker) rather than age per se. When the older workers and younger supervisors worked side by side, the older workers were able to directly show their talents and their ability to perform the job well.

Use of Talents and Optimizing Performance of Mid and Late Career Workers

Today, individuals place greater emphasis on the ability to use their talents in meaningful ways as they complete their work and achieve significant goals for the organization (Buckingham & Clifton, 2001; Buckingham & Coffman, 1999; Csikszentmihalyi, 1997). Talents are defined as a naturally recurring pattern of thoughts and behaviors that, when honed through the ongoing acquisition of knowledge and development of skills, become strengths that optimize the individual's ability to contribute to the achievement of organizational results (Buckingham & Clifton, 2001; Csikszentmihalyi, 1997; Seligman, 2002). Employees who use their talents and strengths regularly are able to achieve higher levels of individual performance and higher levels of satisfaction with their careers and lives overall (Buckingham & Clifton, 2001; Seligman, 2002).

Individuals today also have different expectations about how their managers will interact with them and the type and level of work they will be assigned. For example, individuals expect their managers to be facilitators, mentors, and supporters, rather than planners, organizers, and controllers of the work process and outcomes (Bennis et al., 2008). As a result, the organizational context can directly impact the opportunities given to individuals in their mid and late careers. For example, role autonomy and freedom to make decisions have a direct impact on how well individuals will be able to use their talents on a daily basis to complete their work. The importance of having freedom and being able to measure one's accomplishments was emphasized in the interview with Sara.

CASE STUDY

Sara stated that being able to work on projects and fully use her talents to be creative became more and more important as she became more seasoned in her career. The most meaningful performance discussions she had with her boss focused on generating ideas about how to improve the work she was doing and setting goals so that she could measure how well she was doing. The performance discussions during which her boss told her what to do and how to complete the work were not only meaningless, but very frustrating. An important goal for Sara in any project that she was given was to be able to learn something new and use her talents to achieve important goals for the organization. She consistently sought out projects and assignments that allowed her to learn, have fun, and make a contribution to others in the process.

Learning, achieving specific goals, and having fun and enjoying what you are doing are all important ways to measure individual performance. These concepts of learning have been incorporated as performance indicators that go beyond the traditional quantitative and qualitative measures of individual and team performance to have a performance system that is focused on both short term and long term organizational results.

To be fully integrated, the performance management system needs to have measureable performance indicators that focus on what has been accomplished, but also the practices that will contribute to the long-term future success of the organization (Kaplan & Norton, 1996). Leading indicators of performance (i.e., long-term outcomes) include measures of employee engagement, learning and development opportunities, customer retention, and depth in the talent pool for both employees and managers to ensure that people are ready for promotion opportunities as jobs become available. Buckingham and Clifton (2001) recommend that all employees have a scorecard which clearly describes how their performance will be measured. While it is a logical conclusion that each individual will have clearly defined goals and specific measures of their job performance, research conducted by the Gallup Organization found that 67% of employees stated that they do not know what is expected of them in their role at work (Buckingham & Coffman, 1999).

Designing a Talent-Based Performance Management Process

Performance management systems that are designed to optimize the ability of individuals to use their talents as they complete their work ensures that the specific results to be accomplished are clearly understood by managers and employees. The goals and outcomes need to be clearly defined by the manager, but the individual who is completing the work needs to decide *how* to accomplish the goals. While organizational leaders will express the importance of optimizing each individual's talents in order to achieve higher level results and productivity, organizations rarely make the necessary investments to optimize individuals' talents when assigning them to jobs or projects (Buckingham &

Clifton, 2001). When designing performance management systems, organizational leaders express consistent agreement about the need to:

1. Measure performance objectively so that there is a direct line of sight between the individual's performance and organizational results (e.g., targeted sales, quantity and quality of goods/services, growth in profits);
2. Satisfy customers (both internal and external) to ensure that expectations are met and feedback on how to improve performance is regularly discussed (often done through customer satisfaction surveys and monitoring calls from customers); and
3. Facilitate effective teamwork to ensure high quality working relationships so that when work is passed on to the next individual/team it is complete and meets expectations. Ensuring consistent quality work facilitates positive relationships among colleagues across the organization. This is often measured through 360 feedback processes and organizational culture audits.

However, the majority of performance management processes describe not only what needs to be accomplished but how to accomplish it (via defining "job competencies" or establishing work protocols) (Buckingham & Clifton, 2001; Spencer & Spencer, 1993). To fully utilize individuals' talents, processes need to be designed that gives them the freedom to make their own decisions about what steps need to be taken to achieve their goals. This approach does not imply that safety protocols and other important procedures can be ignored. It does mean that giving employees checklists or telling them how to do their work (e.g., scripts for call center staff to use with customers) will have a negative impact on the individual's ability to integrate his/her talents and fully engage the employee in achieving important organizational outcomes. To facilitate the integration of talents into performance, leaders need to determine what *must be* done in a specific way for safety or other legal reasons, and then define what approaches are recommended to achieve results. The individuals doing the jobs, however, should decide the optimal approaches they will use to achieve the targeted results. In this context, individuals can share best practices that are used but all individuals will ultimately determine how to use their own unique talents and experiences to get the job done.

A key part of the performance management process is the discussions managers have with their employees in order to fully understand their talents and career aspirations. In the traditional approach to the performance discussion, managers tell employees what jobs they should take in the future and what projects they should work on with little or no discussion of employees' talents and how those talents would be utilized in other positions. Managers often assume that all career movement should be upward in the organization in order to have more prestigious titles, bigger offices, more responsibility, and larger total compensation (Arthur & Rousseau, 1996; Ettington, 1997; Loretto & White, 2006; Sullivan & Arthur, 2006). However, upward movement can actually take people out of their talent zone and move them farther away from the activities that they enjoy most and that utilize their talents on a regular basis. When this happens, people often become dissatisfied with their work.

For mid and late career workers who have been moved many times into different positions by managers trying to help them move up in the career ladder, they may be so far out of their talent zone that from someone looking at their performance and behavior, these individuals could appear to be behaving in ways that reinforce the negative stereo-types about older workers. Behaviors that may appear to reflect lack of motivation, lack of interest in learning new skills, and underperforming in one's job are shown by people who are not using their talents regularly in their work.

However, organizations that ensure that their performance management process is effectively used and that each individual has the opportunity to use his/her talents on the job can circumvent this negative outcome and effectively place people of all ages in posi-tions that allow them to use their talents on a regular basis. Doing so, helps to facilitate their ability to contribute to the organization's results and remain fully engaged in ongoing learning and development. When this occurs, workers in their mid and late careers will find it more compelling to continue to seek out training and development opportunities and find new ways to apply what they are learning to achieving their work goals and objectives.

Individuals who choose to work at older ages do so because work provides them with positive social interactions and a sense of meaning that satisfies their needs (Baltes, Rudolph, & Bal, 2012). Leaders who are managing the performance of mid and late career employees need to understand the talents of their direct reports and assign them work and projects that optimize their ability to use their talents. Many large organi-zations use their performance management processes to motivate higher levels of per-formance by offering rewards such as increased pay, opportunities for promotion, and other outcomes that may not be valued by later career workers. Attracting and retaining individuals who are not motivated by the traditional reward structure can be a challenge for leaders. Offering opportunities to work on projects and complete work that mid and late career workers find interesting and engaging can be more meaningful and energizing than offering promotions and other extrinsic rewards. Also, working toward important goals that give the older worker a sense of purpose may have a stronger and more sus-tained impact on the performance outcomes that are achieved by workers in their mid and late careers (Cappelli & Novelli, 2010).

Future Research Directions

Understanding how to manage performance for all employees is important regardless of the age of the individual. Effective performance management processes that are directly related to training and development systems will contribute to the ongoing growth of individuals in their mid and late careers To ensure that these workers can optimize their contributions, however, managers and supervisors have a responsibility to directly address stereotypes that only serve to reinforce negative perceptions reified in the popular press or through anecdotes that reinforce the idea that you "can't teach an old dog new tricks" or "she's too old to change." Creating systems that contribute to everyone's success and effectiveness is the most powerful way to attract and retain the best people regardless of age. In the competitive environments in which most organizations operate, having employees who are fully engaged and using their talents will make a positive impact on the effectiveness of the organization and the individuals who contribute to organizational performance. We need continued research in this area to understand the factors that ensure accurate perceptions of the performance of mid and late career workers.

Performance management processes provide support and clarity to help individuals make choices about how to optimize the use of their talents and achieve goals that are important to the organization. Future research needs to focus on the specific approaches that can be used to assess individual talents and then assign goals that optimize the use of those talents. We also need to understand if the process used to align individual talents with organizational goals is different for individuals early in their careers versus those in their mid and late careers. Research in this area needs to focus on understanding the interaction between chronological age and stage in career. For example, do older workers (those 50 and above) who have been in the same career have a clearer understanding of their talents and the types of projects that they could contribute to most effectively? This could be compared to how effectively individuals who are in their 50s but have just started a new career are able to identify their talents and the types of projects that they would be most able to contribute to in the organization. We then need to compare how effectively individuals in their 20s who are just starting their careers are able to identify their talents and the projects they are most able to contribute to in the organization.

We need to do research to identify if there are specific performance management design and implementation factors that need to be in place in order to optimize the success of mid and late career workers. Specifically, what are the unique challenges that workers face when they are reporting to a younger manager? How does the impact of the performance planning and goal setting processes differ for younger versus older workers? Are there specific implications regarding how mid and late career workers can be engaged in the process of performance management to optimize their performance and use of talents; or is the process the same for workers of all ages?

Since the relationship between the manager and employee is critical in the performance management process, we need to do further research into what factors impact the quality of the relationship, especially between a younger manager and an older direct report. The pattern of having younger managers with older direct reports will persist over time as baby boomers continue to age. As a result, we need a clearer understanding of the factors that impact the relationship between older workers and their younger supervisors as well as the type of communication patterns that emerge in these reverse age reporting relationships. In these age reversed management situations, many seasoned older workers may claim the younger supervisor lacks real world experiences and a track record (Cappelli & Novelli, 2010). Younger supervisors may perceive the questions and feedback they receive from older workers as indicators of resistance to changes that they are attempting to make. Future research needs to focus more attention on the impact of communication styles and feedback dynamics that occur between individuals of different ages in the manager-direct report relationship. How does the type and quality of performance feedback that older workers perceive change when they have younger supervisors? What environmental and personal characteristics impact whether or not this reverse age reporting relationship is successful? Are there specific training and development strategies that both younger supervisors and older employees can use that will facilitate the effectiveness of the performance feedback process? Are there differences in the approaches that younger supervisors need to take in the goal setting process to help older workers be fully engaged in the achievement of those targeted objectives?

Chapter 9

Training, Development, and Mentoring

This chapter focuses on the significance of integrating training, development, and mentoring processes to optimize the growth and retention of employees in their mid and late careers. Maintaining this focus on growth and development for these employees will facilitate the likelihood that these individuals are able to fully use their accumulated experiences and contribute to the organization's key objectives and strategic goals. In this chapter, we will also integrate the concept of talents as developed by Buckingham and Clifton (2001) to underscore the importance of providing ongoing training and development for employees in their mid and late careers. In this model, talents are defined as a naturally recurring pattern of thoughts and behaviors that, when honed through the ongoing acquisition of knowledge and development of skills, facilitate optimal performance (Buckingham & Clifton, 2001; Csikszentmihalyi, 1997; Seligman, 2002). Employees who use their talents regularly at work are able to achieve higher levels of individual performance and experience greater satisfaction with their careers and lives overall (Buckingham & Clifton, 2001; Seligman, 2002). Finally, this chapter will conclude with a discussion of the significance of mentoring and ongoing development for individuals in their mid and late careers. We have also included information on the experiences from the mid and late career individuals we interviewed about the training, development, and mentoring they have received and given over the course of their careers.

Training and Development Overview

Organizational leaders make significant investments in their employees by providing them with training and development opportunities to optimize individual productivity and overall organizational performance (Berman, Bowman, West, & Van Wart, 2006). Organizations develop, purchase, and provide training to employees to ensure that employees have the knowledge, skills and abilities to perform their jobs optimally. Training is offered on a wide range of human resource and job related skills and behaviors. For example, regardless of the age of the worker, most organizations offer training for new employees, training to develop skills related to changes in job tasks, ongoing training to keep skills up-to-date, leadership skills, and sexual harassment and workplace bullying (Aamodt, 2010). Traditionally, organizations have focused the majority of their training resources on the development and continued growth of knowledge, skills, and abilities that are directly related to performing job tasks and accountabilities (Goldstein & Ford, 2002).

To remain competitive, it is essential that organizations attract and retain employees with advanced knowledge and skills to adapt and innovate in ways that facilitate organizational growth (Van der Heijde & Van der Heijden, 2006). The experience gained as their careers unfold can assist mid and late career employees in applying newly acquired knowledge more efficiently and effectively than employees who have less experience (Warr, 2001). The tacit knowledge that mid and late career employees have accumulated often contributes to their ability to complete work more efficiently and effectively because they understand the nuances and interconnections among tasks that less seasoned employees may not (Sternberg, 1986). In addition, in their mid and late career employees have more experience with the political dynamics that impact their ability to accomplish results in the organization. This tacit knowledge facilitates their ability to integrate the newly acquired information learned in training and to apply the information in ways that will be most beneficial to their organizations.

For today's knowledge-based workers, computer-based training applications are widely used to deliver instruction and information to keep employees up-to-date. Using technology has enabled organizations to deliver specific information and knowledge to large groups of geographically separated workers in a consistent manner. Using technology-based tools, however, is very expensive to implement and maintain. When organizations make this investment, the goal is to enhance job performance and ensure compliance with regulatory requirements, and organizational policies. However, just having access to information does not mean that performance will improve. It is *how* the individual integrates and transfers the information that they acquired that makes a difference. For employees in their mid and late careers, the assumption is often that they are less adapt in using technology and, as a result, may not be able to transfer the knowledge from computer-based, on-line training to job performance (Van Vianen, Dalhoeven, & De Pater, 2011).

In our interview with Mack, he addressed the preconceived notion that all mid and late career workers are technology challenged and would not be able to keep up with their younger counterparts in the organization.

CASE STUDY

Mack stated that we need to directly confront the perception that people who are 50 or older were technology dim wits and that people in their 20s were "digital natives" who could solve any problem faster and more efficiently. He gave examples of how he brought together teams of people to solve specific business and technical problems. When choosing who to invite into his group problem solving teams, he purposefully chose the people who were willing to share ideas and learn from each other. He was thoughtful when selecting the younger more technically competent people and the older experts who could quickly solve the problem, but had difficulty using the technology to model it.

> *Mack found that by bringing people together to share ideas and really "see" each other's experience, some of the walls that had been created came down quickly. The younger digital natives saw how the 55-year-old engineer was able to synthesize alternatives developed from several previous projects he worked on to address the challenge the team currently faced. The engineers in their 50s, who preferred to do the work with paper and pencil, were able to have the 20-something engineers translate the model into the program and manipulate the variables in the design more quickly and efficiently test the impact of design changes. By working together, they built relationships and learned from each other and all involved developed meaningful skills. He strongly believed it was his job as their area director to bring people together to solve problems and share ideas using technology to help in the process.*

Research evidence supports that there is a positive stereotype about older workers regarding the belief that due to their age they have more experience (Finkelstein, Higgins, & Clancy, 2000). However, that stereotype does not consistently translate into ongoing training and development opportunities. The willingness and ability for employees in their mid and late careers to participate in and apply what they have learned through training and development initiatives (regardless of the mode in which it is delivered) depends on other situational factors, not just the age of the person. Their willingness can be impacted by the biases and stereotypes held by others about whether or not older workers are willing and able to change and learn.

Biases and Stereotypes: The Impact on Mid and Late Career Employees

One of the most pernicious stereotypes against training older workers is that they will not be able to learn the information being presented and then apply that knowledge on the job to achieve higher levels of performance (Finkelstein, Allen, & Rhoton, 2003; Finkelstein, Burke, & Raju, 1995; Hedge, Borman, & Lammlein, 2006; Isaksson & Johansson, 2000). Over time, as part of the aging process, cognitive functioning can decline As a result of this fact, it is *assumed* that older workers are less able to learn new skills and, therefore, would not be able to apply the information and skills learned in training (Maurer, 2007; Wrenn & Maurer, 2004). When this negative age bias is held by managers, it also impacts how older workers perceive themselves and can directly impact their confidence when participating in training classes or other developmental initiatives (Baldi, 1997; Kite & Johnson, 1988; Maurer, 2001). This becomes a self-fulfilling prophecy if workers in their mid and late careers do not seek out additional training because they believe their managers do not support them. This, in turn, reinforces the belief that organizational leaders may be wasting resources by including older workers in ongoing training and development opportunities. When older workers do not seek out training or if they appear hesitant to participate, it can reinforce negative stereotypes held by some managers (Maurer, 2007; Wrenn & Maurer, 2004).

Kubeck, Delp, Haslett, and McDaniel's (1996) meta-analysis on the impact of training studies showed that when compared with younger individuals, older workers demonstrated somewhat less mastery of training content, took longer to learn the new skills and perform the training tasks, and took longer to complete the training program. These results do not indicate, however, that the older workers did not learn the training content just that it took more time to assimilate and apply the information while in the training class. Using these results to draw the spurious conclusion that older workers are not worth investing in by giving them training and development opportunities reinforces negative stereotypes (and contributes to negative interpersonal relationships and more than likely lower levels of performance). Drawing the conclusion that older workers will receive less benefit from training also does not take into account other contextual factors (e.g., lack of exposure to new technologies that is used to deliver the training content, different learning styles) that impact the ability of older workers to assimilate new information (Hedge et al., 2006; Sterns & Doverspike, 1988). There is no reason to assume that once mid and late career workers become familiar with the content, technology, and equipment that they would not be able to perform at similar levels to those who have more experience using technology and more confidence when experimenting with new tools and approaches to completing their work.

Furthermore, Peterson and Wendt (1995) found that a significant number of older workers did not seek out training programs because they perceived that the content of the training would not be related to their work. For mid and late career workers who have had experience participating in training classes that were essentially a waste of time, they may not be interested in pursuing further training. Unfortunately, this can be interpreted by others (including their supervisors) as a lack of willingness to learn and grow. Kubeck et al. (1996) identified significant challenges in interpreting the outcomes of studies examining how older workers performed in studies conducted on the impact of training. Specifically, the results of laboratory studies showed greater performance differences between older and younger workers than did field studies. One interpretation of this outcome is that simulated laboratory environments did look like the work environment to the older participants in the research but were more familiar to the younger participants, who more recently completed their formal education. In addition, older workers are likely to have more organizational specific knowledge that will enhance their performance in field studies within their organizational context and this knowledge is not usually relevant in laboratory simulations. Again, contextual relevance needs to be considered to ensure that the results of studies on the impact of training are interpreted appropriately.

Research on the relationship between age and training performance has found that older workers often need additional time to complete training and training assessments (Charness & Czaja, 2006; Charness, Szaja, & Sharitt, 2007). One reason that additional time may be required is that older workers are focused on completing the tasks with accuracy rather than completing the training tasks quickly. The tendency to focus on accuracy versus speed would cause older workers to take longer to complete their training exercises and it would (spuriously) look like they did not learn the material as effectively as the younger workers in the training session (Charness & Czaja, 2006; Waldman & Avolio, 1986). Supporting this interpretation, Charness et al. (2001) found that although older workers tended to take longer to complete training exercises in the classroom setting when compared to their younger counterparts who were learning the same material, there were minimal age differences in actual job performance after the training when comparing younger and older workers ability to apply what they had learned in training.

The importance of contextual factors cannot be underestimated when searching for reasons why mid and late career workers may be hesitant about pursuing training and development opportunities. Van Vianen, Dalhoeven, and De Pater (2011) found that the developmental support that was shown by the supervisor had a direct impact on the willingness of older employees to participate in ongoing training and development. Supervisors can show older employees support by verbally encouraging them to identify training and development opportunities and then supporting them as they pursue training to learn and develop the skills and hone their talents. Mid and late career employees who have the willingness to learn and expand their talents and are working for supervisors who encourage them to seek out ongoing training and development activities have the optimal combination to facilitate their own growth and ongoing learning.

CASE STUDY

The integration of training with providing ongoing support, coaching, and mentoring was illustrated in the interview with Phyllis. She emphasized the importance of the role she played in encouraging her direct reports who were over 50 years old to continue to reach for their career goals and stay fully engaged. Phyllis was a master at assessing the talents of people and providing them with opportunities to shine. She found May, a 54-year-old woman in the organization who was exceptionally talented, but floundering in her current role. Phyllis had an opening in her department and reached out to May and invested time to understand her talents and her career aspirations. May had not felt engaged and "heard" for quite some time. She felt that she was being passed over by her current director who selected younger individuals who would more often than not "just do what they were told." After spending time with May, there was no doubt in Phyllis' mind that May could handle the position, but Phyllis knew she would have to actively encourage and develop May to deal with the politics and interpersonal dynamics that were involved in the position promotion she was about to offer May. Phyllis invested in May by sending her to expensive outside training workshops and 360 feedback development coaching (i.e., feedback from multiple sources including supervisors, peers, and subordinates), as well as taking the time every day to discuss the issues that May confronted and offered coaching and mentoring to help May be successful and feel confident in the decisions she made and the actions she was taking. Both the cost of training and the time Phyllis' invested in mentoring paid off in terms of May's success as well as the results she accomplished after only 18 months in her new job.

The practical impact of biases and stereotypes about older workers is that managers less frequently nominate older workers to participate in training workshops in order to save money and achieve a (hoped for) higher return on investment by sending younger employees to training and development opportunities. The reality, however, is that older workers continue to comprise one of the largest segments of the workforce (Alley & Crimmins, 2007). Thus, it is in the best interest of organizations, to retain and retrain these employees, rather than force them into early retirement and then spend more money to select and train new employees (Gutherie & Schwoerer, 1996; Lindbo & Shultz, 1998; Salthouse & Maurer, 1996; Taylor, Shultz, & Doverspike, 2005).

Designing Training and Development to Engage Mid and Late Career Workers

To engage and motivate older workers in the training and learning process, the content needs to be clearly relevant to their work with an emphasis on being practical so that participants see how to apply what they are learning once they return to complete their job tasks and projects (Hale, 1990; Sterns & Miklos, 1995). Given the experience that older workers have accumulated through their working years, they could be more adept at finding and creating linkages between what they are learning through the training and how to apply that information to enhance work performance. Specifically, Buckingham and Clifton (2001) found that individuals who were using their talents to complete their work more easily found approaches to apply the new information in innovative and complex ways to enhance their performance. Those who were not using their talents were less motivated and interested in the information being presented because it was not relevant to them and therefore they were not motivated to learn, retain, or apply it. The principle of demonstrating the relevance of training for all participants, regardless of their age, is essential to help individuals apply the knowledge that was acquired during the training and development activities. Relevance may indeed have a greater impact than age on predicting who will perform at a higher level after the training (Buckingham & Clifton, 2001; Goldstein & Ford, 2002). Emphasizing the specific ways that participants in training can apply what they are learning on the job and giving them the time to practice the new skills will directly impact the return on investment (ROI) of the training for the organization (Fisk & Rogers, 2000).

CASE STUDY

All of the individuals we interviewed emphasized the importance of relevance for any training and development initiative. Without relevance, they believed it was a waste of time for the individuals receiving the training and a waste of money for the organization. Specifically, they all directly stated that you have to make it worth their time to participate in the training and "sell" them on the importance of the training. Those in mid career want more information than being told "just go to training because I tell you to do it." Younger individuals may be more concerned about asking questions to get more information. The older workers that we interviewed also reflected on the possibility that when individuals in their mid and late careers asked questions about the training their questions could be misinterpreted as resistance to training and they did not want to change. That could be related to the perception that older workers are not interested and that "you can't teach an old dog new tricks."

Previous studies that have been conducted on the participation rates of older workers in training have focused on how older workers utilize training delivered by organizations to support the growth of their employees. However, Simpson, Greller, and Stroh (2002) found that older workers were actually more likely to seek out training and learning opportunities outside of the organization (rather than training offered internally) to build and enhance their talents and learning. Their research found that younger workers were more likely to seek out internal training programs, mentors, and apprenticeships to build their skills and talents (Buckingham & Clifton, 2001; Simpson et al., 2002). This result could be related to the fact that having been in their career longer, older workers have a broader network of relationships and know where to go to obtain specific skills and build on their talents. Younger workers, however, may be more reliant on the organization's resources since they have fewer years of experience and possibly a smaller network of professional contacts.

Designing and implementing training and development processes that facilitate learning and retention are important for both younger and older workers (Hedge et al., 2006). There are, however, specific steps that can be taken to be inclusive in the training process so that the learning styles and preferences of both younger and older workers are reflected in the training design and delivery. First, it is essential that the learning objectives are clearly defined and articulated. It is also important to *advertise* the training so that all employees who would benefit from the training are aware of the opportunity and understand how they will benefit from participating in the training. This is a basic principle for designing effective training sessions (Aamodt, 2010), but one often neglected by trainers and human resource professionals who are often focused on filling the seats in the class rather than ensuring that those who would receive the most benefit from the training and learning opportunity are present. Also, having a communication process to advertise the available training would ensure that individuals have access to the information about the training and development opportunities that exist rather than relying on supervisors and managers to share that information with their employees. As part of the communications, the benefits of the training process for older workers need to be clearly articulated (Hedge et al., 2006; Straka, 1998).

Design of training processes needs to include how to engage individuals who have different learning styles to facilitate understanding of the content and the ability to apply what is learned in the training to real world tasks and projects. Learning style is defined as a consistent approach that an individual uses to respond to problem solving and decision making situations (Kolb & Kolb, 2005). Too often, training is not designed to meet the different learning styles of the people receiving the training. To be effective, training programs need to incorporate approaches that account for the diversity of learning styles and preferences that are related to age differences as well. Using active learning methods, such as case studies, peer learning groups, simulations, role plays, and interactive large group discussions to facilitate learning and retention are well established approaches that facilitate learning and retention for employees of all ages (Aamodt, 2010; Sterns & Doverspike, 1988). These active learning approaches are also effective ways to ensure that older, as well as younger, participants are engaged in the learning process and not alienated by classroom oriented lecture training (Hale, 1990; Hedge et al., 2006). As part of the learning process, it is beneficial to include examples in the training that show older workers in situations that demonstrate the skills to be developed. Utilizing older people as positive examples of how to use the skill or demonstrate the application of the knowledge being taught in the training process ensures that they see themselves as valued resources for the organization and valued in the training process. In addition, Warr (2001) suggested that ensuring that older workers are actors demonstrating the principles to be learned during the training provides visible recognition that older workers are willing to learn and have the ability to effectively use the skills that are being taught in the training process.

CASE STUDY

In the interview with Anne, she emphasized the importance of having training in which everyone is actively involved in the learning process, no lectures. Everyone should not only see the relevance of what they are learning to doing their job well, they should have time to practice the skills and receive feedback on how to do it better.

A final recommendation to facilitate the transfer of learning from training to job performance is to ensure that older, as well as younger, workers are encouraged to use what they have learned in training to improve job performance by establishing specific training and development goals (Aamodt, 2010; Cascio, 2006). Far too often, individuals complete the training and development process with no specific plan regarding how they will apply what was learned. The plans that are developed to implement what is learned need to be specific and realistic. Brim and Liebnau (2011) found that developmental goals established to implement what was learned in training need to build on and expand the current talents of the individual. The development plan should focus on behaviors and actions that can be regularly incorporated into one's work and be relevant to improving job performance. More often than not, however, when employees return from training, the supervisor does not work with them to establish plans to apply what was learned to improve performance. As a result, it is often reported that training made little or no difference in job performance (Cascio, 2006; Kanfer & Ackerman, 2004). To be effective, supervisors need to be actively involved in discussions regarding what was learned in the training session and give the employee time to apply what was learned to improve job performance (Sterns & Doverspike, 1988; Warr, 2001). Taking the time to provide encouragement and support will ensure a greater return on investment for the time and money that organizations invest in the ongoing development of employees regardless of their age and career development stage.

Training and Development: Are There Generational Differences?

Both individual employees and their managers have a role in ensuring the effectiveness of training and development initiatives in organizations. Specifically, knowledge workers need to be proactive in managing their own learning and development by staying up-to-date on the latest advances in their specific field of work (Bertolino, Truxillo, & Fraccaroli, 2011). For knowledge workers, this is especially significant as previously acquired skills and abilities can quickly become obsolete. Being aware of one's own talents and strengths and seeking opportunities to continue to develop skills and expand one's learning will likely increase the contributions made by mid and late career worker.

It is also essential that leaders in the organization take their role seriously in terms of actively engaging and developing individuals in all roles, regardless of their age (Luthans & Youssef, 2004). It is important that leaders be aware of the negative biases held by some individuals about older workers and whether or not employees in their mid and late careers have the skills or motivation to continue to contribute to organizational goals. There are many negative anecdotes that are shared repeatedly about older workers and their lack of willingness to learn and keep their skills and knowledge up to date. Many of these anecdotes have been published in popular press articles and news reports highlighting the perceived differences among people based on their demographic designation (e.g., Gen Y, Gen X, Boomers, Traditionalists), but little systematic research has been conducted to determine if there are indeed genuine differences among people in different age groups.

Deal (2007) conducted research to identify whether or not meaningful differences actually exist across people who are categorized into the different *generations* (e.g., Gen Y, Gen X, Boomers, Traditionalists). The findings of her research showed that people from all generations valued similar attributes in their relationships at work and desired similar outcomes, but different behaviors were associated with each valued attribute and outcome. For example, Deal found that people from every generation wanted to feel that they were respected by those they worked with, had trust in their relationships with others at work, had credible leaders, and worked in an organization where negative politics was addressed and discouraged. In addition, workers from all generations expressed the desire for clearly defined and consistent goals and objectives rather than continuous changes in direction. In terms of training and development, the most consistent result was that people from all age groups wanted to learn on an ongoing basis and that the opportunity to continue to learn on an ongoing basis was the most important factor for people at all career stages (Deal, 2007; Twenge, Campbell, Hoffman, & Lance, 2010). Employees in early, mid, and late career stages all expressed that having opportunities to learn and develop were important retention factors, and, if opportunities to grow were not available in an organization, they were more likely to look for another position or become dissatisfied with their work.

In addition, the results of Deal's (2007) research showed that the top five training and development skills that were deemed important across age groups were: leadership skills, technical skills, problem solving and decision making skills, team building skills, and communication skills. There was remarkable consistency in the types of skills that were seen as essential to be effective in organizations regardless of age. There was also consistency across the generations in *how* people wanted to learn. The top five methods across all age groups were: (1) on-the-job training, (2) one-on-one coaching, (3) peer interaction and feedback, (4) discussion groups, and (5) traditional classroom instruction.

CASE STUDY

In the interview with Sara, she also emphasized the importance of the soft skills and the technical skills. These always need to be honed and polished. She stated that you can never know enough about yourself and how to work well with others so that goals can be accomplished collectively. Training and development needs to be designed to reinforce relationships with others and high quality outcomes for the organization. Sara also strongly believed that having people train on the job and work with other experts was the most meaningful way to help people in their 50s and above learn and develop new skills and refine their talents.

Training and development has a positive impact on the effectiveness of the organization when the training is meaningful and relevant for participants whether they are in their early, mid, or late careers. Maurer, Weiss, and Barbeite (2003) found that individuals who were motivated to continue to grow and learn sought out learning opportunities and people who could support their ongoing learning and development so that they could continue to enhance their careers and contribute to the organization's key goals. This training self-efficacy was not related to age. In essence, they were intrinsically motivated to continue to learn and took steps which contributed to their growth without waiting for others to give them training and development opportunities. People from all age groups are interested in learning and especially interested in learning how to do their jobs well to continue to enhance their own effectiveness and productivity. In Deal's (2007) research, respondents consistently described how it was often difficult to obtain ongoing training and development because of lack of time, insufficient resources, and inadequate access to high quality training opportunities. Organizations often do not allocate sufficient budget to support effective training and when economic challenges arise, the training budget is often the first to be cut to reduce costs.

Organizational leaders, therefore, need to continue to identify options to facilitate learning and growth for their employees, even when formal training processes are not available. Using talented and experienced people to provide coaching and mentoring to others in the organization who are less seasoned and experienced is essential at all times, and most valuable when training budgets are cut. Deal (2007) found that people from all age groups valued coaching from others that contributed to their ongoing growth and effectiveness.

Impact of Mentoring Between Employees in Different Career Stages

The processes that organizations use to develop and facilitate leadership effectiveness at all levels of the organization, contributes to its ongoing growth and effectiveness (Noe, Hollenbeck, Gerhart, & Wright, 2009). Individuals who have experience and knowledge to share through providing mentoring and coaching to others can be valuable resources to facilitate knowledge transfer and help others perform more effectively (Drucker, 1989; Lindbo & Shultz, 1998). With the changes that have occurred in career paths and choices (discussed in Chapter 2), we can no longer assume that chronological age will determine who serves in the role of mentor and who is the protégé. Individuals may begin new jobs in their 50s and 60s and seek younger colleagues to provide them with guidance and support as they develop new skills and approaches (Allen, McManus, & Russell, 1999;

Hall & Mirvis, 1995). Also, individuals who have created a protean career may nurture alternative mentoring relationships from peers or other experts (using social media tools) that provide them with informational and emotional support as they develop their skills and optimize their job performance (Allen et al., 1999; Olson, Shultz, & Liu, 2011).

Mentoring has been traditionally defined as the process through which a more senior individual (a mentor) provides a less experienced individual (a protégé) with assistance and support to facilitate the development of the protégé to achieve higher levels of effectiveness (Allen, Eby, Poteet, Lentz, & Lima, 2004; Higgins & Kram, 2001). Researchers and practitioners in the areas of adult and career development have emphasized the significant impact mentors can have on the growth and professional development of their protégés (Allen et al., 2004; Dalton, Thompson, & Price, 1977; Kram, 1985; Levinson, Darrow, Klein, Levinson, & McKee, 1978; Olson & Jackson, 2009). Organizational leaders have designed and implemented mentoring programs to provide employees with opportunities to build their talents and develop relationships with key leaders in the organization. Research and practice have shown that positive mentoring relationships facilitates the career development of protégés by enhancing their political savvy, organizational networks, and interpersonal effectiveness (DeJanasz, Sullivan, & Whiting 2003; Killian, Hukai, & McCarty, 2005; Lankau & Scandura, 2002). Moreover, having multiple mentors over the course of one's career correlates with higher promotion rates for those who have developed effective mentoring relationships (Catalyst, 2002; Finley, Ivanitskaya, & Kennedy, 2007; Ragins, Cotton, & Miller, 2000).

As noted by Zellers, Howard, and Barcic (2008), for mentoring relationships to be effective, both the mentor and protégé need to learn from each other. When their relationship is built on trust and commitment to each other's growth, mentors and protégés respect each other's differences, preferences, and past experiences (Gaines, Gurung, Lin, & Pouli, 2006; Thomas 2001). As a result, differences in age actually contribute to the effectiveness of the mentoring relationship and are valued by protégés (McCall, Lombardo, & Morrison, 1988). Employees in their mid and late careers are uniquely positioned to provide the valuable insights and perspectives that contribute to the development of individuals earlier in their career development.

CASE STUDY

In the interview with Phyllis, she emphasized the importance of the partnership between mentor and protégé, in that both have to learn from each other, and both have to be willing to adjust their approach to be effective. Phyllis has mentored dozens of people over the course of her career, some were much younger than she was and others were very close to her age. Phyllis never saw age as an issue, rather she felt it was consistently the willingness of the protégé to be open to her ideas and for her to be open to fully listening to who each one was uniquely and individually—no generalizations or stereotyping (e.g., all recent grads are technically savvy and believe they know it all).

While not all people who are in their mid and late careers will be effective mentors (Olson & Jackson, 2009), they have unique experiences and perspectives that can facilitate the development of others (Lindbo & Shultz, 1998). Often, they have had more exposure to the political dynamics of the organization and can provide guidance to their younger colleagues regarding how to influence others and what actions to take to optimize their growth and development. Mid and late career individuals can mentor and coach those with less experience by helping them identify opportunities to expand their talents and build relationships that will help contribute to organizational goals as well as their own personal career goals. Mentors in their mid and late careers can assist their colleagues who are in their early career stages in establishing specific, attainable, concrete goals that will give the individual experiences that will expand their self-efficacy around their unique talents (Buckingham & Clifton, 2001).

Mentors can also serve as role models by giving their protégés access to people and situations so that they can learn how to perform more complex tasks and address difficult interpersonal situations. As an example, mentors can include their younger colleagues in meetings and situations so that they can directly observe and experience the complexities of organizational decisions and politics. Providing these opportunities for development in a *real life* context exposes individuals (who can be either chronologically younger—in their 20s—or merely new to the role/career—in their 50s) to dynamics that they have only read about in training classes and case studies.

A specific example would be having less experienced individuals observe their more experienced mentors facilitate an effective meeting that includes difficult business decisions that need to be discussed and agreed upon by a group of key individuals. In this real life situation, the less experienced colleague can learn the skills about how to set a meaningful meeting agenda, send out documents to read in advance, ensure the appropriate people are at the meeting, and establish guidelines to facilitate genuine dialogue and discussion in the meetings. Even with this advanced planning for a meeting, there can still be unforeseen and unpredictable behaviors that can and will arise during the actual meeting. Observing a more experienced mentor facilitate a difficult discussion during the meeting can provide an essential observational learning experience for the individual. This is particularly true when the decisions have significant business implications and it becomes politically important to have a more seasoned and respected individual facilitate the discussions during the meeting. For the early career individual, to directly observe how the more experienced colleague handled the facilitation and then to spend time after the meeting fully discussing all the actions and reactions that occurred are essential to the development of these skills and not something that can be taught in an "Effective Meeting Facilitation" class or even fully described in a one-on-one discussion. These are the types of situations that need to be directly experienced in order to fully comprehend.

Another issue that needs to be carefully addressed is how to match older and younger workers who are able to optimize one another's' talents through the mentorship process. For example, in jobs that are physically demanding (e.g., agility and flexibility in maintenance jobs in manufacturing organizations) older workers can mentor the younger workers in processes and strategies to maintain the equipment and new installations; while the younger protégés can perform some of the heavier lifting and squeezing into tight spaces that may be required to complete the work (Rothwell, Sterns, Spokus, & Reaser, 2008).

Mentoring also helps to ensure the transfer of knowledge from one generation of employees to the next. As employees in their mid and late careers make the decision to retire, organizations need to retain the intellectual capital as well as the important relationships that those individuals have developed. Kaye and Cohen (2008) recommend that employers tap the experience and wisdom of their mid and late career employees by:

- Having the older employees serve as subject matter mentors for new hires or employees with less experience;
- Developing work manuals and protocols describing how to maintain equipment, processes, and business functions;
- Forming innovative, intergenerational teams using experience and new techniques (e.g., simulations) to solve business problems and identify a range of alternatives each of which will address the problems.

Formal Mentoring Programs: Design Guidelines for Individuals at Different Career Stages

Within organizations, individuals are often encouraged to build relationships with others from whom they can learn, share ideas and perspectives, and advise about approaches that can impact their ability to influence others. Mentoring relationships often make a stronger impact on one's growth than either the coaching given by one's direct supervisors or what is learned in structured training programs (McCall et al., 1988). To be effective, organizations need to help facilitate the development of formal mentoring processes to build meaningful relationships among people in all career stages. Formal mentoring and coaching programs that have been designed and implemented to bring together employees in their mid and late careers with those in their earlier careers can be a power way to facilitate growth and the knowledge management process. To be effective however, the formal process steps need to be managed and monitored. Below are a list of steps that are based on the design and effective implementation of a formal mentoring program (Olson & Jackson, 2009).

1. *Matching late and early career colleagues.* To create the optimal matches, identify what each person has to learn from others and what he or she has to teach others. To be effective, those involved need to believe they have something to teach and something to learn. For example, the older worker may be uniquely positioned to help the younger worker understand the political nuances of how decisions are made and how to influence others in the organization. It is that political savvy that has been accumulated over the years that the older worker can share to provide coaching and suggestions to the younger worker. Also, the younger worker can provide the older worker with coaching on how to use various technologies to facilitate their ability to complete their work and increase their efficiency. The younger worker may also be able to share up-to-date technical information and approaches with the older worker to expand effectiveness in completing the technical parts of their work.

2. *Communicating expectations and clarifying roles.* Prior to beginning the formal mentoring meetings, all the employees involved need to receive information on how to share expectations, provide coaching and ideas, give each other feedback, make requests of each other, and clarify the roles. The outcome of the formal process

should be that mutual learning and growth occur for those involved in the coaching and mentoring. Both older and younger workers will be most effective when they understand that they need to adjust their own approaches to ensure that they do not come across as *telling* others what to do and implying that the approaches the other uses are wrong or inadequate. Open and clear communication and feedback become important in this process to ensure that learning can occur. Individuals need to understand their role and appreciate that others may have different learning styles and approaches, but that should not be used to reinforce stereotypes (e.g., older workers are not open to learning, younger workers are impulsive and think they know everything)

3. *Monitor and follow up on the learning process.* The supervisors of the late and early career colleagues need to check in with them regularly to ensure that the process is working and to see if there is any advice or assistance they can provide. This shows the supervisor fully supports the mentoring process so that their employees learn from each other and share ideas and perspectives that contribute to the effectiveness of others and the organization. Also, supervisors can share what is working with others and help them to provide mentoring and support the learning of each other, regardless of the age of the employee.

The steps described here serve as a general set of guidelines. Details of the formal mentoring process would need to be customized to fit the organizational culture and the needs and preferences of the individuals in the mentoring relationship.

Career Scaffolding: Networks of Support

In the contemporary literature on career development, the focus has shifted from the significance of having one mentor to understanding the process that individuals use to develop "relationship constellations" or networks of people who help them learn and develop over the course of their careers (Baugh & Scandura, 1999; Higgins & Kram, 2001; Thomas & Higgins, 1996). As careers unfold, many relationships are developed through the jobs individuals hold in different organizations and the professional contacts they develop and nurture over the course of their careers. Thus, individuals in their mid and late careers have a greater *potential* to have a developed large network of mentors, advisors, and supporters who can facilitate their ongoing growth and development. Many factors, however, will impact the size of the network individuals have developed. These factors include the sociability of the individual, his/her willingness to maintain contact with others as jobs and organizations change, and the culture of the organizations that the individual has worked in (i.e., some organizations encourage relationship building more than others). One of the significant advantages of building mentoring relationships with a wide range of people is the potential for protégés to tap into the networks of their mentors.

Higgins and Kram (2001) developed a framework integrating mentoring and social network theories to introduce the importance of developmental networks. This framework includes both the diversity of individuals in the developmental network and the strength of the relationships among the individuals in those networks. As career development has become much more reliant on social networks and relationships with people who have access and information, a wide range of strong relationships with others has become increasingly important.

As was discussed in Chapter 2, an individual is self-reliant when determining the direction of his or her career and how it will unfold. Now, individuals often focus more on finding jobs that use their talents and ensuring that they have overall life satisfaction when making career and job choices. This concept has been defined by Hall (2004) as the protean career. Those who create a protean career will have different developmental networks and potentially greater variation in the diversity of people in those networks than individuals who have taken traditional career paths that are focused on specific jobs, positions, organizations, or professional affiliations.

Future Research Directions

Training and mentoring provide support and clarity to help individuals make choices about how to optimize the use of their talents and accomplish goals that are important to the organization. To be effective, each of these processes must clearly describe the outcomes that people in each job are expected to accomplish so that individuals at each career stage can optimize the use of their talents. While the results accomplished by people in some roles (e.g., managers) are more difficult to measure than others (e.g., sales people), all jobs exist to produce specific results that are important to the organization.

Understanding how to provide training and development, and facilitate coaching and mentoring opportunities for all employees are important regardless of the age of the individual. Effective performance management processes, as discussed in Chapter 8, need to be directly linked to training and development systems that contribute to the ongoing growth of mid and late career workers. To ensure that these individuals can optimize their contributions, however, managers and supervisors have a responsibility to directly address negative biases and stereotypes that only serve to reinforce negative perceptions reified in the popular press that you "can't teach an old dog new tricks." Creating systems that contribute to everyone's success and effectiveness is the most powerful way to attract and retain the best people regardless of their age.

In the future, research attention needs to be focused on how mid and late career workers transfer knowledge attained through training or mentoring, to on the job performance. Specifically, we need to identify if there are unique training processes or mentoring approaches that facilitate successful transfer of learning to improve job performance. Also, we need to identify whether those workers integrate information in unique ways and use tacit knowledge to incorporate new approaches and concepts learned through formal training programs as well as in mentoring relationships.

Ragins (2007) also notes that most of the research on diversity in mentoring relationships has focused on the impact of race and gender of the mentors and protégés. As a result, we need much more clarity on the impact of age differences on mentoring relationships. Specifically, we need to investigate the impact of reverse age mentorships (i.e., younger workers mentoring workers who are older than they are) to determine what factors impact positive outcomes. Ragins (1997) suggested that positive mentoring relationships, when the protégé was younger and mentor older, were impacted by the perceived competence of the mentor and the level of interpersonal trust and comfort that existed between the protégé and mentor. We need to investigate whether or not these same factors are related to the development of a strong mentorship when the age differences are reversed or if there is a peer mentoring relationship. Also, do younger people tend to receive a different type of mentoring (e.g., focused on actualizing one's talents, interpersonal and political skills) when compared to older workers. Whitely, Dougherty, and Dreher (1992) found that younger individuals tended to receive more career mentoring and role modeling from mentors than did older workers. It is important to look more closely at the expectations of the mentors to understand how their beliefs and biases about what people need who are in their 20s compared to people in their 50s, even if both are just starting a new career path. That is, the age of the person may impact the mentors' perceptions of what the protégé needs.

Finally, we need to study how different career path choices impact the network of relationships and mentorships that individuals in their mid and late careers have established. For example, do individuals who are in their 50s and above and have chosen a protean career have different patterns in the types of training, development, and mentoring that they have received as their career choices have unfolded? What is the impact of staying in one organization for one's entire career on the type and quality of training, development and mentoring that individuals who are 50 and older have received? Are there other factors involved related to individual personal characteristics (Chapter 4), the types of jobs/roles the individual has held (Chapter 5), or unique factors about the organization (Chapter 6) that have impacted the quality and quantity of training experiences, developmental roles/activities, and mentoring relationships that one has developed.

Chapter 10

Work and Nonwork Issues for Individuals in Their Mid and Late Careers

This chapter synthesizes relevant research on work and nonwork and how changing demands impact individuals in general, and those in their mid and late careers in particular. By definition, individuals in their mid and late careers have already faced many turning points and made important choices regarding how to address conflicts between work and nonwork demands. While turning points occur at every stage of development, these individuals face unique choice points when compared to those they confronted earlier in their development. Clausen (1995) defines a turning point as a time when individuals perceive that their work and/or life events have taken a different course or direction. For those in their mid and late careers, changes could have been externally imposed (i.e., lack of promotional opportunities, downsizing in their industry, layoffs) or due to changes they have to address personally (i.e., declining physical abilities, wanting more personal meaning, being able to make a contribution, etc.). On a personal level, those in their mid and late careers face the changes that will naturally occur as their parents' age and children grow older. In some cases, however, individuals have waited to have children until they were older, and now, in mid career, they are responsible for young children (often under the age of 6) at the same time they are faced with increasing work demands, particularly in the current competitive environment and difficult financial position that many organizations face due to the global economic issues that need to be addressed. Individuals in their mid and late careers may also reevaluate their own career goals and seek out more ways to satisfy their personal goals in order to make choices that are consistent with their values.

Salience of Work and Nonwork Issues Addressed by Individuals Over 50

Baltes and Dickson (2001) posit that individual development and change occurs across the lifespan. However, there are significant individual differences regarding when changes occur and how people respond to those changes. Longitudinal empirical studies conducted on lifespan development have supported the viewpoint that the process of aging is not consistent for all people (Baltes, 1993; Schaie, 1996). Also, research has shown that as changes occur, they are accompanied by a combination of both gains and losses for the person who experiences the changes (Baltes, 1997; Dixon & Baltes, 1986; Labouvie-Vief, 1982).

At every stage of development, there are conflicts and the potential for conflicts to occur between expectations placed on individuals at work and the needs and expectations of family members at home (Baltes & Young, 2007). In previous generations, individuals in their 50s and 60s looked forward to downshifting and planning for retirement. This is no longer the case. For example, the specific issue of work and family conflict becomes apparent when we consider the recent data gathered on those adults age 50+ who have responsibilities for children and aging parents. In a national survey, Hewlett et al. (2009) found that 41% of workers over 50 reported having to provide financial support for their adult children, 71% reported having some eldercare responsibilities that impacted their work and finances, and 28% reported having responsibility for both children and aging parents. Thus the importance of understanding the issues related to work and family conflict throughout one's career has never been greater.

In the past, research has shown that work and family conflict tends to be greatest for younger workers who have children under the age of 6 (Moen, Waismel-Manor, & Sweet, 2003). However, with the trend toward deferring having children until a later age, it is no longer unusual for men and women in their late 40s and 50s to have children under the age of 6. As a result, people who traditionally would have been considered in mid career (over 40) or late career (over 50), now have children who are in preschool and elementary school. Having young children at home, has a direct impact on the timeline for retirement from full-time paid employment. For those individuals, working until one's children have graduated from college and are established on their own means continuing to work well into their late 60s or 70s. This leads to the possibility of work and family issues and conflicts to increase in intensity as individuals have dual responsibilities for young children as well as aging parents (i.e., the sandwich generation).

The economic needs cannot be underestimated in this situation. Child care expenses tend to be greatest before children enter primary school (Drago, Wooden, & Black, 2009), and the costs of caring for the needs of aging parents can be even greater. The need for individuals in their mid and late careers to continue to work for economic reasons creates a conflict between the amount of time they can invest at work and the amount of time that is required to meet the needs of their children and parents. When the expectations at work and the needs of a more complex family situation collide, having greater work schedule flexibility becomes essential for meeting the needs at work and at home and for ameliorating the feelings of work and family conflict

Research has shown that as people age, they tend to place a greater emphasis on creating work and family balance in their choices and decisions (Evans & Bartolome, 1984).

Specifically, older workers, in general, focus on strategies and approaches to maintain more balance in their lives (Evans & Bartolome, 1979, 1981, 1984), while younger workers tend to place a greater emphasis on achieving success in their work roles (Moen et al., 2003). This trend is strongest among women and men who have college degrees and who made conscious choices to establish themselves in their careers and create financial stability, before beginning to have children.

Creating Balance: Addressing Role Overload and Conflict

Goode (1960) defined role strain as the impact of potential conflicts that emerge when two significant roles (i.e., work and family) create the feeling of being overloaded due to the obligations and goals associated with each of these important roles. The time that is required to invest in each role to achieve important results can lead to feelings of overload and the perception that the roles are in conflict with each other. When this occurs, feelings of anxiety and strain emerge since there is simply not enough time in the day to achieve the important goals at work and meet the needs of the family (e.g., completing the important report at work by 5:00 p.m. and picking up a sick child from school).

Men and women experience role conflict and overload differently based on the expectations they have for themselves and the extent to which they have internalized the role expectations they learned during their early years of development and socialization (i.e., what men should do and what women should do to be considered successful). These expectations impact how they *believe* they should behave given the norms and roles they have incorporated into their belief system (Schnittger & Bird, 1990). How individuals manage the role conflicts they face will impact their feelings of self-efficacy and perceptions of being able to handle conflicts and challenges in a manner that contributes to their feelings of effectiveness. For older workers, these differences in role perceptions can impact the timing of retirement between couples.

CASE STUDY

In our interviews, Phyllis reflected on the impact of her husband's decision to retire on her work life and experience. While her husband was working full time and traveling extensively as part of his job, Phyllis regularly worked 80 hours a week to meet the demands of her executive role. These long work hours did not cause work/nonwork conflict for her. Once her husband retired however, expectations changed. With her husband at home all day and engaged in his retirement pursuits, they wanted to spend more time together and engage in other activities. These changing expectations that she would spend more time at home (and not work while she was home) put intense pressure on her to meet the continued high level of demands from her boss and to plan activities with her husband. Her discussions to reduce the number of hours she invested in important strategic projects were not well received by her boss. As a result, Phyllis had to confront the escalating demands at work and at home. She had to make some very difficult personal and professional choices to determine what her next step would be. She reflected on this conflict extensively before making the decision to ultimately take an early retirement and spend more time with her husband. This was a decision that caused personal stress for her given the decades of time and energy she had invested to "make it" to an executive position in her industry. She is now two years into her retirement and, in her words, "enjoying every minute of it" and reflects with pride on the success she experienced as her career unfolded.

Bandura (1986, 1991) defines self-efficacy as the judgments individuals make about their ability to develop and implement a course of action that will allow them to successfully respond to situations. Perceiving one's self as being able to respond in an adaptive and effective way to ambiguous, unpredictable and often stressful situations increases an individual's self-efficacy. Research has shown that older individuals have developed more coping strategies to adapt to the stress they face (Schnittger & Bird, 1990). Having faced a wide range of challenges and experienced feelings of success in how one responded to those situations contributes to greater feelings of self-efficacy for individuals in their mid and late careers. This enhanced self-efficacy can contribute to greater effectiveness when responding to difficult and stressful situations related to role conflict.

The Cornell Couples and Careers Study conducted by Moen and her colleagues (2003) offers some understanding of the relationship among self- efficacy, age, and salary levels of workers who experience role overload and conflict. In this study, the job prestige level of younger and older workers was roughly the same. The majority of participants in the study were managers and professionals all in dual career couple relationships. Moen et al. (2003) found that younger employees who did not have children experienced the highest levels of perceived workload and stress, while older workers whose children no longer lived at home were the least likely to describe their jobs as demanding and stressful. One possible explanation for this result is that the individuals in their mid and late careers, who have already experienced conflicts related to work and family as well as high expectations at work, had developed more self-efficacy about their ability to handle the pressures and knew that they could address the issues that emerged. As a result, they did not experience their jobs as stressful.

CASE STUDY

This same pattern emerged through the interviews we conducted with older workers. None of the individuals we interviewed had children currently living at home or for whom they were financially responsible. All of them stated that they continued to work on the projects (both in their paid employment and volunteer pursuits) that they enjoyed and found engaging. They all reported that the role conflict that they had experienced earlier in their work lives had dissipated. They had all experienced success in their careers and have a high level of self-efficacy. The "demands" they experienced now were those that they imposed on themselves, but all reported that it was their choice to continue to work hard and to be involved in projects that they found meaningful and important.

Early in one's career, there are also greater financial challenges. Often, young professionals have student loans, the desire to buy and furnish a house, and own a new(er) car. All of these financial needs and desires can contribute to the feelings of stress and the need to work long hours to meet those financial objectives.

The results of the Cornell Couples study (Moen et al., 2003) also showed that there was a significant difference in earnings related to gender and life stage. Older men, with children no longer living at home, earned the highest income, while men without children earned less, in general, than men with children. The pattern for women's earnings was the opposite: women who did not have children earned the most at each life stage. The amount of money and level of benefits individuals accrue is often used as an objective measure of career success. To make more money, however, usually means that individuals have had to invest more time in their work related responsibilities. Spending more time at work, of course, takes away from time spent with family or to invest time in activities that are related to what they value and find meaningful for themselves. While in the past success at work, and in life, meant making a lot of money, along with achieving higher status positions, now, the meaning of success for many individuals over 50 is more closely related to overall life satisfaction and the experience of living a life filled with meaning and consistent with one's values.

CASE STUDY

The importance of doing meaningful work and the evolution of the "meaning of success" was directly expressed in the interview with Sara. In her 20s and 30s, her definition of success in life was directly tied to pay, promotion, job titles, and increasing levels of responsibility. Now in her 60s, Sara wants to be able to give back to others in meaningful ways that contribute to their ongoing growth. Success is measured by how well her students do in her classes and the feelings that come from watching students take on new challenges and reach their potential.

The Evolving Meaning of Success: The Impact on Work and Nonwork Conflicts

Individuals at different stages of their lives have different expectations, skills, available resources, and goals they would like to accomplish in the future. As a result, individuals at different life stages define success differently (Karasek, 1990; Karasek & Theorell, 1990; Parker, Chmiel, & Wall, 1997). Individual definitions of success are influenced by a number of factors. How individuals establish their definitions of success can be influenced by factors such as when they finished their formal education, when they started working in their career path jobs (vs. jobs that *paid the bills*), when they entered into committed relationships, as well as if and when they decided to have children. Different events and the age of the individual when such events were experienced can have a dramatic impact on the ability to achieve personal and professional goals. These events can in turn impact the criteria individuals use to assess whether or not they have been successful in achieving what they dreamed of both at work and in their life overall.

Defining what success means to an individual is a complex task. The definition of success will indeed evolve and change over the course of each individual's life and career. In general, as we discussed in Chapter 2, success has been operationalized on two planes: (a) objective success, as indicated by number of promotions, salary increases, and level achieved in the organization; and (b) subjective success, as measured by one's overall satisfaction with achievements in one's career as compared to what the individual had hoped to accomplish both personally and professionally. Seibert, Crant, and Kraimer (1999) defined career success as the accumulated positive experiences (both what is accomplished and the psychological outcomes experienced) that are associated with one's work. This definition integrates the importance of both objective and subjective indicators of success. While indicators of objective and subjective career success are different, research has shown that these two factors are positively related (Johns, 1999; Judge, Cable, Boudreau, & Bretz, 1995). Individuals who experience objective career success are likely to experience positive self-perceptions, which in turn will contribute to positive feelings about, and satisfaction with, one's career progression and overall level of accomplishments (Ng, Eby, Sorensen, & Feldman; 2005).

The Cornell Couples and Career Study (Moen et al., 2003) investigated many facets related to family and career issues. Specifically focusing on success in terms of balancing work and family needs in dual income earning couples, Moen et al. (2003) found that at all life stages participants in the study reported feeling reasonably successful. Both the husbands and wives who participated in the study reported higher levels of success with their family than with their work choices. Older men and women in the study whose children were no longer living at home and those with children in college rated themselves highest overall on family success. Men and women under 40 and who were childless, rated themselves lowest on both work and family success (Moen et al., 2003). These results indicate that there may be some cumulative advantages for both men and women as they age in perceiving themselves as more successful in both the work and family spheres.

The results of the study clearly illustrate that the needs of both men and women shift over the course of their career, and as family needs change, work and nonwork goals evolve (Moen et al., 2003). For dual income earning couples, results showed that both the men and women reported feeling less successful in balancing work and family issues. However, older, childless workers reported more success in balancing work and nonwork conflicts than those workers at other stages of their development (Moen et al., 2003).

Mid and late career workers, by definition, have fewer years to invest in their careers and to achieve the goals they had set for themselves. To address the conflict caused by lack of time available to achieve those career goals, these individuals could adjust their goals and personal expectations based on the amount of time that they plan to continue working. With the wisdom and self- understanding that individuals in their mid and late careers have accumulated, they would be more likely to use more effective strategies to address their work and family conflicts and cope with the issues that they will confront at this stage of development.

Coping Strategies to Address Work and Nonwork Conflicts

According to Baltes and Dickson (2001), "Successful development is theoretically defined as the maximization of desirable outcomes and the minimization of undesirable outcomes" (p. 52). Individuals use a range of coping strategies to address conflicts and opportunities that arise in both work and nonwork contexts. In both contexts, individuals experience some combination of both gains and losses as they experience changes over the course of their life and in their work roles (Baltes & Dickson, 2001). How individuals respond to changes will impact their assessment of the level of success they have achieved in their work and nonwork roles and overall self-efficacy.

Individuals tend to use different coping strategies to respond to the challenges they face based on the changes they experience. The Selection, Optimization with Compensation (SOC) model provides a framework describing how individuals respond to the gains and losses they experience as they accommodate to changes. This model focuses on both changes that individuals decide to make in their lives and the changes imposed upon them by others (Baltes & Carstensen, 1996; Baltes & Dickson, 2001; Freund & Baltes, 1998).

There are three primary factors in the SOC model that are related to how mid and late career individuals make decisions and evaluate their level of success in accomplishing work and nonwork goals. The SOC model is based on the assumption that individuals have unique combinations of mental, physical, and environmental resources and they make choices about how to use their resources. Both opportunities (i.e., new jobs/positions, having children, beginning and ending relationships with significant others) and losses (i.e., losing a job, skills that decline with age, physical changes that impact job performance) cause individuals to make choices on how to allocate their mental, physical, and environmental resources. Baltes and Dickson (2001) summarize the strategies of selection, optimization, and compensation, and the importance of each strategy on the impact of success in achieving important developmental outcomes.

Selection is the process that individuals engage in as they decide what goals and outcomes to pursue. There can be two unique types of selection processes. Individuals may choose to focus on many goals simultaneously (e.g., individuals early in their careers may select to take whatever steps are needed to gain promotions in their organization as well as decide to get married and start a family) or they may focus on only those goals that are most important to them at the time (e.g., individuals in their mid and late careers may choose to work in jobs that fully utilize their skills and talents even when those jobs do not lead to promotions or higher levels of pay because they want to do what they enjoy while they are working). There can also be loss-based selection when individuals make choices to minimize the psychological, physical, or economic impact of losses they have sustained because of things outside of their control (e.g., organizational downsizing that more directly impacts mid and late career employees who are receiving higher levels of pay and benefits).

Optimization is the process whereby individuals make choices to invest their resources to achieve those goals that they value most in their current stage of development. For individuals in their mid and late careers, they may choose to invest their energy in their families or volunteer work as a way of experiencing success when they are in jobs that no longer have upward mobility or will help them achieve important career goals. They may choose to focus on the importance of nonwork accomplishments while staying in their current position until they are eligible to receive their full pension or social security benefits. This strategy of optimizing accomplishments in the nonwork domain would allow mid and late career individuals to view their work as an important economic resource to sustain their needs until they reach a specific age.

Compensation is a process whereby individuals use alternative approaches to maintain a specific level of performance within a domain where they may have experienced losses. These compensatory strategies could be external (i.e., mid and late career employees develop partnerships with a younger worker who can complete the more physically demanding work tasks while the older worker focuses on completing the paperwork part of the jobs that are essential but which the younger worker dislikes) or the strategies could be internal (i.e., mid and late career workers who consciously choose to learn new technologies that allow them to keep up to date with changes as well as complete work more efficiently). Using these compensatory strategies would allow those in their mid and late careers to utilize their experience and talents to complete work so that others would not observe a decline in performance or productivity.

Work and family conflicts fit into the model of allocation of limited resources and the need for selection, optimization, and compensation (SOC). When individuals of all ages experience conflicts between work and family roles, they have a negative impact on both job and life satisfaction (Kossek & Ozeki, 1998). A specific, relevant example of this is when a dual career couple chooses to start a family. By definition their available resources (time and energy) will be impacted by that choice. As a result, the couple will need to make choices about how to allocate responsibilities (e.g., housework, caring for the child, exercising, time spent at work/on work). This can be addressed by making the choice to use selection strategies based on clearly identifying the most important goals *to them* at that stage of development.

For example, an individual choosing to start a family when in mid career may have already accomplished some of more important work and personal goals, and thereby *select* to spend time with a new child rather than work long hours or train to run another marathon, or any other activity that would take time away from the family. For individuals in their 40s or 50s who have waited to have children, making these decisions would be easier if the couple already has an established economic base that allows them the freedom to make different financial choices when selecting which goals are most important to them and determining how to invest their time and energy.

Baltes and Dickson (2001) propose that individuals who select to change the relative importance of goals as a strategy to deal with work and nonwork conflicts will experience more success when responding to both work and nonwork demands. Individuals could also address work and nonwork conflicts by *optimizing* how they use their time by making conscious choices about what new projects they will accept at work and setting specific goals about how much time they will spend at work (e.g., I will leave the office no later than 5:30 p.m.) to optimize the amount of time they spend on family related needs. Individuals can also use *compensatory* approaches to address work and family time and resource conflicts. For example, they could do work from home and electronically send documents that need to be completed to their manager and other team members. Individuals could also limit their break time so that they can complete their work and leave once all their work is done.

Wiese, Freund, and Baltes (2000) found that the selection, optimization, and compensation strategies when used to address work and family conflict made a positive impact on satisfaction and well-being levels reported by those who were experiencing work and family conflicts. Using the SOC coping strategies can have a meaningful impact on those workers experiencing work and nonwork conflicts. Mid and late career workers have also had more life changes and experiences using different strategies over the course of their development. The successes and failures they have experienced using different strategies to address previous life changes can make a positive impact on their feelings of self-efficacy when addressing changes (both internally generated and externally imposed) that they confront (i.e., impact of downsizing, new technology skill demands, reduced physical abilities).

Impact of Gender on Work and Nonwork Choices

In research focused on understanding how men and women make decisions that impact turning points in their lives, Wethington, Pixley, and Kavey (2003) found that both men and women made choices to significantly change their career trajectory based on conditions they experienced at work. Specifically, 83% of men and 69% of women reported making career changes due to challenges they encountered at work. These challenges included both positive changes at work (e.g., promotions, honors, self-employment opportunities) and negative ones (e.g., layoffs, overload at work due to downsizing, reorganizations). However, women more frequently identified work and family issues as impacting their decisions to take a different career course to accommodate the changing demands of work and/or family realms than did men.

Specifically, the arrival of children simultaneously escalates the importance of having both time at home and the need for more income to accommodate additional costs (Hamermesh, 1996). This dual need has traditionally led to gender segregation of roles; women would tend to quit work or reduce their working hours and men would simultaneously increase the number of hours they worked in order to make more money to pay for increasing costs associated with having children. The economic pressure of children is greatest before age 5. The cost of child care drops as children enter the primary and secondary school years, so often the desire for women to return to work increases, but women still seek flexible work hours to accommodate children's needs until they are ready to move out of the house (Waldfogel, 2006). Highly educated women expressed a preference for reducing the number of work hours rather than opting out of work completely during the years before children start school (Drago et al, 2009).

Couples develop processes to determine how to make decisions to optimize career success as well as balance work and family needs. There are many different models that have been developed to explain how couples make choices to determine whose career has priority and how to optimally balance work and family needs (e.g., economic, traditional emphasis on male career and women as homemaker, geographic preferences, promotion opportunities, job satisfaction, commitment to career, gender roles). In the Cornell Couples and Careers Study, results showed that the man's career was given priority by both the man and woman. The traditional model of man as breadwinner and woman as taking care of home and family needs was reinforced (Pixley & Moen, 2003). This finding was interesting given that this sample included primarily highly educated, professional, dual income earning couples. Only one sixth of the sample reported that the woman's career was given greater priority than the man's career. This outcome was higher than reported in previous research in which the sample studied had lower educational achievement and nonprofessional career trajectories.

Pixley and Moen (2003) also found that for those couples who began their relationship with a difference in educational level, their careers were prioritized based on the career opportunities of the individual with the higher level of educational attainment. Age of the men and women only impacted how their careers were prioritized when the man was more than two years older than the woman. In those cases, the man's career was prioritized as more important than the woman's. For couples who had more traditional gender role attitudes (i.e., man as breadwinner, woman as homemaker), the man's career opportunities were consistently prioritized as more important than the woman's career opportunities. When this occurred, Pixley and Moen (2003) found that both the man and the woman agreed that this is "how it should be."

Regardless of whose career is prioritized as *more important*, organizational leaders have designed and implemented a wide range of options with the intent of helping to reduce the level of conflict that exist between work and nonwork needs. Organizational leaders are very aware of the fact that their employees provide value resources that are essential to accomplish goals and produce important outcomes. Programs designed to help address the conflicts between work and nonwork focus on the importance of retaining good employees and helping them to be successful both at work and at home. Turnover is expensive, and when top employees leave because of work and nonwork conflicts, it is very expensive in terms of lost productivity as well as the negative impact it may have on the culture of the organization.

Organizational Actions to Reduce the Conflict between Work and Nonwork Needs

It would be logical to predict that organizations offering their employees beneficial programs such as flexible work hours would have the greatest impact on how effectively their employees are able to balance the needs of both work and nonwork responsibilities. Organizational leaders have designed benefit packages and organizational policies to retain employees and offer job security during times when nonwork needs may interfere with work related responsibilities. For example, in a national survey of U.S. employers, Galinsky, Bond, and Sakai (2008) found that 75% of U.S. organizations offered paid or unpaid leave and job security to employees who need to provide eldercare to family members. This study also found that 89% of organizations with more than 100 employees offered 12 or more weeks of job-guaranteed leaves of absence to provide care for a seriously ill family member. Family-friendly policies and benefits demonstrate to employees that organizational leaders honor, support, and acknowledge that each individual has unique family needs and concerns that have to be addressed. For example, policies that include parental leaves of absence for both men and women facilitate employees' ability to balance the needs of their children.

Employees, however, may not use some of these benefits due to how it would be *perceived* by others, both at work and at home. For example, Moen et al. (2003) found that there were gender differences in perceptions of men and women who used parental leave benefits provided by the organization. Specifically, it was found that using parental leave benefits had a stronger relationship with feelings of success at work and in balancing the needs of work and family when *male employees* used organizational leave benefits compared to female employees who used the same benefits. This result may be related to traditional expectations that women would take time off and men would work more hours to supplement the additional financial impact associated with children. The additional support needed at home during the early days of children entering the family may be more important, both physically and psychologically, to create a sense of balance and satisfaction. Work can be put on hold and the father can bond with the child in the early days along with the mother. Using paternal leave benefits could build a stronger family unit and greater feelings of closeness among the members of the family. When parental leave benefits are used by the man, this could also create feelings of gratitude toward the organization that provided the man with the time to be with his child and yet have job security and the certainty that he can return to his work role. This benefit can have a positive impact on loyalty to the organization that provided support to him by meeting his needs to bond with his child and share in the parenting responsibilities.

Effective Implementation of Work and Nonwork Policies and Benefits

Organizational leaders can design and implement a variety of benefits and programs to address the issues and challenges that workers face in their efforts to balance work and nonwork needs and responsibilities. Organizational support for work family roles is defined by Kossek, Baltes, and Matthews (2011) as the degree to which design of the work reduces the conflict between work and family. Kossek (2006) stated that organizations can reduce the conflict through the optimal design of three workplace characteristics: (a) structure of the work (i.e., work hours, designing jobs to give workers control over when and where the work is completed); (b) organizational culture and norms that support work and nonwork integration; and (c) human resource programs and policies that support individuals in managing the interface between their work and nonwork responsibilities. As with all organizational programs, however, it is *how* the program is implemented by managers and supervisors that determines whether or not it is effective. Many of the reasons that work and family benefits are not used by employees are related to the perceptions of others about the people who use programs as well as the potential impact of using these benefits has on the career path. If managers show in some way (in words and actions) that they believe that:

- those people who are telecommuting are usually slackers who are sitting at home surfing the net and not really completing the work in a high quality and efficient way,
- *or* those who do not have regular "face time in the office" are not perceived as serious about their work and therefore not viable candidates for promotions as they become available,
- *or* that those who take time off work to attend their daughter's soccer game are usually "dumping" on those who do not have children and picking up the slack so that the parents can get out of completing their work,

then, work and family programs will fail and organizational leaders will perceive that their employees do not want (or need) family friendly programs. What managers say and how they respond to issues send important messages to other employees. If work and family programs are to have the intended impact, managers and supervisors are the ones who facilitate their success and directly impact whether or not individuals will use and benefit from them.

Valcour and Batt (2003) found that when employees perceived that their supervisors supported the organizations' work and family policies and programs, it significantly reduced employee's perceptions of work and family conflict. Supervisors who had strong relationships with their employees had employees who reported feeling more in control of both their job responsibilities and meeting the needs of their family. These employees also expressed lower levels of intention to leave the organization than those employees who did not have a supportive relationship with their supervisor (Valcour & Batt, 2003).

Managers need to be aware of issues and concerns that are surfacing among their employees when implementing work and nonwork programs. They need to be open in their communications with all employees, whether or not the employees are currently using these programs. They also need to be equitable in monitoring the workloads of all their employees (as an effective manager should) in their department to ensure that those who are not using the leave benefits do not have increased workloads due to the need to cover for those employees who are attending to their nonwork responsibilities. Managers need to address concerns immediately and not allow negative feelings to persist or suspicious concerns (e.g., she is at home in her sweats shopping on-line) to go unaddressed. Leaders who are supportive of their employee's family needs tend to elicit more respect, loyalty, and gratitude from their employees than those who do not. Informal supervisor support works hand in hand with effective work and family programs and policies implemented by organizations to help their employees achieve both their personal and professional goals. (Kossek et al., 2011).

The Desire for Phased Retirement

Drago et al. (2009) found that individuals preferred to have the option for phased retirement rather than complete dissolution of their full-time work schedule which occurs with their decision to retire. This is consistent with the research of Zhan, Wang, Li, and Shultz (2009) who found that reduced hours through a phased retirement process in one's field of expertise or work background led to a more successful retirement transition than for those individuals who stopped working full time or who started working in another completely different job or industry. Also, phased retirement allows individuals to maintain some structure in their days/weeks as they develop their new self-image as a retired person. The flexible work hours that would allow late career employees to make the transition to retirement also has a positive impact on family relationships as there would still be the income stream (meeting economic needs of the family) being generated by the person in the phased retirement work schedule. For individuals who are phasing into their retirement, working fewer hours can also help them make the needed adjustments at home to accommodate their new schedules with the schedule of their partner. This more gradual approach to retirement can also give the individual time to find and expand other activities that they enjoy and that will fill the time that has been created through reducing the number of hours spent at work.

Flexible Work Schedules and Telecommuting

One of the most important benefits that organizations can offer employees of all ages is flexible work hours (Kossek, 2006; Matthews, Bulger, & Barnes-Farrell, 2010; Noe, Hollenbeck, Gerhart & Wright, 2009; Ryan, & Kossek, 2008). Flexibility of hours serves as a retention tool for organizations as it helps support the unique needs and preferences of employees at each stage in their development. Over the last several decades, there has been unprecedented growth in part-time, temporary, and self-employment work arrangements in lieu of traditional, full-time work schedules. It is estimated that 25–30% of workers have an alternative work arrangement. The rate of growth in the number of people in alternative work arrangements is projected to be faster than the overall growth in the workforce (Marler, Tolbert, & Milkovich, 2003; Matthews et al., 2010). The growth in the number of people who have alternative work arrangements reflects workers' increased focus on balancing the needs of work and nonwork time, changing economic conditions (worldwide), and the changing nature of the employment relationships; many companies employ part-time rather than full-time, traditional employees to manage costs. Traditional gender roles appear to be related to the use of part-time work arrangements. Marler et al. (2003) found that for married couples, the woman often chooses part-time positions to accommodate the needs of work and home, whereas when men hold a part-time job, it tends to be involuntarily.

When couples make the decision to use flextime or to work off-site and telecommute, they lose the boundary between work and family and the negative stress from one domain that spills over into the other domain can negatively impact perceptions of both. Keeping the two domains separate can be an advantage when stresses at home mount. While flexible schedules and telecommuting conceptually can make a positive impact on one's ability to balance work and family needs, if there are negative stressors at home, using these flexible work options can actually back fire by tainting the experience of success at work.

These organizational benefits of alternative work arrangements are clearly not the panacea that individuals and organizational leaders had hoped they would be when they were initially designed and implemented. For example, Goff, Mount, and Jamison (1990) studied the impact of onsite childcare on employees' experiences of work and family conflict and employee absenteeism. When onsite daycare was designed as a benefit option, the goal was to make a positive impact by reducing the feelings of work and family conflict as well as absenteeism. The research findings showed that onsite childcare did not reduce either work and family conflict or absenteeism. Also, organizations that offer benefits such as telecommuting and educational seminars on work and family and childcare issues have found that they have not been effective in dealing with the issues they were designed to address.

The lack of positive results may be due to the expectations of employees and managers. With telecommuting as an example, managers may make the assumption that they need to be on-site with their teams and employees who telecommute may receive implicit messages that somehow they are not working hard enough or that they need to be monitored to ensure that they are fully engaged and on their computer during the required work hours. Given that organizational policies and processes do not consistently address the work and family issues that continue to persist, identifying how individuals can engage in strategies (e.g., selection, optimization, compensation) to personally address their unique needs may be of value to both the individual and the organizations in which they work.

The bottom line is that organizations that design and implement work/life programs and policies send a clear message to their employees that their unique needs are valued and important to the organization. Organizational leaders clearly understand that people do not leave who they are and their concerns and problems at the door when they come to work. Organizations that respect the unique needs of the individual retain their employees over time and ensure that the training and development that the employees have received contributes to the productivity for many years (Kossek et al., 2011). Since turnover, particularly of talented people, is always expensive for the organization, integrating work/life programs and policies that show individuals how important they are to the organization can serve as a long-term retention strategy mid and late career workers.

Future Research Directions

Popular press articles and anecdotes posit the view that it is difficult (if not impossible) to experience success in both work and nonwork. These articles emphasize the need to make the difficult choices necessary to be successful in one domain and suggest that by doing so, it is unlikely that individuals will experience success in the other domain, implying that you cannot have it all. The summary of the research in this chapter provides support for the notion that individuals do not *have* to choose between being successful either at work or nonwork goals. Both men and women can and do experience success in both work and nonwork domains, especially as they are in their later career and family stages. It is not a zero sum game that results in the need to focus on accomplishments at work and thereby suboptimizing life at home or vice versa.

The research findings presented in this chapter show that success at work contributes positively to feelings of success at home for both men and women. Feelings of success at work are directly related to feelings of success at balancing work and family responsibilities. This implies that it is not a matter of trading off success in either domain but making choices that create synergy between work and family so that one has a sense of accomplishment in both domains. Further research is needed in this area to more fully understand the impact of work and nonwork decisions on the overall estimation of career success for individuals in their 60s and beyond. Specifically, it is important to understand the impact on overall satisfaction comparing individuals who chose to have children in their 20s and 30s, with those who had children in their 40s and 50s, with those who chose not to have children at all. What is the impact of these choices on their career progression, definitions of career success, feelings of work/nonwork balance at different developmental stages, etc.? We also need further research on how the culture of the organization and support of one's manager impacted the perceptions of work and nonwork conflict and the willingness of individuals to use programs that were designed to address the conflict that employees face when addressing work/nonwork conflicts.

Also, as individuals grow older, the expectations of what can be accomplished at work and at home tends to change based on their earlier successes and failures. With the wisdom gained from experience, individuals can adjust their goal hierarchy and make choices about what they are willing to give up in order to accomplish what is most important to them at work and in their nonwork goals. Future research needs to address how the changes in goal hierarchies impact how people in their mid and late careers invest their time to optimize the balance between their work and nonwork goals. Also, further investigation of how the SOC model of coping is utilized differently by mid and late career individuals compared to those In the early stages of their careers. How to optimize the balance between work and nonwork demands will always be an issue regardless of age.

Further investigatation is also needed on the types of work schedules that optimize job performance and have the greatest impact on individual satisfaction for workers over 50. While flexible scheduling has been offered by organizations for several decades, its impact on performance and satisfaction is unclear. For older workers, other factors that may impact the perception of flextime need to also be considered (e.g., personality, complexity of the work being completed, the number and intensity of nonwork demands that impinge on older workers time at work).

Future research also needs to more thoroughly investigate the impact of technology advancements on the ability to work remotely and give individuals more freedom to choose when and where they will do their work. With the advent of telecommuting, individuals have been given more latitude to work independently using laptops and mobile devices to complete their work. However, the impact of 24/7 contact with work, while making it more convenient to complete the work, also may lead to more role conflict since it is assumed that one will be in constant "touch" with the office. That may actually cause higher levels of stress and difficulty managing the work and nonwork boundaries. Further research on the impact of this is essential to understand how the ongoing need to develop technology skills (as discussed in Chapter 9) may uniquely impact mid and late career workers' ability to manage the stress of maintaining work/life balance using more complex technologies in the process.

Chapter 11

The Transition to Retirement

Greller and Simpson (1999) stated that "One could not reasonably look at late career without examining the literature on retirement. Retirement may be viewed as either the end of late career or an integral part of it" (p. 325). Greller and Simpson concluded, "For the broad population, a successful late career is the most likely prelude to a successful retirement. A frustrating, disrupted, and personally diminishing late career from which one was compelled to exit provides a poor basis for whatever may come next" (p. 328). Thus, it is clear that how older workers wind up their late careers, has significant implications for life after full-time work. It is also clear that the demarcation between late career and retirement has become noticeably blurred (Wang, Adams, Beehr, & Shultz, 2009). As a result, it is important that we better understand how workers make the transition from late career to retirement if we wish to fully appreciate how workers successfully adjust to retirement.

Defining Retirement

While what it means to be retired may seem self-evident at first, it is clear that, particularly today, there is no one definition (Shultz & Olson, 2013; Shultz & Wang, 2011). Denton and Spencer (2009) recently noted that there are many ways to define retirement: (a) lack of paid employment, (b) receipt of pension and/or retirement benefits, (c) exit from one's main employer, (d) reduced work hours, (e) hours worked or earnings received from work below some arbitrary cutoff, (f) changing employers late in one's career, (g) self-assessment of being retired, or (h) some combination of the previous definitions. Traditionally, the first three definitions have been most used to describe someone as "retired," particularly the first definition. Thus, the major focus has traditionally been on *when* to retire (i.e., when to leave paid employment). However, it is becoming more apparent that retirement no longer means simply the lack of paid employment (Wang et al., 2009). In fact, a recent study by the Families and Work Institute, and The Sloan Center on Aging and Work at Boston College (Brown, Aumann, Pitt-Catsouphes, Galinsky, & Bond, 2010) showed that over 20% of workers age 50 and older who define themselves are retired were also working for pay and that 75% of workers aged 50 and older expect to have a paid job during retirement.

As a result of the increasingly amorphous nature of what it means to be retired, it is no longer simply a question of *when* to retire, but also a question of *how* to retire and *what* to do in retirement (Adams & Rau, 2011). Thus, just as individual's career options became much more numerous in the 20th century (as we discussed in Chapter 2), so too have their retirement options in the 21st century. Retirees may engage in complete leisure activities, start an entirely new career, start their own business, or engage in a host of unlimited options in between. Retirees may have multiple exits and entries to and from the workforce; what may have initially appeared to be "retirement" may end up being simply a late career sabbatical between their long-term career employment and their new occupation in a completely different field (Shultz & Wang, 2011). Thus, how we define retirement will have implications for how we study it, particularly in relation to one's late career (Wang et al., 2009).

Many researchers have used the "self-assessment" definition (i.e., let the survey respondents tell you whether they are retired or not) when studying the concept of retirement. While this may be appealing on some levels, there is the risk of defining retired individuals in vastly different personal and work situations; some respondents still working full time, but not in their career jobs, others working part time or seasonally, and some not working at all. Thus, the heterogeneity found in using the self-assessment definition of retirement may make it difficult to find compelling patterns of the antecedents and outcomes in the retirement process which we discuss below. Consequently, researchers need to be explicit in how they are defining retirement in their particular study. Alternatively, we recommend researchers accommodate the specific features of the person's retirement (e.g., paid work hours, nature of the employment, amount of pension/social security received) into their inquiries to better capture the heterogeneity of retirement in their samples. In this sense, retirement can be viewed as a subjective perception of a life stage, which may manifest various kinds of value orientations and behavioral patterns across different individuals.

CASE STUDY

In Chapter 2 we discussed a recent interview with Lupe, a 68-year-old Hispanic mother of seven children. It was clear that her career did not follow the linear, lockstep, age-graded path predicted by many of the earlier career models discussed in that chapter. In addition, it was also clear that Lupe has experienced multiple transitions in and out of the workforce toward the end of her career. She retired for the first time at age 53. However, within a year Lupe was back working in a similar role. She then retired a second time at age 60, only to again find another job within a year, this time as a receptionist at a public sector agency. She is now planning to retire a third (and she says final) time within a few months. Thus, Lupe's experience of multiple retirements serves as a clear example of how many individuals now experience multiple retirements at the end of their careers.

Retirement as a Process versus an Event

When most of us think about retirement, we think of it as a single event. That is, the day when someone stops working and begins to engage in full-time leisure. However, it is clear that this stereotype of retirement is becoming less representative of how most people retire today, as in Lupe's case described above. In fact, Ekerdt (2010) remarked that the boundary between work and retirement is both shifting and becoming more ambiguous. Thus, the line that had traditionally separated work from retirement is becoming more difficult to delineate. This change is also represented in the multiple definitions of retirement we discussed above.

Wang and Shultz (2010), Shultz and Olson (2013), and Shultz and Wang (2011) recently noted that retirement is not just a single event but rather a temporal process that unfolds over time. For most of us, the process begins long before the decision to retire and becomes more prominent as we begin to more vividly envision and plan for what we want from our retirement. For example, this process may begin when one has to make the first decision about opening a 401k or other retirement account, and may take center stage during the late career period. In fact, Wang et al. (2009) view retirement as a new, additional career stage that may well involve bridge employment in order to foster a smooth transition from career employment to a leisure filled retirement. Bridge employment refers to the type of employment between full-time career work and complete leisure retirement. Specifically, bridge employment refers to continued work, either in the same or different field, with a reduced commitment to work (Wang et al., 2009). It represents a transition phase from full-time career employment to alternative employment or retirement that typically involves reduced work hours (e.g., part-time or seasonal) and reduced psychological commitment to work. At some point, a worker must make a decision about continued commitment to a given job, employer, and/or career. If the decision is to begin to disengage from these roles, then he or she will initiate the transition into retirement. Finally, once the transition from full-time work to full-time retirement begins, then retirement adjustment becomes a major focus (Wang, Henkens, & van Solinge, 2011).

We depict the temporal nature of the retirement process in Figure 11.1. Looking at Figure 11.1 from top to bottom, we see how the retirement process unfolds over time. It first begins with planning—both formal and informal. While much of the research focus has traditionally been on the effects of formal (mostly financial) retirement planning on an individual's retirement satisfaction and life satisfaction in retirement, there is much less research on the effects of informal planning (more psychological in nature) in terms of discussions with family, friends, and colleagues about one's retirement goals and aspirations, and its impact on both retirement satisfaction and adjustment (Adams & Rau, 2011). The retirement planning stage is also a time when individuals develop and solidify their hopes and ambitions for retirement. Whether it's continued work on a part-time basis, starting a new business, spending more time with family, or volunteering (or some combination of these), goals become more crystallized and definitive as retirement approaches.

Examining Figure 11.1 further, we see that the next phase in the retirement process is the actual retirement decision. A wide variety of factors go into this decision, including the previously noted retirement planning activities. For example, whether one's retirement is viewed as voluntary or involuntary can have profound effects on how individuals later adjust to retirement (Shultz, Morton, & Weckerle, 1998). Typically, the more voluntary one's retirement is viewed, the more likely that adjustment to retirement will be successful, and higher levels of retirement satisfaction will be obtained (Wang & Shultz, 2010). In addition, whether retirement is partial or complete and early or on-time, can also affect how individuals adjust to retirement. Thus, as Beehr (1986) notes, personal factors (e.g., wealth, health, personality traits, skill obsolescence) and contextual or environmental factors (e.g., job and organizational factors, family life, current economic conditions) lead to retirement preferences, which in turn lead to thoughts about retirement. These thoughts then become intentions, which in turn become actions or behaviors. However, a variety of factors, such as an offer of an early retirement incentive package, may quickly change the relative valence of the various factors and completely disrupt the best laid plans for retirement (Feldman & Beehr, 2011).

One of the major decisions that many older workers in their late career may be facing is whether to engage in bridge employment (Feldman, 1994). Kim and DeVaney (2005) found that self-employed workers and those with college degrees were the most likely to hold bridge jobs. Much of the early research and writings on bridge employment (in the early to mid 1990s) focused on documenting its existence and examining the demographic and socioeconomic factors that predict bridge employment patterns (Shultz, 2003). However, in the last decade or so, there have been more systematic studies examining various antecedents and outcomes associate with engaging in a range of forms of bridge employment.

For example, in summarizing the recent research on bridge employment, Wang and Shultz (2010) note that those older workers who were more satisfied with their financial situation, had flexible jobs, and felt they had control over their retirement decision were all more likely to engage in bridge employment. Additional factors such as health status, job tenure, having a working spouse, and having dependent children were also positively related to engaging in bridge employment. More recent studies of bridge employment have conceptualized it as a career development stage (e.g., Davis, 2003; von Bonsdorff, Shultz, Leskinen, & Tansky, 2009; Wang, Zhan, Liu, & Shultz, 2008), distinguishing career bridge employment, bridge employment in a different field, and full retirement. The results from the various recent studies indicate that men with higher entrepreneurial orientation were more likely to engage in career bridge employment versus retirement, as were those with fewer nonwork interests, wanted to have better use of their skills, and had higher monetary desires, whereas individuals who were married and hand longer organizational tenure were less likely to do so. Meanwhile, having less stress and more satisfaction in one's pre-retirement job distinguishes individuals who engage in career bridge employment versus bridge employment in a different field, while older workers who perceived the job market to be good, wanted to have better use of their skills, and had fewer concerns about changes in their benefits were more likely to engage in bridge employment in a different field versus retirement.

Wang and Shultz (2010) go on to summarize the more limited literature on the outcomes associated with bridge employment to indicate that those individuals who engage in bridge employment are more likely to have better physical and mental well-being, as well as be more satisfied with retirement and have better adjustment to retirement. Again looking at bridge employment as a career stage, Zhan, Wang, Liu, and Shultz (2009) found that those who engaged in career bridge employment experienced both better

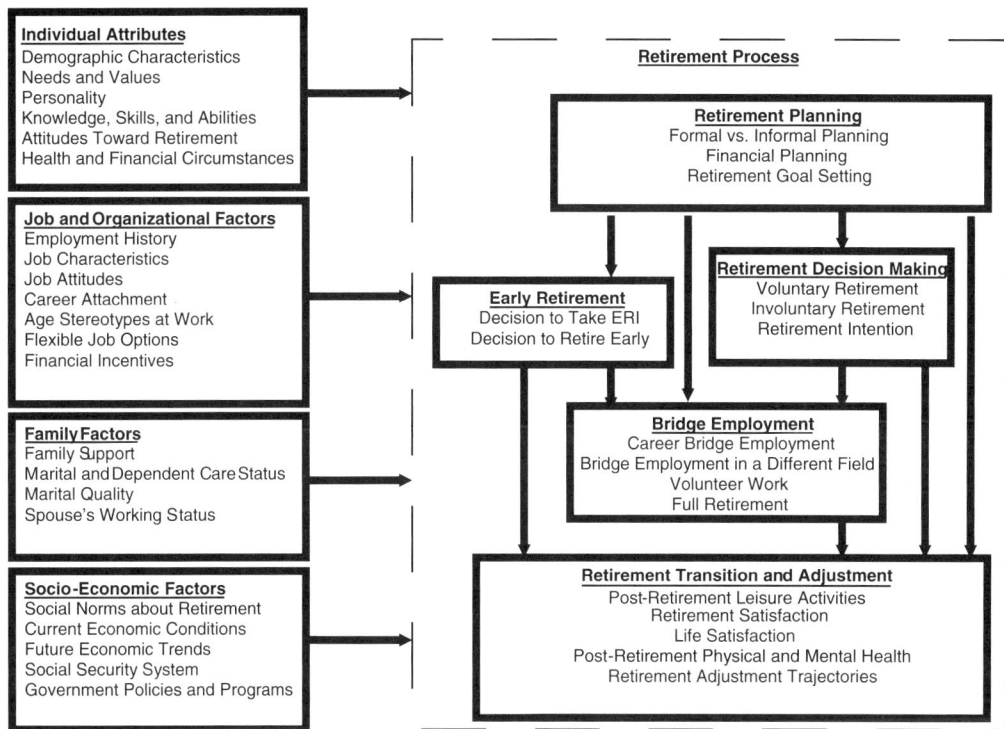

FIGURE 11.1 The Retirement Process as it Unfolds Over Time (From Wang and Shultz [2010]. Employee retirement: A review and recommendations for future investigation. *Journal of Management*, 36, 172–206, Thousand Oaks, CA: Sage Publications Inc.).

physical and mental health, while those who engaged in bridge employment in a different field had only better physical health. In addition, Brown et al. (2010) found on a variety of outcome factors including personal well-being, job satisfaction, job engagement, and work-family spillover that those individuals 50 and older working in retirement are doing just as well, and sometime even better, that those who have not yet retired. Thus, we are just starting to better understand the bridge employment process during older workers' late careers, both in terms of its antecedents and its consequences. In fact, Wang et al. (2009) note that bridge employment is a dynamic process, in that individuals may well move in and out of bridge employment status over time during the late career stage. As a result, just as we need to study retirement as a process and not a static event, we also need to study bridge employment as a process.

The final stage of the retirement process, depicted near the bottom of Figure 11.1, is the transition and adjustment to retirement stage. As with the other phases, there are a variety of factors that can impact how successfully late career workers are able to transition from full-time career employment to retirement (Wang et al., 2011). These factors include the choice of postretirement leisure activities, the quality of martial and family relationships, as well as physical and mental health statuses to name just a few. These can affect retirement satisfaction, life satisfaction in retirement, current retirement adjustment, as well as the post-retirement adjustment trajectory. For example, someone may have high expectations for having a physically active retirement, but if they suffer a major physical set back (e.g., onset of multiple sclerosis, severe stroke), their satisfaction with and adjustment to retirement will likely to be greatly altered.

Finally, looking at left side of Figure 11.1, we see a wide variety of individual attributes (e.g., personality, health issues), job and organizational factors (e.g., employment history, flexible job options), family factors (e.g., marital quality, family support), and socioeconomic factors (e.g., Social Security, pensions, social norms with regard to retirement) that will impact the entire retirement process, from planning, to intentions, to the retirement decision, to deciding whether to engage in bridge employment and, if so, what form it will take, to ultimately, the retirement transition and adjustment process. While all of these factors are present and influence the retirement process, for the present discussion, we are most interested in the individual attributes, and job and organizational factors, as they are most directly related to mid and late career issues.

For example, a worker's employment history relates directly to how his mid and late career has unfolded over the last several decades. If his career history represents a relatively orderly and volitional trajectory, he will be much more likely to transition through the retirement process more smoothly, as compared to someone who has had a more disjointed and disruptive career trajectory. In addition, factors such as organizational and occupational attachment and embeddedness (which we discuss in detail in Chapter 2) will affect not only retirement planning and decision making, but ultimately retirement satisfaction and adjustment. Additionally, mid and late career issues such as employer flexibility, and age stereotypes and biases that older workers face in the workplace will also affect all phases of the retirement process. For example, an older worker who would prefer to continue working, who perceives few alternatives to full-time, year-round employment, and who is experiencing age discrimination at work, may be more likely to retire, but then have a more difficult time adjusting to retirement as he retired much earlier than he wanted to.

Influencing the Retirement Decision

In general, most governments in developed countries have shifted their stance toward retirement in the last several decades from "pro-retirement" to "pro-work" (Shultz & Wang, 2011). By pro-retirement we mean that most government and employer policies traditionally encouraged older workers to retire at a set age (e.g., a mandatory retirement age of 65). However, as we outline below, these policies and incentives have mostly shifted to a pro-work stance, encouraging continued employment (e.g., the removal of mandatory retirement for most workers). However, as van Dalen, Henkens, Henderiske, and Schippers (2010) noted, at least in Europe, most employers are not in line with the official stance of the European Union (EU). That is, not all employers have embraced the pro-work policies espoused by the EU. A similar phenomenon can be observed in the United States, where employer's actions do not necessarily match the government's pro-work stance. This apparent incongruence may be due to the fact that employers are more likely to be pro-retirement toward older workers with long organizational tenure, who are very expensive and whose training may not be up-to-date. However, on the other hand, employers may be seeking out (i.e., a pro-work stance) older workers with higher levels of expertise for part-time or consulting work. Thus, we see employers in most developed countries both encouraging continued work (pro-work) and attempting to entice workers in their late career to retire early (pro-retirement). Below, we outline some of the major components that have been used in promoting each strategy.

Promoting Retirement

Many employers have used early retirement incentive packages (ERIs) to induce older workers to retire earlier than they might have otherwise done, thus reducing labor costs, at least in the short run. Many employers view ERIs as a more humane alternative to massive layoffs and downsizings during times when personnel cuts are necessary to rebalance the workforce. ERIs typically consist of some type of financial inducement (e.g., lump sum payment, increased pension benefits) that organizations use to entice older workers to retire. However, organizations which offer ERIs must balance out various concerns, such as determining how many older workers are likely to accept an ERI, which workers are likely to accept an ERI, and doing this at the right cost to the organization.

Feldman (2003) notes that incentives used in ERIs will differ depending on whether the workers are covered by a defined benefit (DB) or a defined contribution (DC) pension plan. Employers assume the risks with funding DB plans where individuals receive pension benefits based on years of service and final salary. However, in DC plans employers simply contribute funds to the worker's pension account (e.g., 401k) and the employee assumes all the risk for managing and growing their retirement nest egg. As a result, the major incentives that employers with Defined Benefit pension plans can provide include adding years of service or how the final salary is calculated. They can also change eligibility criteria, however, in general, most research shows that employers have a difficult time determining exactly how much to change in order to get the poorer performers to leave while retaining the better employees.

With DC pension plans, however, the employee's years of service and age have no real influence on pension payouts. Rather, a lump sum contribution would be more likely to incent older workers to accept an ERI within a DC pension plan. In addition, employers can increase contributions to employees who meet certain criteria (e.g., 60 and older). Yet, as with the DB pension plans, the incentives that would have to be sufficiently large to incent poorer performers to accept an ERI, are also likely to incent better performers to accept as well. Employers can also offer non-monetary incentives as part of an ERI. For example, they can offer no or low cost pre-retirement counseling, extend fringe benefits, and offer opportunities for phased retirement and/or bridge employment. Of course, the current macro economic climate (e.g., unemployment rate, inflation, stock market appreciation) will also influence how likely individuals will be to accept an ERI offer under either type plan. This was abundantly clear from 2008–2011 as more older workers delayed retirement due to the severe downturn in the economy.

Employers must also examine a wide variety of additional factors such as the estimated acceptance rate, determining how frequently to offer ERIs, the cost of any "free riders" (i.e., individuals who would have retired in a given year anyway regardless of an ERI offer), and whether to offer bridge employment to employees (Feldman, 2003). Thus, there is a wide variety of factors outside the control of the organization, including individual retiree characteristics (e.g., risk aversion, organizational commitment) and macro economic conditions that are likely to influence any ERI offer. As a result, it is difficult to determine the precise influence that any given factor may have on the likelihood of an individual in their late career accepting an ERI and retiring early.

CASE STUDY

We introduced Clarice, a 59-year-older African American female, in Chapter 2. We noted that she had recently decided to accept an offer of earlier retirement. Clarice had served as a secretary and help desk technician for over 30 years with the same agency. This public sector agency, with a defined benefit (DB) pension plan, was offering a "one time only" early retirement incentive offer to workers over age 55 with 20 or more years of service. While Clarice had anticipated working at least another three to five years, she had decided to make her part-time, side job as a full-time Internet travel consultant. She is looking forward to the decreased work hours overall and the increased flexibility in scheduling her time. Yet, Clarice does not anticipate fully retiring until her younger husband retires in at least eight to 10 more years. Thus, Clarice serves as a clear example of how outside interests, nature of the retirement pension plan, and personal characteristics (e.g., having a younger spouse who is still working) can all play a role in determining the likelihood of accepting an ERI offer.

Beyond formal ERIs, both employer and occupational norms regarding retirement can serve as pro-retirement enticements. For example, in most professional sports, by the time an athlete reaches their mid 30s, questions of retirement start to surface, while in many white-collar professional occupations, such questions are unlikely to arise until individuals are in the 60s, and maybe even their 70s. Employers and co-workers may also express subtle, and sometime not so subtle, hints that it is time for individuals to retire. These social pressures may be very effective in encouraging older workers to retire before they are really ready to do so.

Extending Late Careers

Greller and Stroh (2003) note that we may not know as much about extending workers' careers as we might think. The common wisdom has been that if we simply stop doing what were doing before (in terms of inducing older workers to retire) then they will stay and decide not to retire. However, that has not generally been the case. Thus, Greller and Stroh outline several options for increasing the likelihood that older workers will want to extend their work lives. The first option they discuss is implementing various flexible work arrangements that are older worker friendly, such as phased retirement, job sharing, telecommuting, and seasonal employment. These options can be used by the older worker's current employer to retain them, or by other employers who may be looking to hire retirees from other organizations to serve in part-time or contingent employment. Of course, given the various definitions of retirement we discussed at the beginning of this chapter, it may be that flexible options such as phased retirement may actually encourage individuals to reduce their work hours sooner than if such options were not available. Thus, instead of helping to extend careers, they may in fact be cutting them short.

However, what is clear is that many workers in late career do have a desire to remain in the workforce, but in a reduced capacity. As we discussed in Chapter 2, older worker's late career goals and aspirations typically shift from seeking career advancement to working to leave a legacy. Thus, flexible work options would be very appealing to most workers in their late career.

In addition, most late career workers have high firm, industry, and/or occupational specific knowledge. However, they may not be up-to-date on the most recent trends in their field. In addition, with the rapid pace of technology advancement and knowledge generation, it is clear that all workers, but particularly those in their late career, will need continuous training to stay employable and extend their careers (Charness, Czaja, & Sharit, 2007). However, past research has shown that older workers are much less likely to engage in workplace training than those earlier in their early career (Maurer, 2007). Thus, it is important that late career workers continue to seek out training and professional development activities, whether employer sponsored or not. We discussed training issues with regard to mid and late careers in great detail in Chapter 9.

In Europe, the concept of *work ability* has been used for several decades to extend work lives for individuals (Ilmarinen, 2009). At the Finnish Institute of Occupational Health, Ilmarinen (2009) used the Work Ability Index to predict who is at greatest risk for disability in their late career, and then developed intervention strategies (e.g., health screenings, work reassignments, job redesign) to intervene and extend older workers' careers. As a result, older workers who would have otherwise left the workforce due to disability, injury, or illness, are able to extend their work lives. However, the concept of work ability is even broader, in that it helps to create a balance between worker's skill, ability, and attitudes, and the demands of their job and the workplace. Accordingly, work ability includes not only maintaining basic functional capacity (e.g., physical and mental health), but also current competence (e.g., up-to-date knowledge, skills, and abilities), as well as positive attitudes and motivations, so that they match the ever changing nature of work and the workplace, thus allowing older workers in their late career to extend their careers (Shultz & Olson, 2013).

Theories of Retirement

There have been several prominent theories of retirement espoused in the literature. These theories include rational choice theory, role theory, image theory, continuity theory, the theory of planned behavior, and the life course perspective (Wang & Shultz, 2010). Each of these theories posits how individuals make the successful transition from late career to retirement. For example, rational choice theory (prominent in the economics literature) assumes that an individual weighs the relative importance of work versus leisure, and when the balance tips towards leisure, assuming economic conditions permit, that individual will retire. However, much of this is predicated on the fact that retirement really is a voluntary decision. However, as Shultz and Wang (2011) point out, many individuals do not feel that their retirement decision is in fact voluntary. As a result, rational choice theory has not been as prominent outside the economics literature.

Alternatively, role theory delineates the work and non-work roles that individuals engage in and how an individual's roles evolve in late career from predominantly one of worker (representing a role exit) to one of retiree (representing a role entry). Roles are important because they structure our lives and also serve as a source of meaning and self-identity. They can also potentially conflict, for example, when the role of caring for a sickly, elderly parent may interfere with the role of worker. Thus, how we view our roles, and as the roles we engage in change over time, impact how we adjust to retirement and how satisfied we are with retirement. For example, if we are very attached to our worker role and view it positively, we will likely want to continue in that role (i.e., delay retirement). On the other hand, if we are not attached to the work role and find work to be stressful or boring, we may embrace the retiree role and seek as early a retirement as possible (Wang & Shultz, 2010).

Like role theory, image theory focuses on individuals' self-concepts and examines how these self-concepts (e.g., as a worker or retiree) fit with how they perceive themselves in the context of their families and broader society. To the extent that one's self-image matches a given role, then the individual is more likely to desire to be engaged in that role. However, if it is not a good match, the person is unlikely to desire to be in that role and also unlikely to be satisfied in that role. For example, if individuals are having difficulty imagining themselves as retirees, they are going to be less likely to want to retire. Thus, image theory focuses on one's present self-concept or image, whereas role theory focuses more on individual's envisioning their future role of retiree.

Continuity theory suggests that individuals will attempt to maintain as much internal/psychological (e.g., self-concept, ideas, interests, attitudes) and external/social and physical continuity as they can as they make the transition from late career to retirement. Doing so is predicted to lead to better retirement adjustment and higher levels of retirement satisfaction (Wang et al., 2011). Thus, according to continuity theory, the role transitions that individuals make as they transition into retirement are typically relatively minor and consistent with what they have always done (e.g., as the work role diminishes, it is replaced with previously engaged in volunteer activities) in order to achieve satisfactory retirement adjustment. Engaging in career bridge employment would be a good example of continuity theory as individuals are able to maintain continuity by engaging in activities after retirement from their career job that are very similar to their career job (e.g., an accountant who worked for a large employer, who is now doing similar work for a much smaller employer after accepting an ERI from his former employer).

The theory of planned behavior links work and retirement attitudes with workplace and social norms. Thus, older worker's work and retirement-related attitudes are placed in the context of workplace norms (e.g., social pressure to retire or continue in employment from coworkers or administrators), as well as social norms (e.g., one's spouse's desire for an individual to retire). These attitudes lead to intentions, which in turn lead to behaviors. For example, Warren and Kelloway (2010) examined retirement decision making in Canada, after the removal of mandatory retirement, using the theory of planned behavior as their theoretical grounding. The authors attempted to predict retirement timing intentions (i.e., planned retirement age) by examining social policy influences and perceived control over retirement decisions, as well as pre- and post-retirement financial well-being. Older workers' perceptions of age and life satisfaction were also examined, as were attitudes toward work and attitudes toward people at work. Finally, older workers' intentions to work in a similar job post retirement were also examined. The authors found that attitudes toward people at work predicted older workers' attitudes toward work. In turn, attitudes toward work predicted age and life perceptions. Age and life perceptions then predicted perceived control, which then predicted social policy influences, and finally social policy influences predicted planned retirement age. Thus, Warren and Kelloway were able to use the theory of planned behavior to successfully predict planned retirement age from a variety of factors.

The life course perspective may be thought of as a meta-theory that encompasses many of the theories above. It looks at individual life histories and trajectories to provide a context for interpreting an individual's transition from late career to retirement. Thus, all transitions are embedded and interpreted within an individual's unique historical context and experiences, which in turn determine the meaning that an individual ascribes to a given transition (e.g., is retirement considered a life altering event or no big deal?). Of course these life course histories and contexts can be described at multiple levels, including micro (e.g., individual, family), meso (e.g., organizational, community), and macro (e.g., society, governmental). As a result, a successful transition from late career to retirement can take multiple forms depending on the individuals unique set of circumstances.

Future Research on the Transition from Late Career to Retirement

Shultz and Henkens (2010) noted, "To increase our insight into the decisions older workers make at the end of their career, we believe that it is important to acknowledge the importance of several aspects of older workers careers and the implications for current research" (p. 266). They then go on to outline five key issues and directions for future research. The first issue is one we discussed earlier; namely that the nature of retirement itself is changing. Retirement is becoming a much more complicated and less definitive process as individual's careers become less orderly, and the organizational and environmental contexts continue to evolve and become more diverse (Shultz & Olson, 2013). As a result, we see individuals engaged in a variety of forms of bridge and hybrid employment options, self-employment, as well as phased or partial retirement options, while fewer are making the leap directly from full-time employment to full-time leisure retirement. Thus, the retirement transition process itself is becoming blurred, and this must be fully acknowledged and taken into consideration in future research.

Second, there is a growing need for an interdisciplinary perspective on late careers. A wide variety of academic disciplines study retirement (e.g., economics, sociology, psychology, social work, organizational sciences), yet there is often little true integration of the works from various disciplines. Thus, issues around economic and wealth factors, social embeddedness, and psychological processes that proceed late career employment and retirement decisions, need to be integrated. Future research on the retirement transition will need to acknowledge and incorporate these various academic perspectives when investigating how the retirement transition process unfolds over time. For example, economists may emphasize the macro economic and labor market conditions and psychologists may emphasize the micro attitudinal factors, but few have combined these areas. However, by combining the two perspectives, researchers may be better able to identify the labor market and macro economic conditions that would make attitudinal factors such as tolerance for ambiguity or risk avoidance key factors in the successful transition from late career to retirement and the various forms it may take (e.g., engaging in late career entrepreneurial activities).

According to Shultz and Henkens (2010), a third issue that needs to be addressed in future research on the transition to retirement is the need to look at the demand side of the retirement equation. That is, much of the current research focuses on individual attributes (e.g., personality factors, needs and values, and demographic characteristics), however employers and government policy makers are key players in defining the opportunities that late career workers have for working longer and retiring (e.g., early retirement incentive packages). Thus, as Shultz and Henkens (2010) note, "… it is incumbent on us to better delineate the role that employers play in the late career employment-retirement nexus" (p. 266). Again, the macro economic and labor market conditions may have a large influence on how these employer policies play out at any given point in time.

Fourth, there are clear international variations in the contexts and processes surrounding an individual's late career transition from full-time career work to retirement. More international data is becoming available that will allow researchers to determine the impact of various policies and contextual factors on individuals transitioning to retirement. For example, in the United States, we have seen a dramatic drop in the last few decades in the number of workers covered by defined benefit pension plans (i.e., those that pay a fix income based on age, years of service, and final salary), with a concomitant rise in the number of defined contribution pension plans (e.g., 401k plans that basically serve as portable retirement savings accounts). However, many European countries still have predominantly defined benefit pensions. Thus, researchers are able to not only compare U.S. workers over time as the pension landscape changes, but also to make current comparisons with older workers in other countries where there has been little change in the pension systems (e.g., van Dalen, Henkens, & Hershey, 2010).

Finally, Shultz and Henkens (2010) note that future research examining the late career retirement nexus needs to incorporate a wide variety of methodological perspectives. For example, while much of the research has used large scale, quantitatively oriented survey methods to examine these issues, more in-depth qualitative and case study methodologies are needed to compliment these large scale efforts. By doing so, we will obtain a much richer picture of the transition from late career employment to full retirement. In that vein, we present the following example of a case study (see Text Box 11.1).

Wang and Shultz (2010), in their recent review of the retirement literature also provide several directions for future theorizing on the retirement process in the 21st century. Their suggestions include incorporating a person-environment fit framework in studying both retirement and bridge employment decision making, which would allow researchers to examine this transition from multiple levels, as recommended by Beehr and Bennett (2007). In addition, applying a resource perspective to understanding the retirement transition and adjustment process would allow for more generalizable results, in that most previous studies tend to be able to explain the outcomes for only a small subset of retirees, whereas resource theory incorporates many resources (e.g., cognitive, physical, social, emotional, environment) in explaining the retirement transition process from a temporal perspective (Wang et al., 2011). Examining bridge employment from a dynamic perspective treats it as a longitudinal workforce participation process in late career, and as such, better captures the vibrant nature of bridge employment and the influence it has

TEXT BOX 11.1 The Changing Nature of Retirement for Individuals and Society

The concept of retirement is evolving rapidly at both the individual and societal levels. As a result, individuals will need to adjust and adapt to the changing nature of retirement as they age and approach retirement. Thus, each individual needs to customize his retirement based on his own unique set of circumstances and life situation. In a recent interview with John, a 55-year-old high level consultant in the computer industry, he articulated this notion: "I agree that 'retirement'" is a very individual thing. Also, the retirement I envisioned when I was in my 20s is not the retirement I envision now in my 50s. For one thing, I don't think I will ever really retire completely, unless I am unable to work. There is an economic aspect to that decision—being downsized around 2000 and the depressed economy of the last few years have done a number on my 401K. But a large part of that decision is personal as I can't imagine not working. I like working. I have spent the last decade reinventing myself as a consultant and expert in my field. That means I have more freedom to work on my terms, and it is very satisfying. The problem with my plan is that I don't have control over the job environment. While I might like to continue working as long as I can, I don't see a lot of 70 year olds doing what I do. Although age discrimination isn't legal, corporations move their expensive and older employees out the door all the time. So, I also created my back-up plan which is my web design business. That's something I have control over and something I enjoy doing. I keep it active at a low-level now because I may have to fall back on it sometime. Whatever happens, you won't see me as a greeter at Wal-Mart or bagging groceries at the super market."

Clearly, John's conception of retirement has evolved as he has matured and had to deal with decisions imposed on him by the organizations he has worked for and the economic cycles that have impacted everyone. Part of his evolution is due to his own personal and professional growth, however it is clear from John's statement, that part of it is also driven by the evolution of how retirement has changed over time. Organizations no longer offer monthly pension payments for all their retirees that are guaranteed until they die, and even after they die for their surviving spouse. Also, the desire to continue to stay active and engaged, continuing to use one's skills and talents is a change that has occurred among the baby boomers that did not exist (at least not as strongly) among the previous generation. Retirement was conceptualized as a time to engage solely in leisure pursuits with a complete disengagement from activities associated with one's previous work role.

Another interesting aspect of John's comments is the desire for autonomy in future work roles, despite the perception that he may not have as much control over the external work environment as he would like. Thus, in his remarks we see a small glimpse of how older workers' conceptions of retirement can evolve over time and how both internal and external factors can help to shape how one envisions, and ultimately enacts, retirement.

on the retirement adjustment process. This would also allow for better estimates of the influence of more distal factors on the bridge employment process as it unfolds over time.

Shultz and Wang (2011) also outline three key areas for future research on retirement. First, they emphasize the need to examine retirement from a longitudinal perspective. Too often researchers focus on just one component of the process (e.g., retirement planning) using cross-sectional data at one point in time. However, with more large scale, longitudinal data sets now available (e.g., the Health and Retirement (HRS) data set in the United States and the Study of Aging and Retirement in Europe (SHARE) data set in the European Union), researchers have the data they need to examine retirement as a longitudinal process that unfolds over time, often decades, and across many phases. Thus, treating retirement as a longitudinal process, as depicted in Figure 11.1, has strong implications for research and also for practice. For example, when career counselors or coaches provide advice for a worker in late career, they should take a longer term view to incorporate both the factors leading up to the present time, as well as the implications present decisions will have on long-term outcomes for the individual.

Shultz and Wang (2011) also emphasize the need to examine the voluntary nature of retirement when examining the retirement process. While many may assume that retirement is now always voluntary with the removal of forced age-based retirement in the United States and most other developed countries, that perception is not always held by older workers themselves. Thus, for example, while accepting an ERI offer may be technically "voluntary," it is clear that many older workers do not view such acceptances as voluntary, but rather as having no real choice. Basically, either accept the ERI offer or face the uncertainty of being downsized with no such generous inducements. Thus, researchers need to be aware of how their respondents are defining their retirement, as it has strong implications for the results they are likely to obtain. In addition, practitioners need to be aware that to the extent that retirement is not voluntary, an individual's retirement adjustment is likely to be more troublesome and incorporate this into their practice.

Finally, Shultz and Wang (2011) emphasize the need to examine retirement as another career stage, where retirement is no longer viewed as the end of one's working life, but rather as an opportunity to continues one's working life but in a different venue and/or context, usually with a reduced psychological commitment to work. Thus, many individuals are, on the one hand, extending their late careers with bridge employment, but also beginning the transition to retirement by engaging in bridge employment. Consequently, several individuals may decide to accept an ERI offer, but one may continue in the same career, while another begins a new entrepreneurial venture, while yet another may work only part time in a job totally unrelated to their career, but that allows her to continue to bring home a pay check while also allowing for daily structure and the ability to stay engaged and socially connected. Again, as with the other two factors, viewing retirement as another career stage has strong implications for how we research retirement and how retirement plays out in practice.

CONCLUSION

Chapter 12

A Resource-Based Dynamic Perspective on Mid and Late Careers

The major purpose of this book was to review, summarize, and integrate the extant literature on a wide variety of issues related to mid and late careers. Corresponding to this purpose, prior chapters in this book have addressed a wide range of important issues from both the individual and organizational perspectives. In this last chapter, we seek to integrate our writing in three specific ways. First, we aim to summarize common themes that need to be considered to fully comprehend the experiences of mid and late career workers. In particular, we will provide a synthesis of the chapters by introducing a theoretical conceptualization of mid and late career experience that allows us to connect the content we presented in the preceding chapters. Second, using this theoretical conceptualization, we aim to provide a theoretical model that could offer a more comprehensive perspective in understanding mid and late career issues. Third, we discuss the key implications of the current book for older workers, policy makers, organizational decision makers, and society more broadly.

Mid and Late Career Experience as Adjustment to Internal and External Changes

As illustrated in the previous chapters, research on mid and late career issues takes many forms, from in-depth, qualitative interviews with workers, to quantitative analyses of large scale national multi-wave panel studies. In addition, mid and late career experience itself can serve as a predictor (or independent variable) in attempts to understand workforce exits (e.g., retirement), physical and mental health, and financial well-being. Nevertheless, more often mid and late career experience serves as the criterion (or dependent variable) where researchers attempt to predict career actions (e.g., job turnover and career path change) or career quality (e.g., job and career satisfaction). To synthesize the common themes of the previous chapters, we propose to conceptualize mid and late career experience as adjustment to career-related internal and external changes that are experienced by an older worker. In particular, we argue that mid and late career experience indicates an older worker's career-related adjustment to both the intra-individual changes in physical, psychological, and financial conditions, and the quickly evolving and shifting context in which one's career takes place.

Specifically, as illustrated in Chapter 2, multiple theoretical models have explicitly emphasized that mid and late career experience is shaped by either intra-individual changes (e.g., the boundaryless career model and the protean career model), or the context in which the career takes place (e.g., the career and occupational embeddedness model), or both (e.g., the kaleidoscope career model). In addition, in Chapter 4 we discussed the specific intra-individual factors that may shape mid and late career experience, whereas Chapters 3, 5, and 6 we discussed the contextual factors that may influence mid and late career experience. In Chapters 7 through 11, when analyzing mid and late career-related practice regarding career renewal, performance management, training, development and mentoring, work and non-work issues, and transition to retirement, we also organized our discussion by implicitly or explicitly considering the roles played by career-related internal and external factors. In the following paragraphs, we discuss the advantages for applying this adjustment conceptualization to understanding mid and late career experience.

Dynamic Nature of Mid and Late Career Experience

First of all, conceptualizing mid and late career experience as career-related adjustment emphasizes the dynamic nature of mid and late career experience. As we reviewed in Chapter 2, as early as in the 1970s, lifespan researchers (e.g., Gould, 1978; Levinson, Darrow, Klein, Levinson, & McKee, 1978; Sheehy, 1976; Valliant, 1977) started to recognize that mid and late life can be a time of considerable transition. In addition, more contemporary career models all have great appreciation for the continued potential for growth and renewal of workers in their mid to late careers. Even in the retirement literature, it has been recognized that individuals can "un-retire" or "re-retire" by rejoining the workforce and starting a new career after they retire (Alley & Crimmins, 2007; Wang, Adams, Beehr, & Shultz, 2009). For example, there are individuals now who retire multiple times throughout their lifetime (Wang & Chan, 2011). While starting a second career at midlife has always been common in some professions (e.g., professional sports, the military), it is now becoming the norm for many older workers, both professionals and nonprofessionals. As a result, it is not only those in their 60s and 70s who are retiring for the first time, but more and more often those in their 40s and 50s (Shultz & Wang, 2008). All these trends suggest people's career activities in late life (e.g., retirement process) also incorporate multiple dynamic stages and serve multiple functional purposes (i.e., a developmental process).

Heterogeneous Nature of Mid and Late Career Experience

Second, endorsing this adjustment conceptualization for understanding mid and late career experience also emphasizes that this career experience is not homogeneous across individuals. In other words, there is not a formulaic process that all individuals experience in the same lock step way. Large variance exists in terms of how individuals act in mid and late careers, as well as in the consequences they experience from those macro career cycles (Shultz & Wang, 2011). Supporting this point, Chapters 3 to 6 illustrated multiple factors that could impact workers' mid and late career experiences, and it is obvious that there are significant individual differences on each of these factors. As such, the heterogeneity carried by this conceptualization emphasizes the need to examine the interrelations among workers' actions and experiences across different career stages and phases. For instance, workers' experiences in different career cycles are not separate but interrelated, which may influence each other in terms of the length and direction of the cycles (Hall, 2004).

Comprehensive Consideration of Determining Factors

Third, conceptualizing mid and late career experience as adjustment to career-related internal and external changes facilitates the comprehensive examination of determining factors that may influence this experience. As we reviewed in Chapter 2, existing career models often only specify a small set of factors that may shape the mid and late career experience. For example, the boundaryless career model only focuses on two factors (i.e., physical mobility and psychological mobility) in deciding the career boundary crossing or converging. Even the lifespan developmental model, which focuses on a number of individual factors and events, only addresses a limited number of mechanisms (i.e., physical and cognitive aging, as well as unique historical and generational events) in understanding adult career development. However, conceptualizing mid and late career experience as adjustment clearly points to two large categories of factors for empirical examination: career-related internal and external changes. As analyzed in Chapter 4, the career-related internal changes mainly include changes in cognitive ability, physical capacity, work motivation, as well as accumulation of experience and expertise. Further, Chapters 5 and 6 pointed out potential job- and organization-level factors whose changes may also influence mid and late career experience. These external factors include job and financial histories, job characteristics (i.e., traditional motivational job characteristics, knowledge and social job characteristics, and contextual job characteristics), employee-organization relationship (EOR), and human resources management practices. All these external factors help shape the context where one's career actions and experience take place, but have not been extensively acknowledged in previous career models. Finally, Chapter 4 also specified a set of individual dispositions (e.g., core self-evaluation and resilience) that may influence how one adjusts to those internal and external changes. These sets of factors are particularly important to consider because adjustment is an active process, which is heavily influenced by the worker's agency functions. Depending on how individuals deal with changes in internal and external factors, even when the changes they face are similar, they may still end up with vastly different results in terms of their adjustment.

Aligning the Common Career Goal with Diverse Career Outcomes

Fourth, endorsing this adjustment conceptualization for understanding mid and late career experiences also offers an opportunity to reconcile the discrepancy between the common goal held by workers regarding their mid and late careers (i.e., reaching a desirable career state) and the existence of large amount and forms of career outcomes that are used in the empirical research. According to the hedonic approach to change adaptation, also known as the set point theory (e.g., Frederick & Loewenstein, 1999), individual well-being levels are relatively stable over time. Daily life events (both good and bad) only temporarily affect well-being, and people return relatively quickly back to pre-event levels. Following this perspective, daily life adjustment is considered complete whenever the well-being level returns to its set point. However, another principle of this hedonic approach is that the set point may be reset over time depending on the internal goal shift within an individual. This shift is mainly due to the change in the subjective utility in pursuing certain career goals.

Considering individuals typically have different career goals in different career stages, we argue that it is also conceivable that different individuals have different concrete goals (i.e., the set points) for their mid and late careers, and these goals are subjectively determined. Therefore, although the common goal is always to lead to desirable career state, the actual desirable adjustment set points may still be different for different individuals. As such, investigating multiple forms of career criteria becomes a necessity if we would like to truly understand how individuals react to career-related internal and external changes in their mid and late careers. In Chapters 7 through 11, we specifically considered those potential concrete goals in terms of career renewal, performance management, training and development, work and non-work life, and transition to retirement, for mid and late career workers.

Enhancing the Theoretical Development

Finally, endorsing this adjustment conceptualization for understanding mid and late career experience can also facilitate the incorporation of the career development literature and the retirement research literature. According to Wang and Shultz (2010), the retirement process can be conceptualized as an adjustment process that contains both the retirement transition (i.e., from employment to retirement) and postretirement trajectory (i.e., individual development in postretirement life). Following this conceptualization, as we discussed in Chapter 11, retirement literature has largely relied on the life course perspective, role theory, and continuity theory to form concrete hypotheses regarding the underlying mechanisms to understand retirement adjustment as well as factors that would influence retirement adjustment. However, these theories and mechanisms have not been extensively used in the career development literature. As such, by endorsing the adjustment conceptualization for mid and late career experience, it creates an opportunity to directly apply theories that have been used in the retirement literature to understand mid and late career issues. Further, it helps to incorporate retirement as another career development stage when we consider mid and late career issues, which ties retirement experience more closely to the previous career cycles.

In this section, we have proposed to conceptualize mid and late career experience as adjustment to career-related internal and external changes that are experienced by an older worker. This conceptualization provides a good synthesis of the common themes of this book and logically connects different chapters in various ways. In particular, this conceptualization recognizes that one's mid and late career is complex in terms of its purpose, its driving force, its content, and its consequences. As a result, it may be particularly efficient and fruitful for researchers to take a theoretical model that pays specific attention to the dynamic nature of mid and late career experience, as well as the internal and external changes older workers may face, in studying this adjustment process. On the basis of this theoretical conceptualization, we next provide such a theoretical model (i.e., a resource based dynamic model) that could offer a more comprehensive perspective in understanding mid and late career issues.

A Resource-Based Dynamic Model

According to Hobfoll (2002), resources can be broadly defined as the total capability an individual has to fulfill his or her centrally valued needs. Reviewing different types of resources studied in previous research, Wang (2007) suggested that this total capability may include one's physical resources (e.g., muscle strength), cognitive resources (e.g., processing speed and working memory), motivational resources (e.g., self-efficacy), financial resources (e.g., salary and pension), social resources (e.g., social network and social support), and emotional resources (e.g., mood and affectivity). When endorsing the adjustment conceptualization for understanding mid and late career experience, the central premise of this resource perspective for studying mid and late career issues is that the adjustment experience can be viewed as the direct result of the individual's access to resources. Specifically, when people have higher levels of capability (i.e., resources) to fulfill needs they value in their mid and late careers, they will experience less difficulty in adjusting to career-related internal and external changes. On the other hand, negative changes in workers' resources will have an adverse effect on their career experience. Therefore, following this perspective, when considering the internal and external changes that may influence the mid and late career process, researchers may focus on examining changes that have direct impact on different types of resources.

Specifically, consistent with how the mid and late career experience was conceptualized earlier, the resource-based dynamic perspective argues that an individual's mid and late career is a developmental and dynamic process. During this process, workers' levels of adjustment in mid and late careers may fluctuate as a function of individual resources and changes in these resources. Therefore, this perspective focuses on the underlying mechanism through which internal and external changes have their impact. As illustrated in Figure 12.1, incorporating the resource perspective, variation in the level of adjustment (e.g., career satisfaction) along the mid and late career progression process can be viewed as a result of resource changes. In other words, if over time (e.g., t_4 to t_5 in Figure 12.1) a worker's total resource does not change significantly he or she may not experience significant change in career satisfaction. Alternatively, if over time (e.g., t_2 to t_3 in Figure 12.1) a worker's total resource significantly decreases (e.g., due to losing major income source), he or she may experience negative change in career satisfaction. Further, if over time (e.g., t_1 to t_2 or t_3 to t_4 in Figure 12.1) an individual's mid and late career enables him or her to invest significantly more resources (e.g., due to gaining cognitive resources that were previously occupied by a stressful job) in fulfilling centrally valued needs, he or she may experience positive change in career satisfaction. As such, this theoretical framework has the flexibility to accommodate a variety of longitudinal patterns for the mid and late career adjustment. This significantly enriches the theoretical approach to understanding

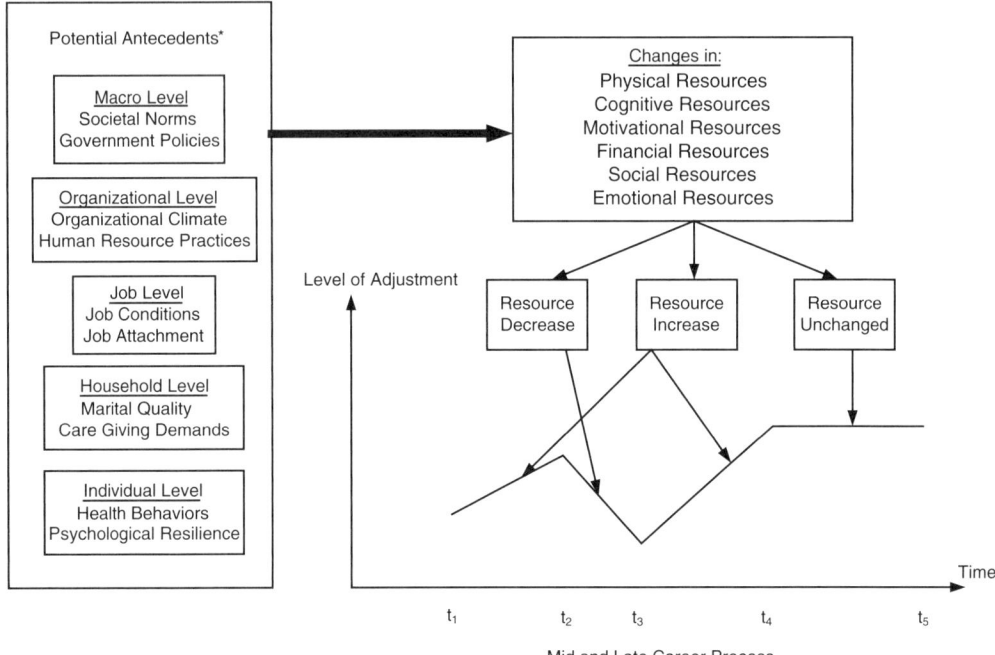

FIGURE 12.1 Illustration of the Resource-Based Dynamic Model for Understanding Mid and Late Career Experience as an Adjustment Process.

how internal and external changes may influence one's experience during the mid and late career process.

Moreover, this resource-based dynamic model can also be linked to the two large categories of factors (i.e., internal and external changes) that were discussed earlier to influence the mid and late career experience. Specifically, this resource-based dynamic model offers a large scope of antecedents that could influence various workers' resources in the mid and late career process, including variables from macro level, organizational level, job level, household level, and individual level. In addition, some central constructs in other theoretical frameworks, such as the immediate circumstance of mid and late career and the interdependent life spheres specified by the life course perspective, can all be viewed as pointing to variables that may influence workers' resources in different time points and aspects of the mid and late career process. As such, adopting the resource-based dynamic model may be complementary to existing theoretical models in terms of integrating the examinations regarding the effects of internal and external changes on the mid and late career process.

Finally, this resource-based dynamic perspective also provides new opportunities for us to understand other characteristics of the mid and late career adjustment process. For example, although other theories may provide specific predictions regarding the downward and/or upward trends in workers' career satisfaction change over time, they may not be as informative in terms of understanding the turning point (e.g., t_2, t_3, and t_4 in Figure 12.1) that connects two different trends (or small developmental segments) in the longitudinal mid and late career development process. However, adopting the resource perspective, it is not difficult to hypothesize that certain individual differences (e.g., openness to change, goal orientation in mid and late career, and need for structure), which may impact workers' motivational resources, and certain environmental factors (e.g., family support, community cohesiveness, and unemployment rate in the local labor market), which may impact workers' financial and social resources, may predict how fast the turning points will be reached for workers who experience negative change first but positive change in their career satisfaction later. This is because these individual differences and environmental factors all facilitate workers obtaining more resources, which makes them more likely to switch from the downward trend to the upward trend in career adjustment. Therefore, in future studies, applying this resource based dynamic model may further improve our understanding about the form and the nature of the mid and late career process.

So far, there exist few empirical studies that directly examine internal and external changes in the mid and late career process. However, several retirement studies (e.g., Kim & Moen, 2001; van Solinge & Henkens, 2008; Wang, 2007) have found that retirees' health decline during the retirement process had a negative impact on their adjustment experience, supporting the argument of the resource based dynamic model. Further, reviewing the empirical findings regarding the predictors of objective or subjective career success criteria, it is important to note that most of them are directly associated with different types of resources that workers have. For example, workers' physical and mental health, work stress and psychological and physical job demands, and recovery activities are associated with their physical and cognitive resources. Workers' financial income, unemployment history, number of dependent children, training and education are associated with their financial resources. Workers' marital status, marital quality, and social network are associated with their social resources. Workers' career role identity, job and career dissatisfaction, and work and career motivations are associated with their motivational resources. Finally, age-related discrimination experienced at work and anxiety associated with entering a new career path are likely linked with workers' emotional resources. All in all, these conceptual linkages between empirically identified variables and different categories of resources suggest that it is feasible to apply the resource based dynamic model to account for the effects of internal and external changes on the mid and late career experience.

Key Implications and Applications

Implications for Older Workers and Retirees

For many individuals, their lives have become increasingly more defined by the work they do as well as the financial freedom and engagement opportunities it provides them. As an example, we interviewed Mack who directly asserted, "Work is my life, it always has been and I love working. I want to work until I am no longer physically or mentally able to work. I can't imagine what I would do without the ability to work every day." Mack, like many individuals, has found meaning and full engagement through work and the success he has experienced. Work gives people both a sense of achievement and expands their social network by giving them the opportunity to be a part of a community in their workplace. These ongoing social relationships provide social support and bonds that can extend personal relationships they have through their friends and family.

Pitt-Catsouphes, Matz-Costa, and Besen (2009) found that work engagement and commitment are highest among workers over 40 years old compared to their younger counterparts doing similar work. Their study also showed that workers 50 and older expressed the highest levels of job satisfaction, and employees between ages 30 and 39 expressed the lowest levels of job satisfaction. Coupled with this, those older workers who are using their talents at work on a regular basis have higher levels of commitment, engagement, and satisfaction in the work they are doing have the possibility of continuing to be productive in the work they are doing.

Related to this, with the delay of child bearing until after one's career is established, older workers often have financial obligations, which can motive them to work longer for both financial reasons as well as the desire to remain actively engaged at work. Since health status has improved and people are living longer in most developed countries, processes to facilitate the ability for individuals to remain actively productive as long as they choose will contribute to the well-being of individuals, the organizations in which they are productive, and for the societies in which they live.

Implications for Organizations

Flexible work arrangements and the ability to choose part-time work has a positive impact on health outcomes for older workers and for those who chose to work even after they retire from their full-time careers (Taylor, 2008). Organizational leaders who provide workers a flexible schedule will be able to attract more older workers (as well as younger ones who have additional goals and obligations) and allow them to contribute positively to work-nonwork balance (as discussed in Chapter 10).

Discrimination against older workers poses one of the largest barriers that needs to be addressed by organizational leaders. Even though, in the United States, the Age Discrimination in Employment Act (ADEA) prohibits *discrimination against people over age 40*, in practice both research and experience show that discrimination and bias against older workers continues across industries. Discrimination in employment opportunities is related to both social perceptions and economic justifications for not training, hiring, or promoting older workers. We covered many of these issues in Chapters 8 and 9 as we discussed the impact of performance ratings, as well as training and development opportunities for older workers and how they were impacted by the biases of their supervisors and organizational decision makers. For economic reasons, organizational leaders may claim that younger workers cost less (in terms of salary and benefits), have more up-to-date knowledge (e.g., technology related skills), will have more working years ahead of them, and, therefore, are a better "investment" when compared to older workers. However, research also shows that older workers have more OCB (organizational citizenship behavior; Ng & Feldman, 2008) and are likely to work longer for the organization than their younger counterparts. From a social perception standpoint, older workers are often passed over during the selection process for a wide range of "reasons" (i.e., they won't fit into the team, they are overqualified, they do not have up-to-date technology skills, they are inflexible, they are slow to or unwilling to learn new skills, they are more likely to get sick and not be available/cost a lot in terms of healthcare benefits).

We will never know exactly how pervasive age discrimination is among organizational leaders as it is illegal and not politically correct. What is clear, however, is that decisions are sometimes made for reasons not related to the worker's ability to perform the job, and biases impact leaders' actions. Ongoing education of organizational managers and the impact of their decisions on both individual effectiveness and the productivity of their organization needs to be consistent. Case studies that describe the impact of older workers on organizational performance as well as the results of empirical studies that demonstrate not only the lack of relationship between age and performance (Ng & Feldman, 2008; Temple, Adair, & Hosseini-Chavoshi, 2011), but also the fact that older workers have more commitment and engagement to their work (Pitt-Catsouphes et al., 2009) may help address and alter these biases and the corresponding discriminatory actions taken in organizations.

Implications for Policy Makers

Worldwide, we are seeing an increase in the age at which workers can collect some form of government-sponsored payment and healthcare benefits. In the United States, the age is increasing from 65 to 67. To facilitate the successful transition, policies need to be established that contribute to the success of older workers to continue to be productive contributors in their organizations. Less physically demanding jobs positively contribute to prolonging the length of time that individuals can continue to be productive. However, ongoing training and development needs to be given and supported by policy makers to ensure that workers have opportunities to engage in low cost retraining to continue to develop the skills needed to perform the types of work that is available in today's job market (Temple et al., 2011). Specifically, with ever greater reliance on use of technology to perform a wide range of jobs across different industries, it is essential that retraining and multi-skilling of older workers be supported through state and federal training programs. For older workers who may have been laid off by organizations, but who still want to be actively engaged in work, this is essential to keeping them employed and employable. Public policy needs to be established to ensure that for all older workers who desire to continue to learn and remain engaged have the opportunity to develop those skills as well as access to employers who are willing to hire older workers. This is directly related to policy that addresses biases and discrimination against older workers. Research and practice have often shown that organizational leaders prefer to hire younger rather than older workers (Macnicol, 2006).

Implications for Society

Clearly, the increasing number of people eligible for retirement benefits and the decreasing number of full-time workers to pay for government-sponsored pensions (e.g., Social Security in the U.S., Superannuation in Australia) has worldwide implications. As a result, increasing the workforce participation of workers over 60 years of age is essential to reducing the economic burden for countries with an aging population (Temple et al.,

2011). Also, when individuals go on a fixed income there is often a corresponding drop in their consumerism. Given the reduction in the overall quality of life that can occur once full-time work ceases, the longer that individuals are able to engage in full-time work, the higher the economic standard they maintain, which in turn causes them to continue to engage in consumer activities that fuel the economy. In the current worldwide recessionary climate, this represents a win for society overall. As a result, maintaining work force productivity and engagement of older workers provides clear benefits for the communities they live in and society overall.

Final Thoughts: The Reality of Older Workers

Our hope in writing this book was to expand the understanding of the significance of the older worker and to challenge stereotypes and practices that limit opportunities that greatly impact individuals, organizations, and societies. The reality of the older worker is that:

- By 2030, 1 in 8 of the world's population will be 65 or older.
- Globally, life expectancy increased from 47 years (in 1950–55) to 65 years (in 2000–05), and is expected to reach 75 by 2045–50.
- In the period from 1950 to 2000, total fertility fell from 5.0 to 2.6 children per woman and is expected to continue falling to 2.0 children per woman by 2050.
- Japan is the world's oldest country with more than 21% of all Japanese aged 65 or older (TAFEP, 2011).

This data clearly shows the importance of fully deploying workers over 50 years of age to facilitate their personal effectiveness and ability to contribute as long as they are able to engage in productive pursuits that impact the success of the organizations they work for and the societies in which they live. We need to move beyond the focus of seeing careers unfolding at certain ages and fully see the tapestry of options that exists for workers of all ages in today's global economy. Underutilization of any group of individuals, including older workers, will undermine the integrity of the entire tapestry.

References

Aamodt, M. (2010). *Industrial and organizational psychology: An applied approach* (6th ed.). Belmont, CA: Thomson-Wadsworth.

Aaronson, S., & Coronado, J. (2005). Are firms or workers behind the shift away from DB pension plan? *Board of Governors of the Federal Reserve System (U.S.),* Finance and Economic Discussion Series. Washington, DC: Federal Reserve Bank (U.S.).

AARP. (2005). *The business case of workers age 50+: Planning for tomorrow's talent needs for today's competitive environment.* Washington, DC: AARP.

Abraham, J. D., & Hansson, R. O. (1995). Successful aging at work: An applied study of selection, organization, optimization, and compensation through impression management. *Journal of Gerontology: Psychological Sciences & Social Sciences, 50B,* 94–103.

Adams, G. A., & Beehr, T. A. (1998). Turnover and retirement: A comparison of their similarities and differences. *Personnel Psychology, 51,* 643–665.

Adams, G. A., Prescher, J., Beehr, T. A., & Lepisto, L. (2002). Applying work-role attachment theory to retirement decision-making. *International Journal of Aging & Human Development, 54,* 125–137.

Adams, G. A., & Rau, B. L. (2011). Putting off tomorrow to do what you want today: Retirement planning. *American Psychologist, 66,* 180–192.

Adams, G. A., Webster, J. R., & Buyarski, D. M. (2010). Development of an occupational embeddedness measure. *Career Development International, 15,* 420–436.

Aldwin, C. M., & Gilmer, D. F. (1999). Immunity, disease processes, and optimal aging. In J. C. Cavanaugh & S. K. Whitbourne (Eds.), *Gerontology: Interdisciplinary perspectives* (pp. 123–154). New York: Oxford University Press.

Allen, T. D., Eby, L. T., Poteet, M. L., Lentz, E., & Lima, L. (2004). Career benefits associated with mentoring for protégés: A meta-analysis, *Journal of Applied Psychology, 89,* 127–136.

Allen, T. D., McManus, S. E., & Russell, J. E. A. (1999). Newcomer socialization and stress: Formal peer relationships as a source of support. *Journal of Vocational Behavior, 54,* 453–470.

Allen, T. D., Russell, J. E. A., Poteet, M. L., & Dobbins, G. H. (1999). Learning and development factors related to perceptions of job content and hierarchical plateauing. *Journal of Organizational Behavior, 20,* 1113–1137.

Alley, D., & Crimmins, E. (2007). The demography of aging and work. In K. S. Shultz & G. A. Adams (Eds.), *Aging and work in the 21st century* (pp. 7–23). Mahwah, NJ: Erlbaum.

Argote, L., & Ingram, P. (2000). Knowledge transfer: a basis for competitive advantage in firms. *Organizational Behavior & Human Decision Processes, 82,* 150–169.

Armstrong-Stassen, M. (2008a). Organisational practices and the post-retirement employment experience of older workers. *Human Resource Management Journal, 18,* 36–53.

Armstrong-Stassen, M. (2008b). Human resource practices for mature workers - And why aren't employers using them? *Asia Pacific Journal of Human Resources, 46*, 334–352.

Armstrong-Stassen, M., & Ursel, N. (2009). Perceived organizational support, career satisfaction, and the retention of older workers. *Journal of Occupational & Organizational Psychology, 82*, 201–220.

Arthur, M. B., Inkson, K., & Pringle, J. K. (1999). *The new careers: Individual action and economic change*. London: Sage.

Arthur, M. B., & Rousseau, D. M. (1996). *The boundaryless career: A new employment principle for a new organizational era*. New York: Oxford University Press.

Bacanli, F. (2006). Personality characteristics as predictors of personal indecisiveness. *Journal of Career Development, 32*, 320–332.

Baldi, R. (1997). Training older adults to use the computer: Issues related to the workplace, attitudes, and training. *Educational Gerontology, 23*(5), 453–465.

Baltes, B. B., & Dickson, M. W. (2001). Using life-span models in industrial-organizational psychology: The theory of selective optimization with compensation. *Applied Developmental Science, 5*(1), 51–62.

Baltes, B. B., Rudolph, C. W., & Bal, A. C. (2012). A review of aging theories and modern work perspectives. In J. W. Hedge, & W. C. Borman (Eds.), *Oxford Handbook of Work and Aging* (pp. 117–136). New York: Oxford University Press.

Baltes, B. B., & Young, L. M. (2007). Aging and work/family issues. In K. S. Shultz & G. A. Adams (Eds.), *Aging and work in the 21st century* (pp. 251–275), Mahwah, NJ: Erlbaum.

Baltes, M. M., & Carstensen, L. L. (1996). The process of successful ageing. *Ageing and Society, 16*, 397–422.

Baltes, P. B. (1993). The aging mind: Potential and limits. *Gerontologist, 33*, 580–594.

Baltes, P. B. (1997). On the incomplete architecture of human ontogeny: Selection, optimization, and compensation as foundations of developmental theory. *American Psychologist, 52*, 366–380.

Bandura, A. (1986). *Social foundations of thought and action: A social cognitive theory*. Englewood Cliffs, NJ: Prentice Hall.

Bandura, A. (1991). Social cognitive theory of self-regulation. *Organizational Behavior and Human Decision Processes, 50*, 248–287.

Baranik, L. E., Roling, E. A., & Eby, L. T. (2010). Why does mentoring work? The role of perceived organizational support. *Journal of Vocational Behavior, 76*, 366–373.

Barnes-Farrell, J. L. (2003). Beyond health and wealth: Attitudinal and other influences on retirement decision-making. In G. A. Adams & T. A. Beehr (Eds.), *Retirement: Reasons, processes, and results* (pp. 159–187). New York: Springer.

Baruch, Y. (2008). Careers in transition. In C. Wankel (Ed.), *21st century management: A reference handbook* (Vol. 2, pp. 120–129). Thousand Oaks, CA: Sage.

Baugh, S. G., & Scandura, T. A. (1999). The effect of multiple mentors on protégé attitudes toward the work setting. *Journal of Social Behavior and Personality, 14*, 503–521.

Becker, T., & Klimoski, R. (1989). A field study of the relationship between the organizational feedback environment and performance. *Personnel Psychology, 42*, 343–358.

Beehr, T. A. (1986). The process of retirement: A review and recommendations for future investigation. *Personnel Psychology, 39*, 31–56.

Beehr, T. A., & Bennett, M. M. (2007). Examining retirement from a multi-level perspective. In K. S. Shultz & G. A. Adams (Eds.), *Aging and work in the 21st century* (pp. 277–302). Mahwah, NJ: Erlbaum.

Beehr, T. A., & Bowling, N. A. (2002). Career issues facing older workers. In D. C. Feldman (Ed.), *Work careers: A developmental perspective* (pp. 214–241). San Francisco: Jossey-Bass.

Benko, C., & Weisberg, A. (2007). *Mass career customization: Aligning the workplace with today's nontraditional workforce*. Boston, MA: Harvard University Press.

Bennis, W., Goleman, D., & O'Toole, J. (2008). *Transparency: How leaders create a culture of candor*. San Francisco: Jossey-Bass.

Bennis, W., & Thomas, R. (2002). *Geeks and geezers: How era, values, and defining moments shape leaders.* Boston: Harvard Business School Press.

Berman, E., Bowman, J., West, J., & Van Wart, M. (2006). *Human resource management in public service.* Thousand Oaks, CA. Sage.

Bernardin, H. J., Buckley, M. R., Tyler, C. L., & Wiese, D. S. (2000). A reconsideration of strategies in rater training. In G. R. Ferris (Ed.), *Research in personnel and human resource management* (Vol. 18, pp. 221–274).Greenwich, CT: JAI Press.

Bertolino, M., Truxillo, D. M., & Fraccaroli, F. (2011). Age as moderator of the relationship of proactive personality with training motivation, perceived career development from training, and training behavioral intentions. *Journal of Organizational Behavior, 32,* 248–263.

Bidwell, J., Griffin, B., & Hesketh, B. (2006). Timing of retirement: Including delay discounting perspective in retirement model. *Journal of Vocational Behavior, 68,* 368–387.

Blau, P. (1964). *Exchange and power in social life.* New York: Wiley.

Bono, J. E., & Colbert, A. E. (2005). Understanding responses to multi-source feedback: The role of core self-evaluation. *Personnel Psychology, 58,* 171–203.

Bond, J. T., Galinsky, E., Kim, S. S., & Brownfield, E. (2005). *National study of employers.* New York: Families and Work Institute.

Borman, W. C. (2004). The concept of organizational citizenship. *Current Directions in Psychological Science, 13,* 238–241.

Boxall, P., & Purcell, J. (2008). *Strategy and human resource management* (2nd ed.). Basingsoke, UK: Palgrave Macmillan.

Brim, B. J., & Liebnau, D. (2011). Does setting major development goals work? *Gallup Management Journal.* Retrieved November 10, 2011 from http://gmj.gallup.com/content/150485/Setting-Major-Development-Goals-Work.aspx?version=print

Briscoe, J. P., & Hall, D. T. (2006). The interplay of boundaryless and protean careers: Combinations and implications. *Journal of Vocational Behavior, 69,* 4–18.

Briscoe, J. P., Hall, D. T., & Frautschy DeMuth, R. L. (2006). Protean and boundaryless careers: An empirical exploration. *Journal of Vocational Behavior, 69,* 30–47.

Broadbent, J., Palumbo, M., & Woodman, E. (2006). *The shift from defined benefit to defined contribution pension plans — implications for asset allocation and risk management.* Report prepared for a Working Group on Institutional Investors, Global Savings and Asset Allocation established by the Committee on the Global Financial System. Retrieved from http://www.bis.org/publ/wgpapers/cgfs27broadbent3.pdf

Brown, M., Aumann, K., Pitt-Catsouphes, M., Galinsky, E., & Bond, J. T. (2010, July). *Working in retirement: A 21st century phenomenon.* Boston: The Families and Work Institute, and The Sloan Center on Aging and Work at Boston College. Retrieved October 20, 2011, from http://familiesandwork.org/site/research/reports/workinginretirement.pdf

Brown-Wilson, D., & Parry, E. (2009). Career plateauing in older workers: Contextual and psychological drivers. In G. A. Baugh & S. E. Sullivan (Eds.), *Maintaining focus, energy, and options through the lifespan* (pp. 75–105). Charlotte, NC: Information Age.

Buckingham, M., & Clifton, D. O. (2001). *Now, discover your strengths.* New York: Simon & Schuster.

Buckingham, M., & Coffman, C. (1999) *First break all the rules: What the world's greatest managers do differently.* New York: Simon & Schuster.

Bunce, D., & Sisa, L. (2002). Age differences in perceived workload across a short vigil. *Ergonomics, 45,* 949–960.

Campion, M. A. (1988). Interdisciplinary approaches to job design: A constructive replication with extensions. *Journal of Applied Psychology, 73,* 467–481.

Campion, M. A., & Thayer, P. W. (1985). Development and field evaluation of an interdisciplinary measure of job design. *Journal of Applied Psychology, 70,* 29–43.

Cappelli, P. (1999). *The new deal at work: Managing the market-driven workforce.* Boston: Harvard Business School Press.

Cappelli, P., & Novelli, B. (2010). *Managing the older worker: How to prepare for the new organizational order.* Boston: Harvard Business School Publishing.

Carstensen, L. L. (1991). Selectivity theory: Social activity in life-span context. In K. W. Schaie (Ed.), *Annual review of gerontology and geriatrics* (Vol. 11, pp. 195–217). New York: Springer.

Carstensen, L. L., Isaacowitz, D., & Charles, S. T. (1999). Taking time seriously: A theory of socioemotional selectivity. *American Psychologist, 54,* 165–181.

Cartwright, S., & Cooper, C. L. (1997). *Managing workplace stress.* Thousand Oaks, CA: Sage.

Cascio, W. F. (1995). Whither industrial and organizational psychology in a changing world of work? *American Psychologist, 50,* 928–939.

Cascio, W. F. (2003). Changes in work, workers, and organizations. In W. C. Borman, D. R. Ilgen, & R. J. Klimoski (Eds.), *Handbook of psychology: Volume 12, Industrial and organizational psychology* (pp. 401–422). Hoboken, NJ: Wiley.

Cascio, W. F. (2006). *Managing human resources: Productivity, quality of work life, profits (7th Ed.)* New York: McGraw-Hill Irwin.

Cascio, W. F. (2007). Trends, paradoxes, and some directions for research in career studies. In H.Gunz & M. Peiperl (Eds.), *Handbook of career studies* (pp. 549–557). Thousand Oaks, CA: Sage.

Catalyst (2002). *Women of color in corporate management: Three years later.* New York; Catalyst.

Cawley, B. D., Keeping, L. M., & Levy, P. E. (1998). Participation in the performance appraisal process and employee reactions: A meta-analytic review of field investigations. *Journal of Applied Psychology, 83,* 615–663.

Chapman, D., Uggerslev, K., Carroll, S., Piasentin, K., & Jones, D. (2005). Applicant attraction to organizations and job choice: A meta-analytic review of the correlates of recruiting outcomes. *Journal of Applied Psychology, 90,* 928–944.

Charness, N., & Boot, W. R. (2009). Age and information technology use: Potential and barriers. *Current Directions in Psychological Science, 18,* 253–258.

Charness, N., & Czaja, S. J. (2006). Older worker training: What we know and don't know. *AARP Public Policy Institute Report,* Washington, DC; AARP.

Charness, N., Czaja, S., & Sharitt, J. (2007). Age and technology for work. In K. S. Shultz & G. A. Adams (Eds.), *Aging and work in the 21st century* (pp. 225–250). Mahwah, NJ: Erlbaum.

Claes, R., & Heymans, M. (2008). HR professionals' views on work motivation and retention of older workers: A focus group study. *The Career Development International, 13,* 95–111.

Clausen, J. A. (1995). Gender, context, and turning points in adults' lives. In P. E. Moen, G. H. Elder, & K. Luscher (Eds.), *Examining lives in context: Perspectives on the ecology of human development* (pp. 365–389), Washington, DC: American Psychological Association.

Cleveland, J. N., & Lim, A. S. (2007). Employee age and performance in organizations. In K. S. Shultz & G. A. Adams (Eds.), *Aging and work in the 21st century* (pp. 109–138). Mahwah, NJ: Erlbaum.

Clifton, D. O., & Harter, J. K. (2003). Investing in strengths. In K. S. Cameron, J. E. Dutton, & R. E. Quinn (Eds.), *Positive organizational scholarship* (pp. 111–121). San Francisco: Berrett Koehler.

Colonia-Willner, R. (1998). Practical intelligence at work: Relationship between aging and cognitive efficiency among managers in a bank environment. *Psychology and Aging, 13,* 45–57.

Committee on Techniques for the Enhance of Human Performance [CTEHP] (1999). *The changing nature of work: Implications for occupational analysis.* Washington, D.C.: National Academies Press.

Corporate Leadership Council. (2004). *Driving employee performance and retention through engagement: A quantitative analysis of the effectiveness of employee engagement strategies.* Washington, DC: Corporate Executive Board.

Coyle-Shapiro, J.A-M., & Shore, L. (2007). The employee-organization relationship: Where do we go from here? *Human Resource Management Review, 17,* 166–179.

Crabtree, S. (2011) Retreived on October 13, 2011, http://gmj.gallup.com/content/149405/

Employees-Worldwide-Common.aspx?utm_source=email&utm_medium=102011&utm_content=morelink&utm_campaign=newsletter

Craik, F. I. M., & McDowd, J. M. (1987). Age differences in recall and recognition. *Journal of Experimental Psychology: Learning, Memory, and Cognition, 13*, 474–479.

Critchley, R. K. (2002). *Rewired, rehired, or retired? A global guide for the experienced worker.* San Francisco: Jossey-Bass/Pfeiffer.

Cropanzano, R., & Mitchell, M. S. (2005). Social exchange theory: An interdisciplinary review. *Journal of Management, 31*, 874–900.

Cross, S. E., & Markus, H. R. (1994). Self-schemas, possible selves, and competent performance. *Journal of Educational Psychology, 36*(3), 423–238.

Csikszentmihalyi, M. (1990). *Flow: The psychology of optimal experience.* New York: Harper & Row.

Csikszentmihalyi, M. (1997). *Finding flow: The psychology of engagement with everyday life.* New York: Basic Books.

Cuddy, A. J., & Fiske, S. T. (2002). Doddering but dear: Process, content and function in stereotyping of older persons. In T. Nelson (Ed.), *Ageism: Stereotyping and prejudice against older persons* (pp. 3–26). Cambridge, MA: MIT Press.

Cummings, T. G. (1978). Self-regulating work groups: A sociotechnical synthesis. *Academy of Management Review, 3*, 625–634.

D'Amato, A., & Herzfeldt, R. (2008). Learning orientation, organizational commitment and talent retention across generations. *Journal of Managerial Psychology, 23*, 929–953.

Dalton, D. W., Thompson, P. H., & Price, R. L. (1977). The four stages of professional careers: A new look at performance by professionals. *Organizational Dynamics, 6*, 19–42.

Daniels, A. C. (2000). *Bringing out the best in people: How to apply the astonishing power of positive reinforcement.* New York: McGraw-Hill.

Davis, B. L., Skube, C. J., Hellervik, L. W., Gebelein, S. H., & Sheard, J. L. (1992). *Successful manager's handbook: Developmental suggestions for today's managers.* Minneapolis, MN: Personnel Decisions, Inc.

Davis, M. A. (2003). Factors related to bridge employment participation among private sector early retirees. *Journal of Vocational Behavior, 63*, 55–71.

Dawis, R. V., & Lofquist, L. H. (1984). *A psychological theory of work adjustment.* Minneapolis: Universitu of Minnesota Press.

Deal, J. J. (2007) *Retiring the generation gap: How employees young and old can find common ground.* San Francisco: Jossey-Bass.

DeFruyt, F., & Mervielde, I. (1999). RIASEC types and Big Five traits as predictors of employment status and nature of employment. *Personnel Psychology, 52*, 701–727.

De Janasz, E., Sullivan, S., & Whiting, V. (2003). Mentor networks and career success: lessons for turbulent times. *The Academy of Management Executive, 17*(4), 78–91.

DeLong, D. (2004). *Lost knowledge: Confronting the threat of an aging workforce.* New York: Oxford University Press.

Denton, F., & Spencer, B. (2009). What is retirement? A review and assessment of alternative concepts and measures. *Canadian Journal on Aging, 28*, 63–76.

Diener, E., & Seligman, M. E. P. (2004). Beyond money: Toward an economy of well-being. *Psychological Science in the Public Interest, 5*, 1–31.

Digman, J. M. (1990). Personality structure: Emergence of the five-factor model. *Annual Review of Psychology, 21*, 417–440.

DiPrete, T. A., & Eirich, G. M. (2006). Cumulative advantage as a mechanism for inequality: A review of theoretical and empirical developments. *Sociology, 32*, 271–297.

Dixon, R. A., & Baltes, P. B. (1986). Toward life-span research on the functions and pragmatics of intelligence. In R. J. Sternberg & R. K. Wagner (Eds.), *Practical intelligence: Nature and origins of competence in the everyday world* (pp. 203–235). New York: Cambridge University Press.

Drago, R., Wooden, M., & Black, D. (2009). Who wants and gets flexibility? Changing work hours preferences and life events. *Industrial and Labor Relations Review, 62,* 394–414.

Drucker, P. F. (1989). *The new realities: In government and politics/in economics and business/in society and world view.* New York: Harper & Row.

Duncan, C. (2001). Ageism, early exit, and the rationality of age-based discrimination. In I .Golver & M. Branine (Eds.), *Ageism in work and employment* (pp. 25–46). Burlington, VT: Ashgate.

Dutton, J. E., & Heaphy, E. D. (2003). The power of high-quality connections. In K. S. Cameron, J. E. Dutton, & R. E. Quinn (Eds.), *Positive organizational scholarship: Foundations of a new discipline* (pp. 263–278). San Francisco: Berrett-Koehler.

Edwards, J. R., Scully, J. A., & Brtek, M. D. (1999). The measurement of work: Hierarchical representation of the multimethod job design questionnaire. *Personnel Psychology, 52,* 305–334.

Edwards, J. R., Scully, J. A., & Brtek, M. D. (2000). The nature and outcomes of work: A replication and extension of interdisciplinary work-design research. *Journal of Applied Psychology, 85,* 860–868.

Eisenberger, R., Huntington, R., Hutchison, S., & Sowa, D. (1986). Perceived organizational support. *Journal of Applied Psychology, 71,* 500–507.

Ekerdt, D. J. (2010). Frontiers of research on work and retirement. *Journal of Gerontology: Social Sciences, 65B,* 69–80.

Erdheim, J., Wang, M., & Zickar, M. J. (2006). Linking the Big Five personality constructs to organizational commitment. *Personality and Individual Differences, 41,* 959–970.

Erodogan, B., Bauer, T. N., Peiro, J. M., & Truxillo, D. M. (2011). Overqualified employees: Making the best of a potentially bad situation for individuals and organizations. *Industrial and Organizational Psychology: Perspectives on Science and Practice, 4(2),* 215–232.

Erez, A., & Judge, T. A. (2001). Relationship of core self-evaluations to goal setting, motivation, and performance. *Journal of Applied Psychology, 86,* 1270–1279.

Ettington, D. R. (1997). How human resource practices can help plateaued managers succeed. *Human Resource Management, 36,* 221–234.

Evans, P., & Bartolome, F. (1979, Spring). Professional lives versus private livers: Shifting patterns of managerial commitment. *Organizational Dynamics,* 2–29.

Evans, P., & Bartolome, F. (1981). *Must success cost so much?* New York: Basic Books.

Evans, P., & Bartolome, F. (1984). The changing pictures of the relationship between career and family, *Journal of Occupational Behavior, 5,* 9–21.

Feldman, D. C. (1994). The decision to retire early: A review and conceptualization. *Academy of Management Review, 19,* 285–311.

Feldman, D. C. (2002a). Advancing research on work careers: A developmental perspective on theory building and empirical research. In D. C. Feldman (Ed.), *Work careers: A developmental perspective* (pp. 346–371). San Francisco: Jossey-Bass.

Feldman, D. C. (2002b). Stability in the midst of change: A developmental perspective on the study of career. In D. C. Feldman (Ed.), *Work careers: A developmental perspective* (pp. 3–26). San Francisco: Jossey-Bass.

Feldman, D. C. (2002c). Second careers and Multiple careers. In R. J. Burke & C. L. Cooper (Eds.), *The new world of work* (pp. 75–94). Oxford, UK: Blackwell.

Feldman, D. (2003). Endgame: The design and implementation of early retirement incentive programs. In G. A. Adams & T. A. Beehr (Eds.), *Retirement: Reasons, processes, and results.* (pp. 115–135). New York: Springer.

Feldman, D. C. (2007). Career mobility and career stability among older workers. In K. S. Shultz & G. A. Adams (Eds.), *Aging and work in the 21st century,* (pp. 179–197). Mahwah, NJ: Erlbaum.

Feldman, D. C., & Beehr, T. A. (2011). A three-phase model of retirement decision making. *American Psychologist, 66,* 193–203.

Feldman, D. C., & Ng, T. W. H. (2007). Careers: Mobility, embeddedness, and success. *Journal of Management, 33,* 350–377.

Ferrin, D. L., Dirks, K. T., & Shah, P. P. (2006). Direct and indirect effects of third-party relation-ships on interpersonal trust. *Journal of Applied Psychology, 91,* 870–883.

Ferris, G. R. (1991). The age context of performance evaluation decisions. *Psychology and Aging, 6,* 616–626.

Fielding, R. A., & Meydani, M. (1997). Exercise, free radical generation, and aging. *Aging, 9,* 12–18.

Finkelstein, L. M., Allen, T. D., & Rhoton, L. A. (2003). An examination of the role of age in mentoring relationships. *Group and Organization Management, 28,* 249–281.

Finkelstein, L. M., & Burke, M. K. (1998). Age stereotyping at work: The role of rater and contex-tual factors on evaluations of job applicants. *Journal of General Psychology, 125*(4), 317–345.

Finkelstein, L. M., Higgins, K., & Clancy, M. (2000). Justifications for ratings of old and young job applicants: An exploratory content analysis. *Experimental Aging Research, 26,* 263–283.

Finley, F. R., Ivanitskaya, L. V., & Kennedy, M. H. (2007). Mentoring junior healthcare admin-istrators: A description of mentoring practices in 127 US hospitals. *Journal of Healthcare Management, 52,* 260–270.

Fisk, A. D., & Rogers, W. A. (2000). Influence of training and experience on skill acquisition and maintenance in older adults. *Journal of Aging and Physical Activity, 8,* 373–378.

Florian, V., Mikulincer, M., & Taubman, O. (1995). Does hardiness contribute to mental health during a stressful real-life situation? The roles of appraisal and coping. *Journal of Personality and Social Psychology, 68,* 687–695.

Frederick, S., & Loewenstein, G. (1999). Hedonic adaptation. In D. Kahneman, E. Diener, & N. Schwarz (Eds.), *Well-being: The foundations of hedonic psychology* (pp. 302–329). New York: Russell Sage Foundation.

Freedman, A. (2006). Balancing values, results in reviews. *Human Resource Executive* (August), 62–63.

Freund, A. M., & Baltes, P. B. (1998). Selection, optimization, and compensation as strategies of life management: Correlations with subjective indicators of successful aging. *Psychology and Aging, 13,* 531–543.

Fried, Y., & Ferris, G. R. (1987). The validity of the job characteristics model: A review and meta-analysis. *Personnel Psychology, 40,* 287–322.

Fronstin, P., Salisbury, D., & VanDerhei, J. (2008). *Savings needed to fund health insurance and health care expenses in retirement: findings from a simulation model* (Issue Brief No. 317). Washington, DC: Employee Benefit Research Institute.

Gaillard, M., & Desmette, D. (2009). Intergroup predictors of older workers' attitudes towards work and early exit. *European Journal of Work and Organizational Psychology, 17,* 450–481.

Gaillard, M., & Desmett, D. (2010). (In)validating stereotypes about older workers influences their intentions to retire early and to learn and develop. *Basic and Applied Social Psychology, 32,* 86–98.

Gaines, S. O., Jr., Gurung, R. A. R., Lin, Y., & Pouli, N. (2006). Interethnic relationships. In J. Feeney & P. Noller (Eds.), *Close relationships: Functions, forms, and processes* (pp. 171–187). New York: Psychology Press.

Galinsky, E., Bond, J. T., & Sakai, K. (2008). *2008 national study of employers.* New York: Families and Work Institute.

Ganzeboom, H. B. G., & Treiman, D. J. (1996). Internationally comparable measures of occupa-tional status for the 1988 International Standard Classification of Occupations. *Social Sci-ence Research, 25,* 201–239.

Gardner, H. (1999). *Intelligence reframed.* New York: Basic Books.

Gelissen, J., & de Graaf, P. M. (2006). Personality, social background, and occupational career success. *Social Science Research, 35,* 702–726.

Giandrea, M. D., Cahill, K. E., & Quinn, J. F. (2008). *Self-employment transitions among older American workers with career jobs*: U.S. Dept. of Labor, U.S. Bureau of Labor Statistics, Office of Productivity and Technology. Retrieved November 18, 2011, from: http://www.bls.gov/osmr/pdf/ec080040.pdf

Goff, S. J., Mount, M. K., & Jamison, R. L. (1990). Employer support child care, work/family conflict, and absenteeism: A field study. *Personnel Psychology, 43,* 793–809.

Goldstein, I. L., & Ford, J. K. (2002). *Training in organizations: Needs assessment, development, and evaluation* (4th ed.). Belmont, CA: Wadsworth.

Goleman, D. (1998). *Working with emotional intelligence.* New York: Bantam.

Goode, W. I. (1960). A theory of role strain. *American Sociological Review, 25,* 483–496.

Gould, R. (1978). *Transformations: Growth and change in adult life.* New York: Simon & Schuster.

Gouldner, A. W. (1960). The norm of reciprocity. *American Sociological Review, 25,* 161–178.

Grant, A. M. (2007). Relational job design and the motivation to make a prosocial difference. *Academy of Management Review, 32,* 393–417.

Grant, A. M. (2008). The significance of task significance: Job performance effects, relational mechanisms, and boundary conditions. *Journal of Applied Psychology, 93,* 108–124.

Greenhaus, J. H. (1971). An investigation of the role of career salience in vocational behavior. *Journal of Vocational Behavior, 1,* 209–216.

Greenhaus, J. (2003). Career dynamics. In W. C. Borman, D. R. Ilgen, & R. J. Klimoski (Eds.), *Handbook of psychology: Volume 12, industrial and organizational psychology* (pp. 519–540). Hoboken, NJ: Wiley.

Greller, M. M., & Stroh, L. K. (2003). Extending work lives: Are current approaches tools or talismans? In G. A. Adams & T. A. Beehr (Eds.), *Retirement: Reasons, processes, and results* (pp. 115–135). New York: Springer.

Greller, M. M., & Simpson, P. (1999). In search of late career: A review of contemporary social science research applicable to the understanding of late career. *Human Resources Management Review, 9,* 309–347.

Gunz, H., Mayrhofer, W., & Tolbert, P. (2011). Career as a social and political phenomenon in the globalized economy. *Organization Studies, 32,* 1613–1620.

Gutherie, J. P., & Schwoerer, C. E. (1996). Older dogs and new tricks: Career stage and self-assessed need for training. *Business Source Premier, 25*(1), 59–91.

Hackman, J. R., & Lawler, E. E. (1971). Employee reactions to job characteristics. *Journal of Applied Psychology Monograph, 55,* 259–286.

Hackman, J. R., & Oldham, G. R. (1976). Motivation through the design of work: Test of a theory. *Organizational Behavior and Human Performance, 16,* 250–279.

Hackman, J. R., & Oldham, G. R. (1980). *Work redesign.* Reading, MA: Addison-Wesley.

Hale, N. (1990). *The older worker: Effective strategies for management and human resource development.* San Francisco: Jossey-Bass.

Hall, D. T. (1976). *Careers in organizations.* Glenview, IL: Scott Foresman.

Hall, D. T. (1996a). Protean careers of the 21st century. *Academy of Management Executive, 10,* 8–16.

Hall, D. T. (Ed.) (1996b). *The career is dead—Long live the career.* San Francisco: Jossey-Bass.

Hall, D. T. (2002). *Careers in and out of organizations.* Thousand Oaks, CA: Sage.

Hall, D. T. (2004). The protean career: A quarter century journey. *Journal of Vocational Behavior, 65,* 1–13.

Hall, D. T., & Mirvis, P. H. (1995). The new career contract: Developing the whole person at midlife and beyond. *Journal of Vocational Behavior, 47,* 269–289.

Hamermesh, D. (1996). *Workdays, workhours, and work schedules.* Kalamazoo, MI: W.E. Upjohn Institute for Employment Research.

Harpaz, I., & Fu, X. (2002). The structure of meaning of work: A relative stability amidst change. *Human Relations, 55,* 639–667.

Harrington, H., & Hall, D. T. (2007). *Career management and work-life integration.* Thousand Oaks, CA: Sage.

Hartman, R. O., & Betz, N. E. (2007). The five-factor model and career self-efficacy: General and domain specific relationships. *Journal of Career Assessment, 15,* 145–161.

Hasher, L., & Zacks, R. T. (1988). Working memory, comprehension, and aging: A review and a new view. In G. H. Bower (Ed.), *The psychology of learning and motivation* (Vol. 22, pp. 193–225). San Diego, CA: Academic Press.

Health and Retirement Study (HRS). (n.d.). Retrieved May 1, 2012. from: http://hrsonline.isr. umich.edu/index.php

Hedge, J. W., Borman, W. C., & Lammlein, S. E. (2006). *The aging workforce: Realities, myths, and implications for organizations*. Washington, DC: American Psychological Association.

Heslin, P. A. (2005). Conceptualizing and evaluating career success. *Journal of Organizational Behavior, 26*, 113–136.

Higgins, M. C. (2001). Changing careers: The effect of social context. *Journal of Organizational Behavior, 22*, 595–618.

Higgins, M. C., & Kram, K. E. (2001). Reconceptualizing mentoring at work: A developmental network perspective. *Academy of Management Review, 26*, 264–288.

Highhouse, S., Brooks, M. E., & Gregarus, G. (2009). An organizational impression management perspective on the formation of corporate reputations. *Journal of Management, 35*, 1481–1493.

Hillgren, J. A., & Cheatham, D. W. (2000). *Understanding performance measures: An approach to linking rewards to the achievement of organizational objectives*. Scottsdale, AZ: WorldatWork.

Hobfoll, S. E. (2002). Social and psychological resources and adaptation. *Review of General Psychology, 6*, 307–324.

Hodgetts, R., Luthans, F., & Lee, S. (1994). New paradigm organizations: From total quality to learning to world-class. *Organizational Dynamics, 2*(3), 5–19.

Holland, J. L. (1985). *Making vocational choices: A theory of careers* (2nd ed.). Upper Saddle River, NJ: Prentice Hall.

Holtom, B. C., Lee, T. W., & Tidd, S. T. (2002). The relationship between work status congruence and work-related attitudes and behaviors. *Journal of Applied Psychology, 87*, 903–915.

House, R., Javidan, M., & Dorfman, P. (2001). Project globe: An introduction. *Applied Psychology: An International Journal, 50*, 489–505.

Hulin, C. L. (2002). Lessons from industrial and organizational psychology. In J. M. Herman & F. Drasgow (Eds.), *The psychology of work* (pp. 3–22). Mahwah, NJ: Erlbaum

Hunter, J. E., Schmidt, F. L., & Judiesch, M. K. (1990). Individual differences in output variability as a function of job complexity. *Journal of Applied Psychology, 75*, 28–42.

Hurtz, G. M., & Donovan, J. J. (2000). Personality and job performance: The Big Five revisited. *Journal of Applied Psychology, 85*, 869–879.

Hutchens, R., & Grace-Martin, K. (2006). Employer willingness to permit phased retirement: Why are some more willing than others?. *Industrial & Labor Relations Review, 59*, 525–546.

Ibarra, H. (2004). *Working identity: Unconventional strategies for reinventing your career*. Boston: Harvard Business Review Press.

Ilmarinen, J. (2009). Aging and work: An international perspective. In S. J. Czaja & J. Sharit (Eds.), *Aging and work: Issues and implications in a changing landscape* (pp. 51–73). Baltimore, MD: The Johns Hopkins University Press.

Isaksson, K., & Johansson, Q. (2000). Adaptation to continued work and early retirement following downsizing: Long-term effects and gender differences. *Journal of Occupational and Organizational Psychology, 73*, 241–256.

Jackson, P. R., Wall, T. D., Martin, R., & Davids, K. (1993). New measures of job control, cognitive demand, and production responsibility. *Journal of Applied Psychology, 78*, 753–762.

James, L. A., & James, L. R. (1989). Integrating work environment perceptions: Explorations into the measurement of meaning. *Journal of Applied Psychology, 74*, 739–751.

James, L. R., Choi, C. C., Ko, C. E., McNeil, P. K., Minton, M. K., Wright, M., et al. (2008). Organizational and psychological climate: A review of theory and research. *European Journal of Work and Organizational Psychology, 17*, 5–32.

Jansen, P. L. (2002). Liver disease in the elderly. *Best Practice and Research in Clinical Gastroenterology, 16*, 149–158.

Jex, S., Wang, M., & Zarubin, A. (2007). Aging and occupational health. In K. S. Shultz & G. A. Adams (Eds.), *Aging and work in the 21st century* (pp. 199–224). Mahwah, NJ: Erlbaum.

Johns, G. (1999). A multi-level theory of self-serving behavior in and by organizations. *Research in Organizational Behavior. 21*, 1–38.

Johnson, R. W., Kawachi, J., & Lewis, E. K. (2009). *Older workers on the move: Recareering in later life.* Washington, DC: AARP Public Policy Institute.

Johnson, R. W., Mermin, G. B. T., & Resseger, M. (2007). *Employment at older ages and the changing nature of work.* Washington, DC: AARP Public Policy Institute Report (2007-02). Retrieved from: http://www.urban.org/UploadedPDF/1001154_older_ages.pdf

Jones, D. A., & McIntosh, B. R. (2010). Organizational and occupational commitment in relation to bridge employment and retirement intentions. *Journal of Vocational Behavior, 77*, 290–303.

Joseph, D. L., & Newman, D. A. (2010). Emotional intelligence: An integrative meta-analysis and cascading model. *Journal of Applied Psychology, 95*, 54–78.

Judge, T. A., Bono, J. E., & Locke, E. A. (2000). Personality and job satisfaction: The mediating role of job characteristics. *Journal of Applied Psychology, 85*, 237–249.

Judge, T. A., Cable, D. M., Boudreau, J. W., & Bretz, R. D. (1995). An empirical investigation of the predictors of executive career success. *Personnel Psychology, 48*, 485–519.

Judge, T. A., Erez, A., & Bono, J. E. (1998). The power of being positive: The relationship between positive self-concept and job performance. *Human Performance, 11*, 167–187.

Judge, T. A., & Hurst, C. (2008). How the rich (and happy) get richer (and happier): relationship of core self-evaluations to trajectories in attaining work success. *Journal of Applied Psychology, 93*, 849–863.

Judge, T. A., & Larsen, R. J. (2001). Dispositional affect and job satisfaction: A review and theoretical extension. *Organizational Behavior and Human Decision Processes, 86*, 67–98.

Kammeyer-Mueller, J. D. (2007). The dynamics of newcomer adjustment: Dispositions, context, interactions and fit. In C. Ostroff & T. Judge (Eds.), *Perspectives on organizational fit* (pp. 99–122). New York: Erlbaum.

Kanfer, R., & Ackerman, P. L. (2004). Aging, adult development, and work motivation. *Academy of Management Review, 29*, 440–458.

Kanungo, R. N. (1982). *Work alienation: An integrative approach.* New York: Praeger.

Kaplan, R. A., & Norton, D. P. (1996). *The balanced scorecard: Translating strategy into action.* Cambridge, MA: Harvard Business Press.

Kaplan, R. E. (1991). *Beyond ambition: How driven managers can lead better and live better.* San Francisco: Jossey-Bass.

Karasek, R. (1990). Lower health risk with increased job control among white collar workers. *Journal of Organizational Behavior, 11*, 171–185.

Karasek, R., Brisson, C., Kawakami, N., Houtman, I., Bongers, P., & Amick, B. (1998). The Job Content Questionnaire (JCQ): An instrument for internationally comparative assessment of psychosocial job characteristics. *Journal of Occupational Health Psychology, 3*, 322–355

Karasek, R., & Theorell, T. (1990). *Healthy work: Stress, productivity and the reconstruction of working life.* New York: Basic Books.

Kaye, B., & Cohen, J. (2008, April). Safeguarding the intellectual capital of baby boomers. *Training and Development, 62*(4), 30–33, 4. Retrieved January 23, 2009, from ABI/INFORM Global database. (Document ID: 1468752891).

Kiggundu, M. N. (1981). Task interdependence and the theory of job design. *Academy of Management Review, 6*, 499–508.

Killian, C. M., Hukai, D., & McCarty, C. E. (2005). Building diversity in the pipeline to corporate leadership *The Journal of Management Development, 24*(1/2), 155–169.

Kim, H., & DeVaney, S. A. (2005). The selection of partial or full retirement by older workers. *Journal of Family and Economic Issues, 26*, 371–394.

Kim, J. E., & Moen, P. (2001). Moving into retirement: Preparations and transitions in late midlife. In M. E. Lachman (Ed.), *Handbook of midlife development* (pp. 487–527). New York: Wiley.

Kim, S., & Feldman, D.C. (2000). Working in retirement: The antecedents and consequences of bridge employment and its consequences for quality of life in retirement. *Academy of Management Journal, 39*, 367–380.

Kite, M., & Johnson, B. (1988). Attitudes toward younger and older adults: An updated meta-analytic review. *Psychology and Aging, 3*, 233–244.

Kite, M. E., Stockdale, G. D., Whitley, B. E., & Johnson, B. T. (2005). Attitudes toward younger and older adults: An updated meta-analytic review. *Journal of Social Issues, 61*, 241–266.

Kolb, A. Y., & Kolb, D. A. (2005). Learning styles and learning spaces: Enhancing experiential learning in higher education. *Academy of Management Learning & Education, 4*(2), 193–212.

Kossek, E. E. (2006). Work and family in America: Growing tensions between employment policy and a changing workforce. A thirty-year perspective. In E. Lawler & J. O'Toole (Eds.), *America at work: Choices and challenges* (pp. 53–72). New York: Palgrave MacMillan.

Kossek, E. E., Baltes, B. B., & Matthews, R. A. (2011). How work-family research can finally have an impact in organizations. *Industrial and Organizational Psychology: Perspectives on Science and Practice, 4*(3), 352–369.

Kram, K. E. (1985). *Mentoring at work: Developmental relationships in organizational life.* Glenview, IL: Scott Foresman.

Kubeck, J. E., Delp, N. D., Haslett, T. K., & McDaniel, M. A. (1996). Does job-related training performance decline with age? *Psychology and Aging, 11*(1), 92–107.

Labouvie-Vief, G. (1982). Dynamic development and mature autonomy: A theoretical prologue. *Human Development, 25*, 161–191.

Langeland, K. L., Jones, C. M., & Mawhinney, T. C. (1998). Improving staff performance in a community mentor health setting: Job analysis, training, goal setting, feedback, and years of data. *Journal of Organizational Behavior Management, 18*, 21–43.

Lankau, M. J., & Scandura, T. A. (2002). An investigation of personal learning in mentoring relationships: Content, antecedents, and consequences. *Academy of Management Journal, 45*, 779–790.

Largey, M. (2011). For older job seekers an even more difficult road. Retrieved frpm http://www.npr.org/2011/10/17/141423015/for-older-job-seekers-an-even-more-difficult-road

Latham, G., Almost, J., Mann, S., & Moore, C. (2005). New developments in performance management. *Organizational Dynamics, 34*, 77–87.

Latham, G., & Wexley, K. (1981). *Increasing productivity through performance appraisal.* Boston: Addison-Wesley.

Lawler, E. E. III, Ledford, G. E., & Chang, L. (1993). Who uses skill-based pay and why. *Compensation & Benefits Review, 25*, 22–26.

Ledford, G. E. (1995). Paying for the skills, knowledge and competencies of knowledge workers. *Compensation & Benefits Review, 27*, 55–62.

Lee, M. D., Kossek, E. E., Hall, D. T., & Litrico, J. B. (2011). Entangled strands: A process perspective on the evolution of careers in the context of personal, family, work, and community life. *Human Relations, 64*(12), 1531–1553.

Lee, T. W., Mitchell, T. R., Holtom, B. C., McDaniel, L. S., & Hill, J. W. (1999). The unfolding model of voluntary turnover: A replication and extension. *Academy of Management Journal, 42*, 450–462.

Lepak, D., & Snell, S. (2002). Examining the human resource architecture: The relationships among human capital, employment, and human resource configurations. *Journal of Management, 28*, 517–543.

Levinson, D. J., Darrow, C. N., Klein, E. B., Levinson, M. L., & McKee, B. (1978). *The seasons of a man's life.* New York: Knopf.

Li, J. T., Tsui, A. S., & Weldon, E. (2000). *Management and organizations in the Chinese context.* New York: St. Martin's Press.

Lindbo, T. L., & Shultz, K. S. (1998). The role of organizational culture and mentoring in mature worker socialization toward retirement. *Public Productivity & Management Review, 22*(1), 49–59.

Litricio, J., Lee, M. D., & Kossek, E. E. (2011). Cross-level dynamics between changing organizations and career patterns of reduced-load. *Organizational Studies, 32,* 1681–1700.

Loher, B. T., Noe, R. A., Moeler, N. L., & Fitzgerald, M. P. (1985). A meta-analysis of the relation of job characteristics to job satisfaction. *Journal of Applied Psychology, 70,* 280–289.

Loretto, W., & White, P. (2006). Employers' attitudes, practices and policies towards older workers. *Human Resource Management Journal, 16,* 313–330.

Lounsbury, J. W., Tatum, H. E., Chambers, W., Owens, K. S., & Gibson, L. W. (1999). An investigation of career decidedness in relation to 'Big Five' personality constructs and life satisfaction. *College Student Journal, 33,* 646–652.

Luchak, A. A., Pohler, D. M., & Gellatly, I. R. (2008) When do committed employees retire? The effects of organizational commitment on retirement plans under a defined-benefit pension plan. *Human Resource Management, 47,* 581–599.

Luthans, F., Avolio, B., Avey, J. B., & Norman, S. M. (2007). Positive psychological capital: Measurement and relationship with performance and satisfaction. *Personnel Psychology, 60,* 541–572.

Luthans, F., & Youssef, C. M. (2004). Human, social, and now positive psychological capital management: Investing in people for competitive advantage. *Organizational Dynamics, 33*(2), 181–173.

Macky, K., Gardner, D., & Forsyth, S. (2008). Generational differences at work: introduction and overview. *Journal of Managerial Psychology, 23*(8), 857–861.

Macnicol, J. (2006). *Age discrimination: An historical and contemporary analysis.* Cambridge, UK: Cambridge University Press.

Maddi, S. R., Kahn, S., & Maddi, K. L. (1998). The effectiveness of hardiness training. *Consulting Psychology Journal: Practice and Research, 50,* 78–86.

Madvig, T. L., & Shultz, K. S. (2008). Modeling individual's post-retirement behaviors toward their former organization. *Journal of Workplace Behavioral Health, 23* (1&2), 17–49.

Mainiero, L. A., & Sullivan, S. E. (2005). Kaleidoscope careers: An alternate explanation for the opt-out revolution. *Academy of Management Executive 19*(1), 1006–123.

Mainiero, L. A., & Sullivan, S. E. (2006). *The opt-out revolt: Why people are leaving companies to create kaleidoscope careers.* Mountain View, CA: Davies-Black.

March, J. G., & Simon, H. A. (1958). *Organizations.* New York: Wiley.

Marler, J. H., Tolbert, P. S., & Milkovich, G. T. (2003). In P. Moen (Ed.), *It's about time: Couples and careers* (pp. 242–258). Ithaca, NY: Cornell University Press.

Martin, R., & Wall, T. D. (1989). Attentional demand and cost responsibility as stressors in shop-floor jobs. *Academy of Management Journal, 32,* 69–86.

Mathieu, J. E., & Zajac, D. M. (1990). A review and meta-analysis of the antecedents, correlates, and consequences of organizational commitment. *Psychological Bulletin, 108,* 171–194.

Matthews, R. A., Bulger, C. A., & Barnes-Farrell, J. L. (2010). Work social supports, role stressors, and work-family conflict: The moderating effect of age. *Journal of Vocational Behavior, 76,* 78–90.

Matz-Costa, C., & Pitt-Catsouphes, M. (2010). Workplace flexibility as an organizational response to the aging of the workforce: A comparison of nonprofit and for-profit organizations. *Journal of Social Service Research, 36,* 68–80.

Maurer, T. (2001). Career-relevant learning and development, worker age, and beliefs about self-efficacy for development. *Journal of Management, 27,* 123–140.

Maurer, T. J. (2007). Employee development and training issues related to the aging workforce. In

K. S. Shultz & G. A. Adams (Ed.), *Aging and work in the 21st century* (pp. 163–178). Mahwah, NJ: Erlbaum.

Maurer, T. J., Weiss, E. M., & Barbeite, F. G. (2003). A model of involvement in work-related learning and development activity: The effects of individual, situational, motivation, and age variables. *Journal of Applied Psychology, 88,* 707–724.

Mayer, J. D., Salovey, P., & Caruso, D. (2000). Models of emotional intelligence. In R. J. Sternberg (Ed.), *Handbook of intelligence* (pp. 396–422). Cambridge, UK: Cambridge University Press.

Mayer, J. D., Salovey, P., & Caruso, D. R. (2008). Emotional intelligence: New ability or eclectic trait? *American Psychologist, 63,* 503–517. doi:10.1037/0003-066X.63.6.503

McAdams, D. P., & Pals, J. L. (2006). A new big five: Fundamental principles for an integrative science of personality. *American Psychologist, 61,* 204–217.

McArdle, A., Vasilaki, A., & Jackson, M. (2002). Exercise and skeletal muscle aging: Cellular and molecular mechanisms. *Aging Research Reviews, 1,* 79–93.

McCall, M. W., Lombardo, M. M., & Morrison, A. M. (1988). *The lessons of experience: How successful executives develop on the job.* New York: Lexington Books.

McCrae, R. R. (1996). Social consequences of experiential openness. *Psychological Bulletin, 120,* 323–337.

McCrae, R. R., & Costa, P. T., Jr. (2008). The five-factor theory of personality. In O. P. John, R. W. Robins, & L. A. Pervin (Eds.), *Handbook of personality: Theory and research* (3rd ed., pp. 159–181). New York: Guilford.

McCrae, R. R., & John, O. P. (1992). An introduction to the five-factor model and its applications. *Journal of Personality, 2,* 175–215.

McEvoy, G. M., & Cascio, W. R. (1989) Cumulative evidence on the relationship between employee age and job performance. *Journal of Applied Psychology, 74,* 11–17.

Mckee-Ryan, F. M., Song, Z., Wanberg, C. R., & Kinicki, A. J. (2005). Psychological and physical well-being during unemployment: A metaanalytic study. *Journal of Applied Psychology, 90,* 53–76.

Meaning of Work International Research Team (MOWIRT). (1987). *The meaning of working.* London: Academic Press.

MetLife. (2009). *The emerging retirement model study.* New York: Metropolitan Life Insurance Company.

Meyer, J. P., & Allen, N. J. (1997). *Commitment in the workplace: Theory, research and application.* Thousand Oaks: CA: Sage.

Mills, M., Blossfeld, H-P., Buchholz, S., Hofacker, D., Bernardi, F., & Hofmeister, H. (2008). Converging divergences: An international comparison of the impact of globalization on industrial relations and employment careers. *International Sociology, 23,* 561–595. doi: 10.1177/026850908090728

Mirvis, P. H., & Hall, D. T. (1994). Psychological success and the boundaryless career. *Journal of Organizational Behavior, 15,* 365–380.

Mischel, W., & Shoda, Y. (1995). A cognitive-affective system theory of personality: Reconceptualizing situations, dispositions, dynamics, and invariance in personality structure. *Psychological Review, 102,* 246–268.

Mitchell, T. R., Holtom, B. C., Lee, T. W., Sablynski, C. J., & Erez, M. (2001). Why people stay: Using job embeddedness to predict voluntary turnover. *Academy of Management Journal, 44,* 1102–1121.

Moen, P. (2003). *It's about time: Couples and careers.* Ithaca, NY: Cornell University Press.

Moen, P. (2005). Beyond the career mystique: "Time in," "time out," and "second acts". *Sociological Forum, 20,* 189–208. doi: 10.1007/s11206-005-4100-8

Moen, P., & Han, P. (2001). Reframing careers: Work, family and gender. In V. M. Marchall, W. R. Heinz, H. Krueger, & A. Verma (Eds.), *Restructuring work and the life course* (pp. 424–445). Toronto, Ontario: University of Toronto Press.

Moen, P., Waismel-Manor, R., & Sweet, S. (2003). In P. Moen (Ed.) *It's about time: Couples and careers* (pp. 242–258). Ithaca, NY: Cornell University Press.

Molleman, E. (2005). Diversity in demographic characteristics, abilities, and personality traits: Do faultlines affect team functioning? *Group Decision and Negotiation, 14,* 173–193.

Morgeson, F. P., & Campion, M. A. (2003). Work design. In W. C. Borman, D. R. Ilgen, & R. J. Klimoski (Eds.), *Handbook of psychology: Vol. 12, Industrial and organizational psychology* (pp. 423–452). Hoboken, NJ: Wiley.

Morgeson, F. P., & Humphrey, S. E. (2006). The Work Design Questionnaire (WDQ): Developing and validating a comprehensive measure for assessing job design and the nature of work. *Journal of Applied Psychology, 91,* 1321–1339.

Morris, J. R., Cascio, W. F., & Young, C. E. (1999, Winter). Downsizing after all these years: Questions and answers about who did it, how many did it, and who benefited from it. *Organizational Dynamics,* 78–87.

Morrison, E. W. (2002). The school-to-work transition. In D. C. Feldman (Ed.), *Work careers: A developmental perspective* (pp. 126–158). San Francisco: Jossey-Bass.

Motowidlo, S. J., Borman, W. C., & Schimitt, M. J. (1997). A theory of individual differences in task and contextual performance. *Human Performance, 10,* 71–83.

Motowidlo, S. J., & Van Scotter, J. R. (1994). Evidence that task performance should be distinguished from contextual performance. *Journal of Applied Psychology, 79,* 475–480.

Naglieri, J. A., & Das, J. P. (1997). Intelligence revised: The planning, attention, simultaneous, successive (PASS) Cognitive Processing Theory. In R. F. Dillon (Ed.), *Handbook on testing* (pp. 136–163). Westport, CT: Greenwood Press.

Neal, M. B., & Hammer, L. B. (2007). *Working couples caring for children and aging parents: Effects on work and well-being.* Mahwah, NJ: Erlbaum.

Neapolitan, J. (1980). Occupational change in mid-career: An exploratory investigation. *Journal of Vocational Behavior, 16,* 212–225.

Ng, T. W. H., Eby, L. T., Sorensen, K. L., & Feldman, D. C. (2005). Predictors of objective and subjective career success. A meta-analysis. *Personnel Psychology, 58,* 367–408.

Ng, T. W. H, & Feldman, D. C. (2007). Organizational embeddedness and occupational embeddedness across career stages. *Journal of Vocational Behavior, 70,* 336–351.

Ng, T. W. H., & Feldman, D. C. (2008). The relationship of age to ten dimensions of job performance. *Journal of Applied Psychology, 93,* 392–423.

Ng, T. W. H., & Feldman, D. C. (2009). Occupational embeddedness and job performance. *Journal of Organizational Behavior, 30,* 863–891.

Ng, T. W. H., & Feldman, D. (2010). The relationships of age with job attitudes: A meta-analysis. *Personnel Psychology, 63,* 677–718.

Noe, R. A., Hollenbeck, J. R., Gerhart, B., & Wright, P. M. (2009). *Fundamentals of Human Resource Management* (3rd ed). New York: McGraw-Hill Irwin.

O'Reilly, C. A., & Caldwell, D. F. (1979). Informational influence as a determinant of perceived task characteristics and job satisfaction. *Journal of Applied Psychology, 64,* 157–165.

O'Reilly, C. A., & Chatman, J. A. (1994). Working smarter and harder: A longitudinal study of managerial success. *Administrative Science Quarterly, 39,* 603–627.

O'Reilly, C., & Pfeffer, J. (2000). *Hidden value: How great companies achieve extraordinary results with ordinary people.* Cambridge, MA: Harvard Business School Press.

Olson, D. A., & Jackson, D. A. (2009). Expanding leadership diversity through formal mentoring programs. *Journal of Leadership Studies, 3*(1), 47–60.

Olson, D. A., Shultz, K. S., & Liu, J. (2012, April). *Social media's influence on social support, efficacy, and life satisfaction.* Paper presented at the Society for Industrial/Organizational Psychology Conference, San Diego, California.

Ostroff, C., Kinicki, A. J., & Tamkins, M. M. (2003). In W. C. Borman, D. R. Ilgen, & R. J. Klimoski (Eds.), *Handbook of psychology: Vol. 12, Industrial and organizational psychology* (pp. 565–593). Hoboken, NJ: Wiley.

Park, D. C. (2000). The basic mechanisms accounting for age-related decline in cognitive function. In D. C. Park & N. Schwarz (Eds.), *Cognitive aging: A primer* (pp. 3–22). Philadelphia: Psychology Press.

Parker, S. K., Chmiel, N., & Wall, T. D. (1997). Work characteristics and employee well-being within a context of strategic downsizing. *Journal of Occupational Health Psychology, 2,* 289–303.

Pearlman, K., & Barney, M. F. (2000). Selection for a changing workplace. In J. F. Kehoe (Ed.), *Managing selection in changing organizations: Human resource strategies* (pp. 3–72). San Francisco: Jossey-Bass.

Peiperl, M., & Baruch, Y. (1997). Back to square zero: The post-corporate career. *Organizational Dynamics, 25,* 7–22.

Perry, E. L., Kulick, C. J., & Bourhis, A. C. (1996). Moderating effects of personal and contextual factors in age discrimination. *Journal of Applied Psychology, 81,* 628–647.

Perry, E. L., Kulick, C. J., & Zhou, J. (1999). A closer look at the effects of supervisor-subordinate age differences. *Journal of Organizational Behavior, 20,* 341–357.

Peterson, C. M., & Seligman, M. E. P. (2003). Positive organizational studies: Lessons from positive psychology. In K. S. Cameron, J. E. Dutton, & R. E. Quinn (Eds.), *Positive Organizational Scholarship.* (pp. 14–28). San Francisco: Berrett Koehler.

Peterson, D. A., & Wendt, P. A. (1995). Training and education of older Americans as workers and volunteers. In S. A. Bass (Ed.), *Older and active: How Americans over 55 are contributing to society* (pp. 217–236). New Haven, CT: Yale University Press.

Peterson, D. A., & Hicks, M. D. (1996). *Leader as coach: Strategies for coaching and developing others.* Minneapolis, MN: Personnel Decisions Inc.

Peterson, N. G., Mumford, M. D., Borman, W. C., Jeanneret, P. R., Fleishman, E. A., Levin, K. Y., et al. (2001). Understanding work using the occupational information network (O*NET): Implications for practice and research. *Personnel Psychology, 54,* 451–492.

Pinder, C. C. (2008). *Work motivation in organizational behavior* (2nd ed.). New York: Psychology Press.

Pitt-Catsouphes, M., Matz-Costa, C., & Besen, E. (2009). *Age & generations: Understanding experiences at the workplace, 6,* 1–43. Boston: The Sloan Center on Aging & Work at Boston College.

Pixley, J. E., & Moen, P. (2003). Prioritizing careers. In P. Moen (Ed.), *It's about time: Couples and careers* (pp. 168–182). Ithaca, NY: Cornell University Press.

Podsakoff, P. M., MacKenzie, S. B., Paine, J. B., & Bachrach, D. G. (2000). Organizational citizenship behaviors: A critical review of the theoretical and empirical literature and suggestions for future research. *Journal of Management, 26,* 513–563.

Pogson, C., Cober, A., Doverspike, D., & Rogers, J. (2003). Differences in self-reported work ethic across three career stages. *Journal of Vocational Behavior, 62,* 189–201.

Porter, M. E. (1985). *Competitive strategy.* New York: The Free Press.

Posthuma, R. A., & Campion, M. A. (2009). Age stereotypes in the workplace: Common stereotypes, moderators, and future research directions. *Journal of Management, 35,* 158–188.

Power, S. J. (2009). Midcareer renewal: A research agenda for the twenty-first century. In S. G. Baugh & S. E. Sullivan (Eds.), *Maintaining focus, energy, and options over the career.* Charlotte, NC: IAP, Inc.

Pratt, M. G., & Ashforth, B. E. (2003). Fostering meaningfulness in working and at work. In K. S. Cameron, J. E. Dutton, & R. E. Quinn (Eds.), *Positive organizational scholarship* (pp. 309–327). San Francisco: Berrett Koehler.

Pritchard, R., Jones, S., Roth, P., Stuebing, K., & Ekeberg, S. (1989). The evaluation of an integrated approach to measuring organizational productivity. *Personnel Psychology, 42,* 69–115.

Pulakos, E. D. (1984). A comparison of rater training programs: Error training and accuracy training. *Journal of Applied Psychology, 69,* 581–588.

Pulakos, E. D., & O'Leary, R. S. (2011). Why is performance management broken? *Industrial and Organizational Psychology: Perspectives on Science and Practice, 4,* 146–164.

Pulakos, E. D., & Wexley, K. N. (1983). The relationship among perceptual similarity, sex, and performance ratings in manager-subordinate dyads. *Academy of Management Journal, 26,* 330–342.

Ragins, B. R. (1997). Antecedents of diversified mentoring relationships. *Journal of Vocational Behavior, 51,* 90–109.

Ragins, B. R. (2007). Diversity and workplace mentoring relationships: A review and positive social capital approach. In T. D. Allen & L.T. Eby (Eds.), *The Blackwell handbook of mentoring: A multiple perspectives approach* (pp. 305–325). Malden, MA: Blackwell.

Ragins, B. R., Cotton. J. L., & Miller, J. S. (2000). Marginal mentoring: the effects of type of mentor, quality of relationship, and program design on work and career attitudes. *Academy of Management Journal, 43,* 1177–1194.

Rau, B., & Adams, G. (2005). Attracting retirees to apply: Desired organizational characteristics of bridge employment. *Journal of Organizational Behavior, 26,* 649–660.

Rhoades, L., & Eisenberger, R. (2002). Perceived organizational support: A review of the literature. *Journal of Applied Psychology, 87,* 698–714.

Richards, O. C. (2000). Racial diversity, business strategy, and firm performance: A resource-based view. *Academy of Management Journal, 43,* 164–177.

Ritti, R. R. (1994). *The ropes to skip and the ropes to know* (4th ed.). New York: Wiley.

Robinson, C., & Clark, R. (2010). Retiree health insurance and disengagement from a career job. *Journal of Labor Research*, 31(3), 247–262.

Robson, S. M., Hansson, R. O., Abalos, A., & Booth, M. (2006). Successful aging: Criteria for aging well in the workplace. *Journal of Career Development, 33,* 156–177.

Rosen, B., & Jerdee, T. H. (1976). The influence of age stereotypes on managerial decisions. *Journal of Applied Psychology, 61,* 428–432.

Rosen, C., Levy, P., & Hall, R. (2006) Placing perceptions of politics in the context of the feedback environment: Employee attitudes and job performance. *Journal of Applied Psychology, 91,* 211–220.

Rosen, S. (1972). Learning and experience in the labor market. *Journal of Human Resources,* 7(3), 326–342.

Rothwell, W. J. (2001). *Effective succession planning, 2nd Edition.* New York: AMACOM.

Rothwell, W. J., Sterns, H. L., Spokus, D., & Reaser, J. M. (2008). *Working longer: New strategies for managing, training, and retaining older workers.* New York: AMACOM.

Rousseau, D. M. (1989). Psychological and implied contracts in organizations. *Employee Responsibilities & Rights Journal, 2,* 121–139.

Rousseau, D. M. (1995). *Psychological contracts in organizations.* Thousand Oaks, CA: Sage.

Ryan, A., & Kossek, E. E. (2008). Work-life policy implementation: Breaking down or creating barriers to inclusiveness. *Human Resource Management, 47,* 295–310.

Ryan, M. R., & Deci, E. (2001). On happiness and human potentials: A review of research on hedonic and eudaimonic well-being. *Annual Review of Psychology, 52,* 141–166.

Sackett, P. R., & Laczo, R. M. (2003). Job and work analysis. In W. C. Borman, D. R. Ilgen, & R. J. Klimoski (Eds.), *Handbook of psychology: Volume 12, Industrial and organizational psychology* (pp. 21–37). Hoboken, NJ: Wiley.

Salancik, G. R., & Pfeffer, J. (1978). A social information processing approach to job attitudes and task design. *Administrative Science Quarterly, 23,* 224–253.

Salgado, J. F. (1997). The five-factor model of personality and job performance in the European community. *Journal of Applied Psychology, 82,* 30–43.

Salmela-Aro, K., & Nurmi, J. (2007). Self-esteem during university studies predicts career characteristics 10 years later. *Journal of Vocational Behavior, 70,* 463–477.

Salthouse, T. A. (1996). The processing-speed theory of adult age differences in cognition. *Psychological Review, 103,* 403–428.

Salthouse, T. A., & Maurer, T. J. (1996). Aging, job performance, and career development. In J. E.

Birren & K. W. Schaie (Eds.), *Handbook of the psychology of aging* (4th ed., pp. 353–364). New York: Academic Press.

Sanchez, J. I., & Levine, E. L. (1999). Is job analysis dead, misunderstood, or both? New forms of work analysis and design. In A. I. Kraut & A. K. Korman (Eds.), *Evolving practices in human resource management* (pp. 43–68). San Francisco: Jossey-Bass.

Sanders, M. J., & McCready, J. W. (2010). Does work contribute to successful aging outcomes in older workers? *International Journal of Aging and Human Development, 71,* 209–229. doi:10.2190/AG.71.3.c

Schaie, K. W. (1996). *Adult intellectual development: The Seattle longitudinal study.* New York: Cambridge University Press.

Schein, E. H. (1990). *Career anchors.* San Diego, CA: Pfeiffer.

Schmidt, F. L., & Hunter, J. E. (1998). The validity and utility of selection methods in personnel psychology: Practical and theoretical implications of 85 years of research findings. *Psychological Bulletin, 124,* 262–274.

Schneider, B., Goldstein, H. W., & Smith, D. B. (1995). The ASA framework: An update. *Personnel Psychology, 48,* 747–773.

Schneier, C. E., Shaw, D. G., & Beatty, R. W. (1991). Performance measurement and management: A tool for strategy execution. *Human Resource Management, 30,* 279–301.

Schnittger, M. H., & Bird, G. W. (1990). Coping among dual-career men and women across the family life cycle. *Family Relations, 39,* 199–205.

Schuler, R. S., & Jackson. S. E. (1987). Linking competitive strategies with human resource management practices. *The Academy of Management Executive, 1*(3), 207–219.

Segers, J., Inceoglu, I., Vloeberghs, D., Bartram, D., & Hendrickx, E. (2008). Protean and boundaryless careers: A study on potential motivators. *Journal of Vocational Behavior, 73,* 212–230.

Seibert, S. E., Crant, J. M., & Kraimer, M. L. (1999). Proactive personality and career success. *Journal of Applied Psychology, 84,* 416–427.

Seligman, M. E. P. (2002). *Authentic happiness: Using the new positive psychology to realize your potential for lasting fulfillment.* New York: Free Press.

Shalley, C. E., Gilson, L. L., & Blum, T. C. (2000). Matching creativity requirements and the work environment: Effects on satisfaction and intentions to leave. *Academy of Management Journal, 43,* 215–223.

Shaw, K. L. (1987). Occupational change, employer change, and the transferability of skills. *Southern Economic Journal, 53*(3), 702–719.

Sheehy, G. (1976). *Passages.* New York: Dutton.

Shuey, K. M. (2004). Worker preferences, spousal coordination, and participation in an employer-sponsored pension plan. *Research on Aging, 26,* 287–316.

Shultz, K. S. (2003). Bridge employment: Work after retirement. In G. A. Adams & T. A. Beehr (Eds.), *Retirement: Reasons, processes, and results* (pp. 214–241). New York: Springer.

Shultz, K. S., & Adams, G. A. (2007). *Aging and work in the 21st century.* Mahwah, NJ: Erlbaum.

Shultz, K. S., & Henkens, K. (2010). Introduction to the changing nature of retirement: An international perspective. *International Journal of Manpower, 31,* 265–270.

Shultz, K. S., Morton, K. R., & Weckerle, J. R. (1998). The influence of push and pull factors on voluntary and involuntary early retirees' retirement decision and adjustment. *Journal of Vocational Behavior, 53,* 45–57.

Shultz, K. S., Olson, D. A., & Wang, M. (2011). Overqualified employees: Perspectives of older workers. *Industrial and Organizational Psychology, 4,* 247–249.

Shultz, K. S., & Olson, D. A. (2013). The changing nature of work and retirement. In M. Wang (Ed.), *The Oxford handbook of retirement.* New York: Oxford University Press.

Shultz, K. S., & Wang, M. (2008). The changing nature of mid and late-careers. In C. Wankel (Ed.), *21st century management: A reference handbook* (Vol. 2, pp. 130–138). Thousand Oaks, CA: Sage.

Shultz, K. S., & Wang, M. (2011). Psychological perspectives on the changing nature of retirement. *American Psychologist, 66,* 170–179.

Shultz, K. S., Wang, M., Crimmins, E. M., & Fisher, G. G. (2009). Age differences in the demand-control model of work stress: An examination of data from 15 European countries. *Journal of Applied Gerontology, 29,* 21–47.

Shultz, K. S., Wang, M., & Olson, D. A. (2010). Role overload and underload in relation to occupational stress and health. *Stress and Health, 26,* 99–111.

Sicherman, N., & Galor, O. (1990). A theory of career mobility. *Journal of Political Economy, 98*(1), 169–192.

Simpson, P. A., Greller, M. M., & Stroh, L. K. (2002). Variations in human capital investment activity by age. *Journal of Vocational Behavior, 61,* 109–138.

Sims, H. P., Szilagyi, A. D., & Keller, R. T. (1976). The measurement of job characteristics. *Academy of Management Journal, 19,* 195–212.

Slagter, F. (2007). Knowledge management among the older workforce. *Journal of Knowledge Management, 11,* 82–96.

Snijders, T. A., & Bosker, R. J. (1999). *Multilevel analysis: An introduction to basic and advanced multilevel modeling.* Thousand Oaks, CA: Sage.

Sowers, M. F. (2001). Epidemiology of risk factors for osteoarthritis: Systemic factors. *Current Opinion in Rheumatology, 13,* 447–451.

Spencer, L. M., & Spencer, S. M. (1993). *Competence at work: Models for superior performance.* New York: Wiley.

Sternberg, R. J. (1986). *Intelligence applied.* New York: Harcourt Brace Jovanovich.

Sterns, H. L., & Doverspike, D. (1988). Training and developing the older worker: Implications for human resource management. In H. Dennis (Ed.), *Fourteen steps in managing an aging workforce* (pp. 97–110). Lexington, MA: Lexington Books.

Sterns, H. L., & Huyck, M. H. (2001). The role of work in midlife. In M. E. Lachman (Ed.), *Handbook of midlife development* (pp. 447–486). New York: Wiley.

Sterns, H. L., & Kaplan, J. (2003). Self-management of career and retirement. In G. A. Adams & T. A. Beehr (Eds.), *Retirement: Reasons, processes and results* (pp. 188–213). New York: Springer.

Sterns, H. L., & Miklos, S. M. (1995). The aging worker in a changing environment: Organizational and individual issues. *Journal of Vocational Behavior, 47,* 248–268.

Sterns, H. L., & Patchett, M. (1984). Technology and the aging adult: career development and training. In P. R. Robinson & J. E. Birren (Eds.), *Aging and technology* (pp. 261–277). New York: Plenum Press.

Sterns, H. L., & Sterns, A. A. (2005). Past and future directions for career development theory. In P. T. Beatty & Roemer M. S. Visser (Eds.), *Thriving on an aging workforce: Strategies for organizational and systemic change* (pp. 81–91). Malabar, FL: Krieger.

Sterns, H. L., & Subich, L. M. (2002). Career development in midcareer. In D. C. Feldman (Ed.), *Work careers: A developmental perspective* (pp. 186–213). San Francisco: Jossey-Bass/ Wiley.

Stevens, R. (2010). Managing human capital: How to use knowledge management to transfer knowledge in today's multigenerational workforce. *International Business Research, 3,* 77–83.

Stone, E. F., & Gueutal, H. G. (1985). An empirical derivation of the dimensions along which characteristics of jobs are perceived. *Academy of Management Journal, 28,* 376–396.

Straka, C. A. (1998). Organization, self-directly learning, and chronological age. In K. W. Schaie & C. Schooler (Eds.), *Impact of work on older adults* (pp. 186–194). New York: Springer.

Strumpf, E. (2009). Employer-sponsored health insurance for early retirees: impacts on retirement, health, and health care. *International Journal of Health Care Finance and Economics, 10,* 105–147.

Sturman, M. C. (2003). Searching for the inverted U-shaped relationship between time and performance: Meta-analyses of the experience/performance, tenure/performance, and age/performance relationships. *Journal of Management, 29,* 609–640.

Sullivan, S. E., & Arthur, M. B. (2006). The evolution of the boundaryless career concept: Examining physical and psychological mobility. *Journal of Vocational Behavior, 69,* 19–29.

Sullivan, S. E., & Baruch, Y. (2009). Advances in career theory and research: A critical review and agenda for future exploration. *Journal of Management, 35,* 1542–1571.

Sullivan, S. E., & Crocitto, M. (2007). The developmental theories: A critical examination of their continuing impact on careers research. In H. Gunz & M. Peiperl (Eds.), *Handbook of career studies* (pp. 283–309). London: Blackwell.

Sullivan, S. E., Forret, M. L., Carraher, S. M., & Mainiero, L. A. (2009). Using the kaleidoscope career model to examine generational differences in work attitudes. *Career Development International, 14,* 284–302.

Super, D. E. (1957). *The psychology of careers.* New York: HarperCollins.

Super, D. E. (1980). A life-span, life-space approach to career development. *Journal of Vocational Behavior, 16,* 282–298.

Super, D. E. (1982). The relative importance of work. *The Counseling Psychologist, 10,* 95–103.

Super, D. E. (1990). A lifespan-life-space approach to career development. In D. Brown & L. Brooks (Eds.), *Career choice and development* (2nd ed., pp. 197–261). San Francisco: Jossey-Bass.

Swann, W. B. Jr., Stein-Seroussi, A., & Giesler, R. B. (1992). Why people self-verify. *Journal of Personality and Social Psychology, 62,* 392–401.

Tripartite Alliance for Fair Employment Practices (TAFEP). (2011). *Leading practices for managing mature employees.* Technical Report. Retrieved on May 1, 2012, from: http://www.dinosaur-exchange.com/FTP/leading_practices_for_managing_mature_employees-tafep-Singapore.pdf

Takeuchi, R., Wang, M., Marinova, S. V., & Yao, X. (2009). Role of domain-specific facets of perceived organizational support during expatriation and implications for performance. *Organizational Science, 20,* 621–634.

Tapinos, E., Dyson, R. G., & Meadows, M. (2005). The impact of performance measurement in strategic planning. *International Journal of Productivity and Performance Management, 54,* 370–384.

Taylor, M. A., & Shore, L. F. (1995). Predictors of planned retirement age: An application of Beehr's model. *Psychology and Aging, 10,* 76–83.

Taylor, M., Shultz, K., & Doverspike, D. (2005). Academic perspectives on recruiting and retaining older workers. In P. Beatty & R. Visser (Eds.), *Thriving on an aging workforce,* (pp. 43–50) Malabar, FL: Krieger.

Taylor, P. (2008). *Ageing labour forces: Promises and prospects.* Cheltenham, UK: Edward Elgar.

Temple, J., Adair, T., & Hosseini-Chavoshi, M. (2011). *Ageing and the barriers to labour force participation in Australia.* Canberra, Australia: Productive Ageing Centre.

Tett, R. P., & Burnett, D. D. (2003). A personality trait-based interactionist model of job performance. *Journal of Applied Psychology, 88,* 500–517.

Thomas, D. (2001). The truth about mentoring minorities: race matters. *Harvard Business Review, 79*(4), 98–107.

Thomas, E. A., & Higgins, M. C. (1996). Mentoring and the boundaryless career: Lessons from the minority experience. In M. B. Arthur & D. M. Rousseau (Eds.), *The boundaryless career: A new employment principle for a new organizational era.* New York: Oxford University Press.

Thompson, A. M., & Bono, B. A. (1993). Work without wages: The motivation for volunteer firefighters. *American Journal of Economics and Sociology, 52,* 323–343.

TIAA-CREF Institute. (2006). *The retiree health care challenge.* New York: Author.

Toossi, M. (2006). A new look at long-term labor force projections to 2050. *Monthly Labor Review, 129,* 19–39.

Trist, E. L. (1981). The sociotechnical perspective. In A. H. Van de Ven & W. F. Joyce (Eds.), *Perspectives on organization design and behavior* (pp. 19–75). New York: Wiley.

Trist, E. L., & Bamforth, K. M. (1951). Some social and psychological consequences of the long-wall method of coal-getting. *Human Relations, 4,* 3–38.

Tsui, A. S., Pearce, J. L., Porter, L. W., & Tripoli, A. M. (1997). Alternative approaches to the employee-organization relationship: Does investment in employees pay off? *Academy of Management Journal, 40,* 1089–1121.

Twenge, J. M., Campbell, S. M., Hoffman, B. J., & Lance, C. E. (2010). Generational differences in work values: Leisure and extrinsic values increasing, social and intrinsic values decreasing. *Journal of Management, 36,* 1117–1142.

U.S. Bureau of Labor Statistics. (2009, March). Retirement benefits: Access, participation, and take up rates data table. *Employee benefits survey.* Retrieved from http://www.bls.gov/ncs/ebs/benefits/2009/ownership/civilian/table02a.htm

U.S. Bureau of Labor Statistics. (2010, December 8). Employer costs for employee compensation news release text. *Economic news release.* Retrieved from http://www.bls.gov/news.release/ecec.nr0.htm.

Valcour, P. M., Bailyn, L., & Quijada, M. A. (2007). Customized careers. In H. Gunz & M. Peiperl (Eds.), *Handbook of career studies* (pp. 188–210). London: Blackwell.

Valcour, P. M., & Batt, R. (2003). Work-Life integration: Challenges and organizational responses. In P. Moen (Ed.), *It's about time: Couples and careers* (pp.168–182). Ithaca, NY: Cornell University Press.

Valliant, G. (1977). *Adaptation to life.* New York: Little, Brown.

van Dalen, H. P., Henkens, K., Henderikse, W., & Schippers, J. (2010). Do European employers support later retirement? *International Journal of Manpower, 31,* 360–373.

van Dalen, H. P., Henkens, K., & Hershey, D. A. (2010). Perceptions and expectations of pension savings adequacy: A comparative study of Dutch and American workers. *Ageing and Society, 30,* 731–754.

Van der Heijden, C. M., & Van der Heijden, B. I. J. M. (2006). A competence-based and multi-dimensional operationalization and measurement of employability. *Human Resource Management, 45,* 449–476.

Van Knippenberg, D., De Dreu, C. K. W., & Homan, A. C. (2004). Work group diversity and group performance: An integrative model and research agenda. *Journal of Applied Psychology, 89,* 1008–1022.

van Solinge, H., & Henkens, K. (2008). Adjustment to and satisfaction with retirement: Two of a kind? *Psychology and Aging, 23,* 422–434.

Van Vianen, A. E. M., Dalhoeven, B. A. G. W., & De Pater, I. E. (2011). Aging and training and development willingness: Employee and supervisor mindsets. *Journal of Organizational Behavior, 32,* 226–247.

Veiga, J. F. (1983). Mobility influences during managerial career stages. *Academy of Management Review, 8,* 23–32.

von Bonsdorff, M. E., Shultz, K. S., Leskinen, E., & Tansky, J. (2009). The choice between retirement and bridge employment: A continuity and life course perspective. *International Journal of Aging and Human Development, 69,* 79–100.

Waldfogel, J. (2006). *What children need.* Cambridge, MA: Harvard University Press.

Waldman, D. A., & Avolio, B. J. (1986). A meta-analysis of age differences in job performance. *Journal of Applied Psychology, 71,* 33–38.

Wall, T. D., & Jackson, P. R. (1995). New manufacturing initiatives and shopfloor job design. In A. Howard (Ed.), *The changing nature of work* (pp. 139–174). San Francisco: Jossey-Bass.

Wanberg, C. R., Glomb, T. M., Song, Z., & Sorenson, S. (2005). Jobsearch persistence during unemployment: A 10-wave longitudinal study. *Journal of Applied Psychology, 90,* 411–430.

Wang, M. (2007). Profiling retirees in the retirement transition and adjustment process: Examining the longitudinal change patterns of retirees' psychological well-being. *Journal of Applied Psychology, 92,* 455–474.

Wang, M. (2012). Health, fiscal, and psychological well-being in retirement. In J. Hedge & W. Borman (Eds.), *Oxford handbook of work and aging* (pp. 570–584). New York: Oxford University Press.

Wang, M., Adams, G. A., Beehr, T. A., & Shultz, K. S. (2009). Bridge employment and retirement: Issues and opportunities during the latter part of one's career. In G. A. Baugh & S. E. Sullivan

(Eds.), *Maintaining focus, energy, and options through the lifespan* (pp. 135–162). Charlotte, NC: Information Age.

Wang, M., & Chan, D. (2011). Mixture latent Markov modeling: Identifying and predicting unobserved heterogeneity in longitudinal qualitative status change. *Organizational Research Methods, 14,* 411–431.

Wang, M., & Chen, Y. (2004). Age differences in the correction processes of context-induced biases: When correction succeeds. *Psychology and Aging, 19,* 536–540.

Wang, M., & Chen, Y. (2006). Age differences in attitude change: Influences of cognitive resources and motivation on responses to argument quantity. *Psychology and Aging, 21,* 581–589.

Wang, M., Henkens, K., & van Solinge, H. (2011). Retirement adjustment: A review of theoretical and empirical advancements. *American Psychologist, 66,* 204–213.

Wang, M., Liao, H., Zhan, Y., & Shi, J. (2011). Daily customer mistreatment and employee sabotage against customers: Examining emotion and resource perspectives. *Academy of Management Journal, 54,* 312–334.

Wang, M., & Shultz, K. (2010). Employee retirement: A review and recommendations for future investigation. *Journal of Management, 36,* 172–206.

Wang, M., Sinclair, R. R., & Deese, M. N. (2010). Understanding the causes of destructive leadership: A dual process model. In T. Hansbrough & B. Schyns (Eds.), *When leadership goes wrong: Destructive leadership, mistakes and ethical failures* (pp. 73–97). Charlotte, NC: Information Age.

Wang, M., & Takeuchi, R. (2007). The role of goal orientation during expatriation: A cross-sectional and longitudinal investigation. *Journal of Applied Psychology, 92,* 1437–1445.

Wang, M., Zhan, Y., Liu, S., & Shultz, K. (2008). Antecedents of bridge employment: A longitudinal investigation. *Journal of Applied Psychology, 93,* 818–830.

Wang, M., Zhan, Y., McCune, E., & Truxillo, D. (2011). Understanding newcomers' adaptability and work-related outcomes: Testing the mediating roles of perceived P-E fit variables. *Personnel Psychology, 64,* 163–189.

Wang, S., & Noe, R. (2010). Knowledge sharing: A review and directions for future research. *Human Resource Management Review, 20,* 115–131.

Ward, A. J., Sonnenfeld, J. A., & Kimberly, J. R. (1995). In search of a kingdom: Determinants of subsequent career outcomes for chief executives who are fired. *Human Resource Management, 34,* 117–139.

Warr, P. (1997). Age, work, and mental health. In K. W. Schaie & C. Schooler (Eds.), *The impact of work on older adults* (pp. 252–296). New York: Springer.

Warr, P. (2001). Age and work behaviour: Physical attributes, cognitive abilities, knowledge, personality traits, and motives. *International Review of Industrial and Organizational Psychology, 16,* 1–36.

Warren, A. M., & Kelloway, E. K. (2010). Retirement decisions in the context of the abolishment of mandatory retirement. *International Journal of Manpower, 31,* 286–305.

Watson, D., & Clark, L. A. (1997). Extraversion and its positive emotional core. In S. R. Briggs, W. H. Jones, & R. Hogan (Eds.), *Handbook of personality psychology* (pp. 767–793). San Diego, CA: Academic Press.

Weiss, H. M., & Shaw, J. B. (1979). Social influences on judgments about tasks. *Organizational Behavior and Human Performance, 24,* 126–140.

Werner, J. M., & Bolino, M. C. (1997). Explaining US courts of appeals decisions involving performance appraisal: Accuracy, fairness, and validation. *Personnel Psychology, 50,* 1–24.

Westerman, J., & Sundali, J. (2005). The transformation of employee pensions in the United States: Through the looking glass of organizational behavior. *Journal of Organizational Behavior, 26,* 99–103.

Wethington, E., Pixley, J. E., & Kavey, A. (2003). Turning points in work careers. In P. Moen (Ed.), *It's about time: Couples and careers* (pp. 168–182). Ithaca, NY: Cornell University Press.

Whitely, W., Dougherty, T. W., & Dreher, G. F. (1992). Correlates of career-oriented mentoring for early career managers and professionals. *Journal of Organizational Behavior, 13,* 141–154.

Whyte, W. H. (1956). *The organization man.* New York: Simon and Schuster.

Whyte, W. H. (2002). *The organization man* (rev. ed.). Philadelphia: The University of Pennsylvania Press.

Wiesenfeld, B. M., Swann, Jr., W. B., Brockner, J., & Bartel, C. A. (2007). Is more fairness always preferred? Self-esteem moderates reactions to procedural justice. *Academy of Management Journal, 50,* 1235–1253.

Wilson, T. (1997). *Diversity at work: The business case for equity.* New York: Wiley.

Wong, M., Gardner, E., Lang, W., & Coulon, L. (2008). Generational differences in personality and motivation: Do they exist and what are the implications for the workplace? *Journal of Managerial Psychology, 23,* 878–890.

Wood, J. V., Heimpel, S. A., & Michela, J. L. (2003). Savoring versus dampening: Self-esteem differences in regulating positive affect. *Journal of Personality and Social Psychology, 85,* 566–580.

Wood, J. V., Heimpel, S. A., Newby-Clark, I. R., & Ross, M. (2005). Snatching defeat from the jaws of victory: Self-esteem differences in the experience and anticipation of success. *Journal of Personality and Social Psychology, 89,* 764–780.

Wood, S. (1999). Human resource management and performance. *International Journal of Management Reviews, 1,* 367–413.

Wrenn, K., & Maurer, T. (2004). Beliefs about older workers' learning and development behavior in relation to beliefs about malleability of skills, age-related decline and control. *Journal of Applied Social Psychology, 34,* 223–242.

Wrzesniewski, A. (2003). Finding positive meaning in work. In K. S. Cameron, J. E. Dutton, & R. E. Quinn (Eds.), *Positive organizational scholarship* (pp. 296–308). San Francisco: Berrett Koehler.

Wrzesniewski, A., Dutton, J. E., & Debebe, G. (2003). Interpersonal sensemaking and the meaning of work. In R. M. Kramer & B. M. Staw (Eds.), *Research in organizational behavior* (Vol. 25, pp. 93–135). Amsterdam: Elsevier.

Wrzesniewski, A., McCauley, C., Rozin, P., & Schwartz, B. (1997). Jobs, careers, and callings: People's relations to their work. *Journal of Research in Personality, 31,* 21–33.

Yeatts, D. E., Folts, W. E., & Knapp, J. (2000). Older workers' adaptation to a changing workplace: Employment issues for the 21st century. *Educational Gerontology, 26,* 565–582.

Zack, M., McKeen, J., & Singh, S. (2009). Knowledge management and organizational performance: An exploratory analysis. *Journal of Knowledge Management, 13*(6), 392–409.

Zappala, S., Depolo, M., Fraccaroli, F., Guglielmi, D., & Sarchielli, G. (2008). Early retirement as withdrawal behavior: Postponing job retirement? Psychological influences on the preference for early or late retirement. *Career Development International, 13,* 150–167.

Zeitz, G., Blau, G., & Fertig, J. (2009). Boundaryless careers and institutional resources. *The International Journal of Human Resource Management, 20,* 372–398.

Zellers, D. F., Howard, V. M., & Barcic, M. A. (2008). Faculty mentoring programs: Reevisioning rather than reinventing the wheel. *Review of Educational Research, 78,* 552–589.

Zhan, Y., Wang, M., Liu, S., & Shultz, K. (2009). Bridge employment and retirees' health: A longitudinal investigation. *Journal of Occupational Health Psychology, 14,* 374–389.

Author Index

Aamodt, M., 132, 133
Aaronson, S., 86
Abalos, A., 37
Abraham, J. D., 52
Ackerman, P. L., 61, 68, 88, 133
Adair, T., 181, 182
Adams, G. A., 27, 31, 38, 49–50, 67, 79–91, 81, 90, 91, 105, 115, 157, 158, 174
Aldwin, C. M., 58
Allen, T. D., 43, 60, 135, 136
Alley, D., 87, 130, 174
Almost, J., 118
Argote, L., 87
Armstrong-Stassen, M., 90, 91
Arthur, M. B., 3, 19, 20, 21, 23, 43, 123
Aumann, K., 157
Avey, J. B., 57
Avolio, B. J., 57, 115, 116, 129

Bacanli, F., 53
Bachrach, D. G., 117
Bailyn, L., 6
Bal, A. C., 109, 124
Baldi, R., 128
Baltes, B. B., 109, 124, 143, 147, 148, 149, 152
Baltes, M. M., 148
Baltes, P. B., 71, 143, 148
Bamforth, K. M., 70
Bandura, A., 145
Baranik, L. E., 81
Barbeite, F. G., 135
Barcic, M. A., 136
Barnes-Farrell, J. L., 9, 50, 105, 154
Barney, M. F., 83
Bartel, C. A., 54
Bartolome, F., 142, 143, 144
Bartram, D., 24
Baruch, Y., 14, 15, 17, 18, 21, 24–25, 30, 31, 99
Batt, R., 153

Bauer, T. N., 105
Baugh, S. G., 139
Beatty, R. W., 63, 113
Becker, T., 112, 114, 118
Beehr, T. A., 160
Beehr, T. A., 31, 38, 49–50, 67, 79–80, 81, 90, 99, 105, 157, 160, 174
Benko, C., 3
Bennis, W., 98, 119, 121
Berman, E., 126
Bernardin, H. J., 115
Bertolino, M., 133
Besen, E., 90, 180
Betz, N. E., 53
Bidwell, J., 68
Bird, G. W., 144, 145
Black, D., 143
Blau, G., 18
Blum, T. C., 72
Bolino, M. C., 119
Bond, J. T., 90, 151, 157
Bono, B. A., 75
Bono, J. E., 53, 54
Boot, W. R., 100
Booth, M., 37
Borman, W. C., 114, 117, 118, 128
Bosker, R. J., 93
Boudreau, J. W., 147
Bourhis, A. C., 115, 116
Bowling, N. A., 160
Bowman, J., 126
Boxall, P., 86
Bretz, R. D., 147
Brim, B. J., 133
Briscoe, J. P., 22, 23, 24
Broadbent, J., 86
Brockner, J., 54
Brooks, M. E., 90
Brown, M., 157, 160

Subject Index

Page locators in *italics* indicate figures and tables.